The Excellence of Falsehood

The Excellence of Falsehood

Romance, Realism, and Women's Contribution to the Novel

DEBORAH ROSS

THE UNIVERSITY PRESS OF KENTUCKY

Library of Congress Cataloging-in-Publication Data

Ross, Deborah, 1954-
    The excellence of falsehood : romance, realism, and women's
contribution to the novel / Deborah Ross.
        p.   cm.
    Includes bibliographical references and index.
    ISBN 0-8131-1764-X
    1. English fiction—Women authors—History and criticism.
2. Women and literature—Great Britain.   3. Romanticism—Great
Britain.   4. Realism in literature.   5. Literary form.   I. Title.
PR830.W6R67   1991
823.009′9287—dc20   91-22068

The world's male chivalry has perished out,
But women are knights-errant to the last;
And, if Cervantes had been greater still,
He had made his Don a Donna.

—Elizabeth Barrett Browning,
Aurora Leigh

Contents

Acknowledgments

I WOULD like to thank the following colleagues and friends for reading parts of this project in manuscript and discussing it with me: Mark Fratzke, Philippe Gross, Tibbie Lynch, Alan MacGregor, Susan Staves, Claudia Thomas, and above all Kathy Phillips, whose support of all kinds has been invaluable. Thanks to Syril and William Ross for their library detective work. I would also like to thank John O'Neill for first introducing me to Fanny Burney, and J.W. Johnson for his insights on women novelists, on the eighteenth century, and on the nature of literary criticism.

A version of chapter four of this study originally appeared in *Studies in English Literature* 27 (1987); I wish to thank the editors for permission to publish it.

Abbreviations

E	*Emma*
ED	*The Early Diary of Frances Burney*
FQ	*The Female Quixote*
L	*Letters*
MP	*Mansfield Park*
MW	*Minor Works*
NA	*Northanger Abbey*
NAt	*The New Atalantis*
P	*Persuasion*
PP	*Pride and Prejudice*
PW	*Prose Works*
R	*The Adventures of Rivella*
SS	*Sense and Sensibility*
"TD"	"Mary de la Rivière Manley, Tory Defender"
"WB"	"Mrs. Manley, an Eighteenth-Century Wife of Bath"

Introduction
A Secret History of the English Novel

The only excellence of falsehood . . . is its resemblance to truth.
—Charlotte Lennox

A STUDENT in an introductory literature course put a plain brown cover on his copy of Willa Cather's *My Ántonia* because he was afraid the feminine title and woman author would make everyone on the bus think he was reading a "romance novel." The cover was meant to prevent attacks on his taste and, more important, on his masculinity. How did "romance," a category that includes works as serious and carefully wrought as Spenser's *Faerie Queene,* come to suggest something both trivial and feminine?

Triviality, or "vanité," was a basis for attacks on romance almost from its first appearance in the Middle Ages (Douglas Kelly 79-80).[1] It was "feminine" in the sense that it chronicled a cultural shift of interest from war to love, and so contained important female characters.[2] During the Renaissance romances were increasingly designed for women readers; Sir Philip Sidney wrote his *Arcadia,* which he called a "trifle," for his sister (Nelson 57). Yet the word and the dedication seem more an excuse for not writing a learned treatise in Latin than a denial of artistic purpose. Not until the late seventeenth century were triviality and femininity linked in serious critical condemnations of the romance.

To understand this development, we will have to go back, briefly, to the fourteenth century, when the word "romance" first came into use in English to denote vernacular, and particularly French, narratives. These stories—at first usually in verse and by the late Renaissance in prose—had two main ingredients: adventure and love.[3] Love became the more prominent theme during the seventeenth century. From the beginning, the religious establishment considered these writings "vain" because, unlike the Bible, they were untrue. According to William Nelson, the early Church fathers criticized writers of the classical period for carelessness in separating fact and fiction (6-7). During the Renaissance this criticism became increasingly severe from both Puritan and counter-Reformation quarters (92), culminating in the late sixteenth century in what critics have called a "historical revolution"—a demand for truth about the past.[4] This concern could be difficult to reconcile with enthusiasm for newly rediscovered classical texts such as Aristotle's *Poetics;* for although Aristotle did distinguish "historical truth" from "poetic truth," he accorded more importance to the latter (Chapter IX). In contrast, sixteenth-century critics valued Greek epics, especially over contemporary romances such as Ariosto's, because they were supposed to be based on historical events (Parker 44-45).[5]

To parry accusations of falsehood, romance writers such as Ronsard, Ariosto, and Tasso were driven to one of two defensive postures to gain respect for their art (Nelson 55): they could avoid lying by not pretending to historical truth—deriving dignity from the Greek tradition and its reverence for poetic invention—or they could assert their truthfulness, in either a historical or an allegorical sense (12-13). Somewhere between these two choices was a third: they could make their romances unverifiable and hence possibly true, like the Apocrypha. One way to do that was to set the stories in the distant past and in faraway lands (43-45); another was to write about present-day, ordinary people whose lives were not a matter of public record (107).[6] This latter category roughly corresponds to what we now think of as the "novel," a form of prose narrative that began to be distinguished from the romance in the later seventeenth century and that gradually, over the next hundred years—in theory, at least—came to replace it.

In France the term "nouvelle" began to be used instead of "roman" (though not consistently) to denote shorter works of fiction dealing with more recent times, written in plainer style (Davis 33-34); in English the cognates "novel" and "novella" also had associations with "news," or current events.[7] "Novels" (even when still called romances) established their veracity through expressed contrast with older romances, which now appeared false in a new way— in their lack of immediacy.[8] When, in the 1660s, the immensely influential critic Nicolas Boileau attacked the French romances of his century, he condemned them for inaccuracy about both the past and the present—for making old Roman warriors self-analytical and love-sick and for turning "excessively ugly" real contemporary figures into perfect beauties (*Dialogue des Héros de Roman* 444-45).[9] English critics of this period and after tended to swallow Boileau's pronouncements whole; his judgments are implicit in William Congreve's attempt, in 1692, to define "romance" and "novel" to emphasize the superior truth, or at least verisimilitude, of the latter.[10]

Such was the official evaluation of romances in the late seventeenth century. Yet often their most severe detractors—including

Boileau (444) and, later, Samuel Johnson, who blamed his boyhood habit of reading romances for "that unsettled turn of mind which prevented his ever fixing in any profession" (Boswell 36)—confessed, off the record, to a guilty fondness for them as children. From Shakespeare's time through the eighteenth century, romance maintained a "subliterary" life and popularity, and among its most faithful adherents were women.[11] During the seventeenth century women's enthusiasm for romance grew to such a pitch that they began to write them as well as read them, in more or less open defiance of anti-romantic criticism that was becoming increasingly anti-feminist as well.

Romance appealed to seventeenth-century women of the upper classes, and gradually to women of the middle class as well, for many reasons—most obviously because it provided an imaginative escape from what for most of them, in a time of arranged marriages, must have been an emotionally dreary life. Romance was associated with imagination by later writers such as Joseph and Thomas Warton, Richard Hurd, and Clara Reeve, who felt their favorite literature had been nearly killed off in the late seventeenth century by an epidemic of "good sense" (Hurd 120).[12] Even then there were those who stated openly that the move away from romance was not a sign of progress toward scientific clarity, or of return to the clean Attic prose of the Greeks, but of cultural decline, the triumph of ugly old merchants over ideally beautiful nymphs and swains. But imagination and reality are not necessarily opposites; it was not at all clear to women readers that romances were any less true than what was normally called reality.

To understand how this could be so, we must examine some of the assumptions behind the critical distinction between romance and novel, particularly the meaning of the "resemblance to truth" that was supposed to separate them. "Novel" and "romance" overlapped during this period in more than terminology, for the claim to exclusive truth in narrative could never be met. It was easy enough for the critic to call a romance false, but it was the romance writer or novelist who then had to try to find out what would make a narrative true; their solutions were many and various, and all unsatisfactory.

As far back as Chrétien de Troyes, romance writers were claiming a degree of historical truth, usually a greater degree than their relatively "false" predecessors.[13] Even verisimilitude (or "vraisemblance") had a number of contradictory meanings in both romances and novels. It might mean observing probability—that is, omitting miracles or coincidences that obscure the workings of natural law, most often what is now meant by "realism."[14] Or it might mean observing laws of moral order, a concept relating to "bienséance" or decorum, usually associated with romance (Davis 32-33)—although the "bad morality" of romance was one of Boileau's chief objections to it (445). Or it might mean failing to observe either set of laws and thus including the fantastic coincidences and unfinished justice of "real life," a commonly stated intention of early novels such as Aphra Behn's *Oroonoko,* which she called a "history." Both romance and novel writers sometimes claimed that their works were literally true while expecting the reader to know that they were fictional; both were also capable of claiming that their stories were fictional while expecting the reader to recognize in them references to current events.[15]

Critical definitions were therefore bound to be simpler and cleaner than the works they were supposed to describe, and no fiction writer completely escaped romance.[16] Male writers generally took greater care than women to avoid the style and themes of seventeenth-century French romance, its pastoral settings and preoccupation with love, but in doing so they simply went back to the earlier, less feminine quest romance and reserved love for the comic ending. Some, such as Richardson, studiously avoided the external trappings of both older and more recent romance, "a hermit and a wood, a battle and a shipwreck" (Samuel Johnson 3:20); but many did not (Fielding's hermits and Smollett's shipwrecks immediately come to mind). None avoided the romance's basic ingredients—adventure and love.

"Romance" and "novel" were difficult to separate, not only because every narrative wound up being a "falsehood," but because the "truth" that "excellent" fiction was supposed to resemble was neither absolute nor universal. Whether truth meant history or current events, women, as members of a subculture, were equally removed from it. History could seem to them a rather boring study, as Jane Austen's Catherine Morland would later remark, with "the men all so good for nothing, and hardly any women at all" (*NA* 108). Nor did women frequent the coffee houses that J. Paul Hunter describes as important centers for the dissemination of "news" ("News" 501).[17] In a sense, official truth was merely verisimilitude for women, something lived second hand.[18]

Romance, however, could seem true to women in several ways. "Adventure" literally denotes events that come to one from without, and therefore the lives of the unempowered are full of it. Though real women were probably not carried off as often as they were in stories, they were commonly given or sold into matrimony—a trend that only became worse as the class of romance writers and readers shifted down from the French nobility to the English bourgeoisie. As for the other main ingredient of romance, love, in "reality" women were supposed not to feel it, for it was a manifestation of self-will that could only be obstructive in a patriarchal courtship system. The marriage for love that by this time formed the standard ending of romance, though "unreal" in the sense that it rarely happened to actual women, was accurate to women's emotional life.

The concentration on love in seventeenth-century French romances made them especially appealing to the female reader; one romance in particular, Honoré d'Urfé's *L'Astrée* (1610-1627), was an important source of inspiration for Madeleine de Scudéry, and hence an important text in the history of women's fiction. This romance puts forth a morality of love, one of the key tenets of which is that a lady by rights belongs to the man who loves her most. Yet, surprisingly, it does not teach the female reader to see herself as a mere object; that was rather the lesson of her experience. In *L'Astrée* the feelings she was not supposed to have are the basis of a whole world and a topic of endless metaphysical discussion.

The intensity of male love in the story endows the female will with a sort of divinity: Astrée and Queen Galathée are immensely powerful, and even the hero, Céladon, is powerless until he dresses in women's clothes. The rampant cross-dressing in *L'Astrée*, according to Louise K. Horowitz, represents an important step in a historical "feminization" process in fiction: "once knights, then shepherds, now transvestites" (254). Céladon spends a considerable portion of the story as the heroine's "female" friend, and when he casts off his disguise his behavior toward her changes very little. Friendship between women is thus a model for romantic love, and the differences between the sexes, both physical and psychological, are minimized.[19] This feature mitigates the effects of the symbolic "otherness" of the romance heroine; it became an important creed in women's "anti-anti-romantic" fiction later in the century.

Of course, the powerful women and sensitive men of *L'Astrée* must have been an escape fantasy for seventeenth-century women readers—and thus, like other romances, it has been seen as a tool used by the patriarchal establishment to support the status quo by "mak[ing] the lives of the dispossessed seem fulfilled" (Perry x).[20] Identifying with the heroine as beloved could be self-defeating, as feminists from Mary Wollstonecraft onward have noted.[21] Exceptional rather than commonplace, above the rest of her sex, the romance heroine competes with her reader, and in imitating her, readers compete with each other rather than joining forces to bring about social change. In any case the heroine cannot be imitated, for as a symbol she has no real character to imitate. Because she is supposed to be unconscious of her beauty and power, the reader, who displays her own consciousness in the act of reading, cannot resemble her.[22] Nevertheless, this heroine could be turned into somebody who would be useful in bringing about gradual improvement in women's lives. When women began writing instead of only reading romances, they were able to make this woman-as-beloved embody their own feelings and perceptions—a necessary step if those feelings were ever to form the basis for action.[23]

When Scudéry took up the pen, she wrote romances that women readers could enter—both literally, in veiled portraits, and through imaginative projection. Scudéry herself appears as Sappho in *Artamenes, or the Grand Cyrus,* thus becoming one of a long line of female "moderns" who, for better or for worse, would bear that classical nickname.[24] Even the heroines of her romances, while retaining their symbolic perfection, possess a consciousness not unlike that of the author, or of the reader, thus opening up new possibilities for "friendship" among the women inside and outside the text.

Clelia, for example, like her male-created predecessors, rarely initiates action (though she does swim the Tiber, an act of heroism that is later disastrously imitated by Charlotte Lennox's Female Quixote); but she does see, and what she sees is her romance's reality. In fact, not being able to act gives her the vantage point that makes her perception reliable, and that makes the male view of reality look skewed. Clelia's father is a Roman despot (not unlike a French or English bourgeois papa) who claims total authority to dispose of his daughter in marriage. She is pursued by two men but obediently refrains from encouraging either. Yet her father blames her for their attention, casting on her all the responsibility for "adventures" over which she has no control (1:46). This tendency to blame the victim was one of the most persistently exposed injustices in women's fiction for more than a century afterward as women writers revealed their own, alternative truth.

Because the heroine does not control the events of her life, the plot of *Clelia* lacks the "realism" of cause and effect that novel readers later came to require. Instead, it is loosely held together by the heroine's feelings and perceptions, as presented in the allegorical picture of her heart, the famous Map of Tender—a highly detailed representation of the psychology of a woman trying to preserve her dignity under the pressures of a patriarchal courtship system. The map assumes, as Clelia's father does not, that her suitors want her real regard and not just her hand and person. Thus it shows how a man may reach the most honored place in Clelia's heart: tender friendship; "for those I beautifie [beatify?] with the title of tender friends, they are but few in number, and they are before so firmly seated in my heart, that they can hardly make any farther progress" (1:41).[25]

As Clelia's friend Celeres interprets the allegory: "You see she hath imagined tenderness may proceed from three different causes, either from a great Esteem, Recognizance or Inclination, which hath obliged her to establish three Cities of Tender upon three Rivers, which derive their names from them, and to make three different ways to go thither, so as we say, Cumes on the Ionian, and Cumes on the Tyrrhene Sea, she makes us say, Tender on Inclination, Tender on Esteem, and Tender on Recognizance" (1:42).[26] The routes to Tender on Esteem and Tender on Recognizance are dotted with villages, as the progress is by slow stages, requiring, for Esteem, "pleasing verses, amorous and gallant Letters . . . Sincerity, Great Heart, Honesty, Generosity, Respect, Exactness, and Goodness," and for Recognizance, "complaisance," "Submission," "small cares," "Assiduity," "Empressement," "great services," "Sensibility," "Divine [obedience]," and "constant friendship" (1:42).[27] A wrong turn leads either to the "Lake of Indifference . . . which by its calm streams without doubt lively presents the thing of which it bears the name in this place," or to the "Sea of Enmity . . . which by the agitation of its waves, fitly agrees with that impetuous passion" (1:42)[28]

To reach Tender on Inclination, on the other hand, one simply proceeds down a river "which runs with such a rapid course, that there can be no lodging along the shore to go to [from] new Amity to Tender" (1:42).[29] "Inclination," then, is a shortcut to Clelia's highest and fondest regard. But the map also makes a contrary statement, for Celeres cites her intention "to describe to us in the Map that she never had love, nor would ever have any thing but tenderness in her heart." She "makes the River of Inclination cast it self into the Sea which is called the dangerous Sea, because it is dangerous for a woman to exceed the limits of friendship, and she makes in pursuit that beyond this Sea is that we call unknown Lands, because in effect we know not what they are . . . to make us understand in a peculiar manner, that she never yet loved, nor could ever receive any" (1:42).[30] Inclination may lead to tender friendship, but it is mysterious and threatening because it may lead beyond it. Its sexual meaning is clearly hinted, both by the danger and by the rapidity of the current, which flows into areas of Clelia's mind which no one, including herself, has explored. By claiming to want friendship rather than love, Clelia sets a limit to the power and importance of sex and hints that she may be happier without it.

But inclination means more than sex; in contrast to tenderness, a passive receptivity that also has sexual overtones, inclination is an active "leaning toward."[31] Though potentially self-destructive, it is paradoxically an expression of will. By refusing to surrender to her own inclinations—like George Eliot's Maggie Tulliver when she refuses to go any further down the Floss with Stephen Guest—Clelia means to avoid being conquered. But in the end, despite her denials, she marries for love, and therefore for inclination, choosing the man whose respect allows these various aspects of her will to harmonize. Aronces's inclination, though strong, is subdued by his even greater tenderness; in contrast, the villain Horatius believes he loves Clelia more because he feels compelled to carry her off by force. As in *L'Astrée,* the heroine is awarded to the man who loves her most; but the man who wins her must be above regarding her as a prize.

The Map of Tender helps to show how the marriage that ends romance could assert the existence and importance of the feminine will. Feminist criticism often points out that the denouement of romance promulgated a myth of romantic love that prevented women from rebelling against matrimony.[32] But since romance heroines marry by their own inclination, often in direct opposition to parental authority, fathers had reason to complain about their daughters' reading habits. Clelia's map could be interpreted as recommending cooperation in arranged marriage, for if a woman is obliged to "recognize" or repay the attentions of her suitors, then the parentally selected candidate was bound to succeed in time, with a little effort. But what Clelia does makes a stronger impression than what she says, and the reader who wished to imitate her by marrying only for love might well oppose her father's plans—or she might imitate Scudéry herself and decline to marry at all. Though known to her friends as the "Princess of Esteem, Lady of Recognizance, Inclination, and Adjacent Lands," Scudéry rejoiced in her "strong propensity against marriage," as she had one of her characters comment in *Artamenes:* "I know quite well that there are many decent men, but when I think of them as husbands I also think of them as masters, and since masters have a tendency to become tyrants, I can, from that moment, only hate them" (Aronson 43-45).

The subversive tendency of Scudéry's romance caused Boileau, who disapproved of romances in general, to single hers out for special censure. In his *Satire X,* he describes what happens to the would-be Clelia in real life:

> At first you will see her, as in *Clelia,*
> Receiving her lovers under the soft title of friends,
> Holding herself back with them to small, permissible
>   attentions:

Then, soon in high water on the River of Tender,
Sail where she will, say everything, hear (understand)
    everything.
And do not presume that Venus, or Satan
Will let her remain within the terms of the romance.[33] [67]

Boileau here helps to establish the French romance's smutty reputation for future generations of English critics. Although Scudéry wrote about love in the chastest and most platonic manner—and although Boileau, kinder to her than later English critics would be to English women novelists, admitted that she was personally untainted by "the bad morality taught in her romances" (445)—he warns that the young girl following her directions in Clelia would find Venus only in the form of Satan: looking for love, she would find sex.[34] This cynical reduction of love to sex was common in much male anti-romantic writing and continually elicited romantic opposition from the women writers in this study. Attacks such as this surprised Scudéry, who thought her version of love too obviously idealized for anyone to try for it (Aronson 146). But as we have seen, Boileau was right to sense danger in that "say everything, and understand everything," in the power of the Map of Tender to give form to women's vague desires and discontents.

Further satire of Scudéry in this poem suggests that she threatened more than male domestic authority. For Scudéry was not only a romance writer but a précieuse, a prominent member of several salons in which women as well as men set up for critics and judged the merits of literary works, both ancient and modern. The affected "Belle" of the tenth satire, for example,

Laughs at the vain amateurs of Greek and of Latin;
Places Aristotle and Cotin in a scale;
Then, with a hand still more delicate and more skilful
Coldly weighs Chappelain and Virgil;
Points out many weaknesses in the latter;
However admitting he has some merit.[35] [74]

The précieuses are condemned for being on what Boileau considers the wrong side of the "ancients vs. moderns" controversy; although they praise the ancients, they prove themselves deplorably modern by presuming to weigh ancient and modern works in the same balance—an error they cannot help because the ancients were available to most women only in modern translations. On the same grounds romance writers were also deplorably modern, for however much they invoked classical ancestors, their own works were written in the vernacular.[36] Scudéry's claim that her works imitated Virgil's epics (Aronson 55-56) was therefore doubly discounted. Yet if she had avoided this criticism by learning Greek and Latin, she would have resembled the female pedant who is also condemned in Boileau's satire. Thus, Boileau permitted women neither to seize the keys to the magic kingdom of criticism by force, nor to earn them by hard work.

As we have seen, romance had long been considered trivial, and it was increasingly being considered feminine; but it was Boileau's satire that first damned both women and romance by mutual association. His attack on Scudéry marks the beginning of a long struggle between male critics and female romance writers and novelists that has yet to be fully resolved—a struggle that will be chronicled in the following chapters.[37] Of course, gender aside, it is arguably the theorist's job to create distinctions and the practitioner's job to blur them.[38] But this particular battle was clearly, in part, a battle of the sexes, a continued attempt to fortify serious literature against the encroachment of women's writings, which were becoming ever more abundant and popular. When novels were the preferred form, writers such as Henry Fielding scornfully classed Eliza Haywood's productions with French romances. And later, when romance was enjoying a new respectability, writers such as Sir Walter Scott wrote patronizingly of the "realist" Jane Austen. The need to draw and redraw lines that would keep women on the wrong side added zest to critics' attempts to use "resemblance to truth" to separate "romance" from "novel." For their part, women writers often accepted the critical categories in theory; but in practice they showed themselves more interested in combining and harmonizing than in separating and excluding.

The women in this study never fully severed their connection with the d'Urfé-Scudéry tradition. Their works cross categories, not only because romance and novel were not really separable, nor only because, to them, romance had a kind of reality, but because by maintaining some allegiance to a discredited style they could set alternative realities side by side in their fictions and permit them to comment on each other. As a result they revealed large gaps between what women wanted, what they had a right to demand, and what they were likely to receive—especially in love and marriage.[39] The attempt to depict in fiction a believable world in which women may love and be respected encouraged readers to claim their basic human right to choose, or not choose, a husband. Thus fiction affected life; and life in turn affected fiction. For as the conditions of women's lives improved, romance and realism could more fully coalesce, creating more consistent narratives. Jane Austen's works may strike readers of today as "modern" in a way those of her foremothers do not, not only because of her own talent, but because the struggles of the previous century created the conditions that permitted her talent to operate.

In the following chapters I will discuss the interplay of romance and realism in selected texts, not to give a comprehensive history of romance during this period, nor of women's fiction, nor even of English women's fiction, but to mark important stages of development. In the earlier works, the relationship between romance and realism is simplest. An ideal romance hero or heroine is brought into contact with the real world and is destroyed by its corruption. The romance world provides love, which the real world tries to kill, and the result is adventure—that is, suffering. Thus Aphra Behn's Oroonoko and Imoinda perish at the hands of European capitalists, and women in Delarivière Manley's romantic-satiric allegories sacrifice their reputations and lives to love in a world dominated by heartless, power-seeking men.

By the mid-eighteenth century, tragedy begins to give way to comedy as heroines such as Eliza Haywood's Betsy Thoughtless and Charlotte Lennox's Harriot Stuart attempt to succeed at life by renouncing love and romance. But tragedy nearly overtakes them as they learn that love is essential to their happiness and goodness. Thus an ambivalence about the romance emerges. These novels, along with Lennox's *The Female Quixote,* are partly anti-romances; they endorse love while warning against the adventure it brings. Haywood's and Lennox's objection to the romance is moral as well as practical; the heroines' desire for attention—their willingness to *be* heroines—stems from the sin of vanity. In Fanny Burney's novels, the sin seems even greater: there romance becomes a symbol of the selfish individualism that threatened to destroy the social order. Burney almost recommends the sacrifice of love to prevent painful and wicked adventure; but in the end she too gives her heroines their romantic denouement.

Burney ultimately found that, despite her literary and moral objections to the romance, she was unable to describe the isolated and adventure-filled lives of her heroines, or to reward them as they deserve, without it. Like Alice's Looking-Glass House, romance was there to greet her at the end of every path that seemed to lead away from it. Each of her novels is more romantic than the one before, so that Ann Radcliffe was able to build a Gothic romance, *The Italian,* on a plot very similar to that of Burney's *Cecilia.* Though Radcliffe rejected the realistic novel of manners, her message is similar to Burney's: both novels associate love and adventure, passion and imagination, with insanity. Yet realism seemed less necessary to Radcliffe

because in the later eighteenth century critics were showing a renewed interest in older romances, particularly those of the Eliz-
abethan period. This change in the critical climate also affected the
novels of Jane Austen by reminding readers that romance, though
superficially "false," had once been used to express sacred truths.
Austen both satirized and welcomed romance elements in her realistic fictions, using them to describe the relationship between the real
lives of ordinary individuals and the encompassing romance, or religious allegory, that to a Christian gave that life meaning.

The progression I will describe is not exactly a "female tradition"
of the novel. Most of the writers in this study were less interested in
literary sisterhood or daughterhood than in trying to make their own
separate peace with critical authority. Haywood renounced the novel
as practiced by Manley (and by herself in the first half of her career),
Lennox attacked Haywood's morals, and Burney named only men as
her literary ancestors in the preface to *Evelina*. When Radcliffe took
up romance instead of the Burneyan novel of manners, Austen re-
sponded with a novel of manners that satirized Radcliffean Gothic.
Often these writers denied the romance aspects of their writing in
order to win intellectual respect as rational creatures, unable to
anticipate that once they were finally believed they would simply be
dismissed on new grounds. Nevertheless, in affecting and being affected by the conditions of life, these women writers (along with
others too numerous to include in this study) did create an important
line of development not traced in standard courses and texts on the
history of the novel. Despite the efforts of feminist criticism, those
courses and texts still mainly consider Defoe, Fielding, Richardson,
Smollett, and Sterne, though the stretches that are often required to
lead students from one to the next should suggest that something
important has been left out of the picture.

In contrast, the line of development I see, though it moves the
canonical novelists to the periphery, has a logic of its own. I have
called the work a "secret history" of the novel in this introductory
chapter in part to pay my respects to the popular women writers of
romans à clef—Scudéry, Behn, Manley, and Haywood—but also to
borrow something of their self-consciously different, perhaps even
perverse, "feminine" angle on reality. Just as Behn would describe
Monmouth's rebellion in terms of the Duke's affairs of the heart, and
just as Manley would characterize the Duke of Marlborough by his
amours rather than his campaigns, I have chosen here to describe the
history of the novel through the works of a few women novelists. The
result is no more comprehensive than male-centered studies—but
neither is it less so. Furthermore, whereas women's novels rarely fit

well into the theoretical structures designed to explain male novelists, the structure of my own study leaves room for the inclusion of the more standard "major" works in all their complexity. In that sense it is a step toward the more complete, integrative history of the novel that still needs to be written.

One would think that that history would have been written already, given the new availability of editions of neglected women's novels, the proliferation of scholarly discussion of those novels, and the dazzling historicist criticism of the last decade. Studies by Lennard Davis, J. Paul Hunter, and Michael McKeon, for example, subtly and convincingly show the novel rising, or being born, out of social and ideological instabilities of the early eighteenth century. All, reacting against Northrop Frye's archetypal approach (among other approaches), distinguish the novel sharply from the romance; Davis even questions whether romances such as Scudéry's were a substantial influence on the novel at all (25, 41). Yet the social and intellectual currents each of these critics describes did not affect women in the same way that they affected men; nor do the novels of Aphra Behn, a woman who is sometimes called the first novelist, depart as radically from the French tradition as those of Daniel Defoe, the man who is usually called the first novelist.[40] These studies break down generic barriers by showing the interrelatedness of novels and other kinds of writing, and other manifestations of popular culture; but while exhaustively explicating one period in history, they play down connections with the past, the similarity between the impulses toward truth and verisimilitude that produced what they call novels and those that affected the earliest romance writers.[41] (A broader historical sweep may be found in Nelson's *Fact or Fiction,* and in Adams's *Travel Literature and the Evolution of the Novel.*) And though all these writers make serious efforts to include women novelists, they continue to make theoretical distinctions that do not accurately describe those novelists' practices.

That these and other "mainstream" studies do not fully incorporate the work of feminist scholarship may be due in part to assumptions inherent in some of that scholarship. Since the days of Mary Wollstonecraft, heightened awareness of the impossible conditions under which women artists attempted to create has led to the almost inescapable conclusion that their works must be seriously flawed—especially, as John Stuart Mill believed, with respect to originality.[42] Since the 1970s, many writers have been pointing out that women have not been completely powerless—though to prove this they have sometimes had to redefine "power" in some very tricky ways (Newton xiii-xv). Today, as Janet Todd notes in her survey, many branches of feminist criticism denigrate or simply ignore the works of early women writers because they inhabited an unenlightened age, or failed to illustrate Lacan's version of Freudian mythology, or belonged to a privileged class. The American style of feminist literary analysis, best illustrated by Sandra Gilbert and Susan Gubar, favors nineteenth-century novels such as Brontë's *Villette,* which can be made to reveal subtexts containing something like current feminist awareness, but this "double text" approach works less well with earlier authors whose values are more alien to our own (*Feminist Literary History* 29).[43] By regarding these early women's novels with "double vision," some critics conclude that romance elements are a sign of the crushing effects of patriarchy and so perpetuate the sense of their unoriginality, their "minor" status, and their marginality.[44]

My approach, both historicist and feminist, differs from those summarized above. First, with respect to historicism: Though I believe that more work needs to be done to provide a fuller sense of the novel's social milieu, I have not attempted to provide that "gyno-critical" context here; this study is historical in the sense that the texts discussed are recognized as existing in history rather than as trans-historical myths, whether Frye's or Lacan's.[45] At the same time, I do argue here that "novel" and "romance" are not the completely distinct categories they have appeared to be in recent historicist criticism, particularly when those terms are applied to women's fiction.

In the chapters that follow, I will use "novel" to describe the works of the English women writers discussed—though that term was not used consistently at the time—because all of them show at least some of the characteristics that are now usually considered novelistic. When I wish to bring out the relationship between these novels and earlier romances, I will speak of their "romance characteristics" or "romance conventions." However, my use of these terms rests on the basic conviction that the novel never has fully separated itself from the romance—perhaps, as Frye wrote, it never can (*Secular Scripture* 15)—and that it can best be understood, as Clara Reeve understood it, as a variety of romance that aims at a particular kind of "resemblance to truth" (*Progress* 1:14). In later chapters I will further distinguish "romance," a type of prose narrative, from "Romanticism," the late eighteenth-century movement in the arts.

Second, with respect to feminist criticism: I hope that my emphasis on textual analysis in the context of history will lead beyond the awareness that women novelists were forced to lead a double life, to an understanding of the ways these women chose to use the conventions and traditions that were available to them. That is, romance will not appear here as an imposition of patriarchy that was rebelliously subverted by realism, but as a potential means of self-expression.[46]

I believe that this approach helps prepare the way for a more positive evaluation of these women's achievements—an evaluation that should be possible now that we have been taught to appreciate "heteroglossia" and to praise works for their inconsistencies and tensions.[47] Until such a reevaluation takes place, no amount of women's studies courses or separate Norton Anthologies or cheap editions of nearly-lost novels will affect the way "the novel" is understood and taught. Dale Spender gives a timely reminder about the fate of Julia Kavanaugh, a nineteenth-century scholar of early women's fiction who thought her findings would lead to a revision of the canon, but whose work has now been forgotten (222). When editors of women's novels no longer have to disclaim the novels' "greatness" like the writers of the blurbs found at the end of Virago paperbacks, we may be on the way to achieving for these pioneers the respect and inclusion they were usually unable to secure for themselves.

The women writers in this study used romance to assert the legitimacy of feminine "truth"; yet an important tenet of that alternative truth was that, in various ways, women and men were more alike than men knew. Their truth may or may not accord with our own theories of sexual difference, and it certainly does not accord with the present belief in the partial and provisional nature of truth itself.[48] Yet it had its moment in history; and at this moment in our understanding of the novel, it is an excellent truth to remember.

1

Oroonoko
A Pastoral History

> Young I'd have him too, and fair,
> Yet a man; with crisped hair
>
> . . . .
>
> Even nose and cheek withal
> Smooth as is the billiard ball;
>
> . . . .
>
> Till he cherished too much beard,
> And make Love or me afeard.
>
> —Ben Jonson

WHEN Aphra Behn wrote *Oroonoko* in 1688, the novel was still "fresh" in the way romance had been in the Middle Ages: that is, free from the "ballast of theory" (Erich Auerbach 132-33). If one were going to be that strange and new phenomenon—a professional woman writer—one would very likely be drawn to pitch one's tent in this open territory. Behn first turned to prose fiction in 1684 during a lull in her successful career as a playwright, poet, and translator, no doubt to earn the money she desperately needed (Duffy 226-28, Goreau 255-56, Woodcock 169-70). Not surprisingly, she brought to the novel many of the materials of her earlier works, all of which had links with the French romance, and particularly with its pastoral ancestors. By combining romance elements with true, topical stories, Behn may have founded the English novel.[1]

Just as the seventeenth-century romance had become "feminine" in the hands of Scudéry, the novel as Behn practiced it was ideally suited to the expression of women's perceptions and concerns. And it was much needed for that purpose, for the literary tradition it helped to keep alive was dying out quickly in the more established genres. In the late seventeenth century, anti-romantic writing was found not only in misogynist religious tracts and sermons, but in decadent, satiric forms of what had once been the literature of love. Women were used to seeing themselves as harlots in the writings of both high and low church clergy; they were now also seeing themselves as whores in the satiric romances, mock-pastoral lyrics, and stage comedies of Restoration wits.[2] A wave of sexual disgust, it seems, was making the romance's glorification of love, and of women along with it, seem absurdly or wickedly unrealistic. When Behn took her nickname, Astrea, from Honoré d'Urfé's *L'Astrée* (simultaneously invoking his sources: Spenser's *The Faerie Queene* and Ovid's *Metamorphoses*), she asserted that romance still had meaning.[3] In her pastoral lyrics and plays, and finally in her prose fiction, she used the romance to express the sentiment that love was the greatest and purest source of joy available to men and women.

Behn's writings invite men to join her in celebrating love; they attempt to minimize the gender differences that anti-feminist, anti-romantic literature exaggerated. But by going against the current Behn became involved in the old controversy of ancients vs. moderns, which Boileau had connected with the even older controversy of men vs. women. Although today one would probably see most of Behn's sources as high culture and Behn herself as highly educated, her inability to read Greek and Latin made her of necessity a "modern," cut off from the classical sources of true taste.[4]

One may sense some anger at women's educational disadvantage beneath Behn's boast that it is in fact an advantage: "for I have heard the most of that which bears the name of Learning, and which has abused such quantities of Ink and Paper, and continually employs so many ignorant, unhappy souls for ten, twelve, twenty years in the University (who yet poor wretches think they are doing something all the while) as Logick etc. and several other things (that shall be nameless lest I misspell them) are much more absolutely nothing than the errantest Play that e'er was writ" (1:221). And so women have an opening: "For waving the examination why women having equal education with men, were not as capable of knowledge, of whatsoever sort as well as they: I'll only say as I have touch'd before, that Plays have no great room for that which is men's great advantage over women, that is Learning . . . and as for our Modern ones, except our most unimitable Laureat, I dare to say I know of none that write at such a formidable rate, but that a woman may well hope to reach their greatest heights" (*The Dutch Lover, Works* 1:224). Behn's view of masculine erudition was rather like Virginia Woolf's cynical alphabetizing of Mr. Ramsay; she believed in intellectual equality to men without their learning, using Cowley's example to defend her practice of "translating" Sappho and Ovid by paraphrasing literal translations.[5] In her works, women who try to substitute Greek and Latin for native wit and modern languages (such as Lady Knowell in *Sir*

Patient Fancy) make themselves as ridiculous as Ben Jonson's "masculine" Lady Would-be.

Men's classical education was the basis of their critical authority. Though Behn does not question the predominance of the "unimitable Laureat" Dryden, her remarks strike at the roots of his power and give the old controversy a new dimension: ancient vs. modern, man vs. woman, becomes also critic vs. artist. The peculiar nature of the novel almost necessarily makes rebels of its practitioners, for it is the novelist's job to convince readers that fiction is true, and the critic's job to identify and label fiction as fiction. Thus the first novelists had to keep a step ahead of the definitions that gave the game away: if romances were false, they wrote novels; and if novels were also exposed—what then?

When critics were themselves novelists, their definitions tended to spoil the game only for others while reserving "truth" for themselves. Such a motive may have inspired William Congreve's well-known definition of novel and romance in his preface to *Incognita,* published in 1692 (three years after Behn's death). As a "modern" fiction writer it was in Congreve's interest to make his categories absolute, to show the new as believable and the old as fantastic; but in doing so he overlooked some of the novel's main ingredients. Romance, he says, is "generally composed of the Constant Loves and invincible Courages of Hero's, Heroins, Kings and Queens, Mortals of the first Rank, and so forth; where lofty Language, miraculous Contingencies and impossible Performances, elevate and surprize the Reader into a giddy Delight, which leaves him flat upon the Ground whenever he gives of [*sic*], and vexes him to think how he has suffer'd himself to be pleased and transported, concern'd and afflicted at the several Passages which he has Read . . . when he is forced to be very well convinced that 'tis all a lye." Novels, on the other hand, "come near us, and represent to us Intrigues in practice, delight us with Accidents and odd Events, but not such as are wholly unusual or unpresidented, such which not being so distant from our Belief bring also the pleasure nearer us." The passage concludes with a deceptively neat antithesis: "Romances give more of Wonder, Novels more Delight" (*Works* 1:111). Deceptive, because by this definition *Incognita* itself is more a romance—or, perhaps, a satiric anti-romance—than a novel.[6]

Behn's practice in *Oroonoko* (and in her earlier novel, *Love Letters between a Nobleman and His Sister*) points to the problem with Congreve's theory. Behn too is all for "bringing the pleasure nearer us" by making her story seem true; she claims it is not only realistic, but real:[7] "I do not pretend, in giving you the History of this Royal

Slave, to entertain my Reader with Adventures of a feign'd Hero, whose Life and Fortunes Fancy may manage at the Poet's pleasure; nor in relating the truth, design to adorn it with any Accidents, but such as arrived in earnest to him: And it shall come simply into the World, recommended by its own proper Merits, and natural Intrigues; there being enough of Reality to support it, and to render it diverting, without the addition of Invention" (*Works* 5:129). But the purpose of these facts is hardly to weaken "wonder"; she goes on to say that she has left out any facts that "might prove tedious and heavy to my Reader" and has retained only the most exciting adventures. Even from Congreve's own descriptions it is clear that the goal of the novelist was not really to replace wonder with delight (Richetti 175). The romance had simply ceased to provide wonder, apart from the reader's wonder at himself for being taken in by such nonsense; as Henry Fielding would say much later in *Tom Jones,* the new realism was merely an attempt to get wonder back (Hunter, "Novels," 484-85).

The new readers of fiction had, in McKeon's phrase, an "omnivorous empiricist appetite for 'real events'" (63); they wanted "news"—that paradoxical combination of the wonderful and the factual (Hunter, "News," 510). Unlike Fielding and the other male novelists McKeon describes, however, Behn was not ashamed to admit that her main purpose was to entertain her readers; education was a minor, secondary goal. Though she praised common sense and direct experience over scholasticism, empiricism—and the reportage that developed from it—was for her not so much a moral ideology as a new means to an old end.[8]

The distinction between novel and romance was not as clear for Behn as for Congreve; she casually associated "novel" with "conquests" in love, "rarity," and "comedy" (*Love Letters* 118-19). Her idea of a "novel" shows how easily the term could have become outmoded almost before it was really current, a casualty in the never ending struggle for the illusion of truth. Although novels were supposed to be more believable than romances, the label Behn preferred for *Oroonoko* was "history"—a label both historians and romance writers had long employed as a way of claiming to be factual (Adams 30). As narrator of *Oroonoko* Behn refers to an incident within the "history" as a "Novel": the coincidental meeting of the hero with his wife, who is supposed to be dead (5:173). This label sets off by contrast the greater probability of the surrounding narrative, as the romances *Don Quixote* reads make his "real life" relatively plausible.[9] Paradoxically, the term also makes the "Novel" incident itself more believable—in McKeon's formulation, "strange, therefore true" (47, 111-12)—for if real life can sometimes be "Novel" in this way, then there is no reason a novel such as *Oroonoko* can't be real.[10] But the story ends, not with the lovers' reunion, but with their death. Perhaps the biggest difference between a "novel" and life, in Behn's view, is that life is not a comedy.

Behn's shifting terminology blurs the distinctions that critical theory attempts to sharpen; her "history" is as romantic as any romance, not only in its wonderful adventures, but in its glorification of love. The rest of this chapter will explore Behn's view of love as the natural uniter of genders and literary genres—though ultimately it falls martyr to the forces of controversy and artificial division. First, I will discuss this view as it is set forth in her pastoral lyrics; second, I will show how the same ideas shape and inform *Oroonoko*.

Though modern readers are accustomed to viewing the pastoral as a highly artificial form, there is a sense in which it shares with the novel the paradox of realism, or believable wonder. Pastoral presents ideal beauty against a highly detailed, natural background. The beauty seduces the imagination, and the background makes surrender easy. The natural setting of Behn's poems is not essentially different from the countryside of Kent where she grew up (Duffy 27, Goreau 18). By peopling it with the gods and goddesses, swains and nymphs of traditional pastoral, she removes the unnecessary surface details of daily life to isolate "nature" in its more typical seventeenth-century sense—the essential qualities of life, and of man. Pastoral allows Behn to explore the "nature" of love before its corruption by modern cynicism.

The most complete exploration of this theme occurs in "The Golden Age," a pastoral lyric published in 1684 but probably written in 1679 (Duffy 176). Here we see Behn's vision of erotic love in its ideal state, when sex was not a sin, and when therefore there was no need to fear snakes, "With whom the Nymphs did Innocently play,/No spightful Venom in the wantons lay;/But to the touch were Soft, and to the sight were Gay" (*Works* 6:139).

> The flowry Meads, the Rivers and the Groves,
> Were fill'd with little Gay-wing'd Loves:
>   That ever smil'd and danc'd and Play'd,
> And now the woods, and now the streames invade,
> And where they came all things were gay and glad:
> When in the Myrtle Groves the Lovers sat
>   Opprest with a too fervent heat;
> A Thousand Cupids fann'd their wings aloft,
> And through the Boughs the yeilded Ayre would waft:

Whose parting Leaves discovered all below,
And every God his own soft power admir'd,
And smil'd and fann'd, and sometimes bent his Bow;
Where e'er he saw a Shepherd uninspir'd. [6:140-41]

Maureen Duffy's use of the word "baroque" for this type of description helps legitimize it by placing it correctly within a continental movement in the arts (Intro. to *Love Letters* x), although the word was not applied in this way until the late nineteenth century, and then usually with reference to architecture; it is a word rarely applied to English literature of any period.[11] Duffy no doubt means to suggest a comparison between the mannered ornamentation of the poem and that of the music of Bach or, more important, the paintings of Claude Lorraine, famous for depicting scenes from the romances of Ariosto and Tasso. Behn's pastoral is pictorial (as Claude's painting is poetic) in its paradoxical ability to freeze characters in action, as on a Grecian urn.[12] But "baroque" is also used disparagingly to suggest oddity, garishness, and bad taste. Long before the term itself was current, those negative connotations were already associated with baroque art, particularly with elaborate and highly wrought prose; one might say that Scudéry seemed baroque in this negative sense to Boileau. In Behn's poem the defense of love is also a defense of the baroque, because both were threatened by empiricism, with its emphasis on facts, its worship of reason, and its denial of the imagination.

The more fashionable, plainer prose, though "modern" and scientific like the writings of the Royal Society, was also "ancient" and Attic, well supported by critical tradition. Romantic prose, on the other hand, though becoming passé, was "modern" in the sense Boileau deplored because it resisted Aristotelian classification. If Behn's shepherds were less idealized, the celebration of eroticism in "The Golden Age" might belong to the "mythos" of comedy (Frye, *Anatomy of Criticism*, 164). But the conventions of pastoral allow Behn to portray them as innocents who can revel in erotic love without comedy's traditional coarseness or loss of dignity. The high ornamentation also adds a grandeur Aristotle deemed appropriate to tragedy—and the poem does end tragically; but the fall is made to appear "unnatural," perhaps avoidable. And until the fall occurs, the categories of "comic" and "tragic" are irrelevant.

Gender distinctions are also minimal in Behn's pastoral. Though men are described as "conquerors" in the Golden Age, their aggressiveness does not amount to a tragic flaw; their desires are really no different from, and no greater than, those of the women they conquer:

> The Nymphs were free, no nice, no coy disdain; [*sic*]
> Deny'd their Joyes, or gave the Lover pain;
> The yielding Maid but kind Resistance makes;
> Trembling and blushing are not marks of shame,
>   But the Effect of kindling Flame:
> Which from the sighing burning Swain she takes,
> While she with tears all soft, and down-cast-eyes,
> Permits the Charming Conqueror to win the prize. [6:140-41]

Gender is comparatively insignificant because both the shepherds and the shepherdesses are primarily aesthetic objects—and, as in *L'Astrée,* they look very much alike.[13] Céladon, the hero of d'Urfé's romance, disguises himself as the woman Alexis so that he may live with Astrée in the greatest possible intimacy. When he finally reveals his true identity, he merely says who he is, without even changing his costume; the embarrassed Astrée is "astonished" at the "blindness"— the mere presumption of his femininity—that had prevented her from seeing the truth before (300). Similarly, in Behn's *Love Letters,* a pastoral roman à clef, Philander could easily be female: "but your face! your lovely face, inclining to round, large piercing languishing black eyes, delicate proportion'd nose, charming dimpled mouth, plump red lips, inviting and swelling, white teeth, small and even, fine complexion, and beautiful turn!" (19).

Love between such identical beautiful objects—if one can imagine them loving—is a form of narcissism.[14] In *Love Letters,* in which the pastoral names are merely thin covers for real people, this self-love degenerates into ordinary, comic vanity, a debased version of romance's traditional "vanité." One laughs at Sylvia's bombastic hymn to her own reflection—"Gods! Can this beauty be despised? This shape! This face! This youth! This air!" (158; see also 163)—as later readers would laugh at the conceited Harriot Stuart, Betsy Thoughtless, and Arabella, the Female Quixote. But in the not-yet-fallen world of "The Golden Age," narcissism is still noble and innocent because the nymphs and swains lack the reader's, or viewer's, consciousness; beauty is part of their landscape, of the air they breathe—if one can imagine them breathing.

The resemblance between the shepherds and shepherdesses in Behn's pastorals suggests bisexuality as well as narcissism. Just as Astrée permitted "Alexis" to "kiss my throat, my mouth and my eyes" (300), Behn's Sylvia observes that "both sexes were undone with looking on" Philander (19); Octavio falls for Sylvia without knowing whether she is a man or a woman (114). Bisexuality was common, though not quite respectable, in Behn's day, in life as well as in literature—though on this subject life and literature are not easy to separate. Behn wrote many semi-erotic poems to women during her life, including Lady Morland and Elizabeth Barry (Amoret) (6:175, 157). The apparent homosexuality in these poems may be merely a new twist acquired by an old convention when seventeenth-century women (Katherine Philips as well as Behn) began writing in what had been a male genre, with Sappho as their only female predecessor. But her poem "To the fair Clarinda, who made Love to me, imagin'd more than Woman" seems to suggest something further:

> In pity to our Sex sure thou wer't sent,
> That we might Love, and yet be Innocent:
> For sure no Crime with thee we can commit;
> Or if we shou'd—thy Form excuses it. [6:363]

These lines seem to support Lillian Faderman's suggestion that erotic love between women in the seventeenth century was not considered fornication, for "without a proper tool the job cannot be done" (34). Apparently, however, the toleration was not absolute; Behn's supposed lesbian affair with the actress Emily Price added to her profligate image (Duffy 128-29).[15]

In seventeenth-century life, as opposed to literature, homosexual attachments were not a sign of sexual equality or proximity. Duffy and Angeline Goreau both suggest that Behn may have become romantically interested in women after her miserable affair with John Hoyle (Duffy 277, Goreau 205). The "unisex" standards of beauty made love of one's own sex easy, but it was the war between the sexes—apparent in Behn's relationship with Hoyle—that made such love desirable. This tragic affair, fully described in a series of letters to Lycidus, subsisted on pain caused by Hoyle's unwillingness or incapacity to see resemblance between the sexes.[16] Whereas Behn's possible homosexuality was based on a sense that genders are interchangeable, Hoyle's actual homosexuality (he was tried for sodomy) seems to have accompanied a view of woman as an alien and inferior species.

The affair followed the stereotypical pattern that would later become central to the novels of Delarivière Manley: after making love Behn became more fond, Hoyle less; he insisted on her devotion, yet refused his own. Her letters reveal a constant, unsuccessful attempt to bring his behavior in line with that of romance heroes such as Sylvandre in *L'Astrée,* who asks a cynical roué, "Why do you want the woman you will love a little to want you to love a lot?" (49).[17]

Apparently unable to grasp that Hoyle wanted mastery rather than equality, Behn asked him the same question: "Greedy Lycidus!" she wrote to him, "Unconscionable and ungenerous! You would not be in love for all the world, yet wish I were so. Uncharitable!—Would my fever cure you? or a curse on me make you blessed? Say Lycidus, will it? I have heard, when two souls kindly meet 'tis a vast pleasure, as vast as the curse must be, when kindness is not equal; and why should you believe that necessary for me, that will be very incommode for you?" (Goreau 200).

Like many women of her time—and of the somewhat similar period of the 1960s—Behn found that "free love" was not really "free" for women as long as the sexes were viewed as polar opposites.[18] Behn traces the history of this unnatural polarization in "The Golden Age." Though love and beauty are as natural to men as to women, men (like Lycidus) are "Greedy"; they have sacrificed their better nature in order to overdevelop their instinct to "conquer," until finally they can only "rape" both women and the earth instead of enjoying them. "Right and Property" have evolved from this aggressiveness, and from them the "Tyrant Honour"—in the sense of a woman's reputation for chastity—which she curses throughout two whole stanzas (6:140-43). Because men have made women their property, women must now be ashamed of their desires. Hence they cover themselves with veils, "all the Charmingst part of Beauty hid." In natural retaliation, women become coquettes:

> It [Honour] gathers up the flowing Hair
> That loosely plaid with wanton Air.
> The Envious Net, and stinted order hold,
> The lovely Curls of Jet and shining Gold;
> No more neglected on the Shoulders hurl'd:
> Now drest to Tempt, not gratify the World. [6:142]

When love becomes barter, men and women are on opposing sides of a business transaction; men have the demand, women the supply. Those lovers who do not consent to be vulgarized into comedy become tragically ennobled, when they want merely to be innocently happy. Behn's vision of reality is thus darkened by her sense that, in destroying love, men have brought unnecessary tragedy to both sexes.

As the alienation of the sexes pushed Behn's romantic vision into tragedy, it had the opposite effect on the works of male wits such as Rochester. The difference between these two poets' visions of love is so extreme that one is tempted to induce from it (as Goreau nearly does) a "universal," natural antagonism between men and women (178).

But Behn believed that at heart men and women—and she and Rochester—were more alike than different.

Rochester deliberately subverted and uglified pastoral, as in this satiric persuasion to love "Song":

Phillis, be gentler I advice,
    Make up for time mispent,
When Beauty on its Death-Bed lyes,
    'Tis high time to repent.

Such is the Malice of your Fate,
    That makes you old so soon,
Your pleasure ever comes too late
    How early e're begun.

Think what a wretched thing is she,
    Whose Stars contrive in spight,
The Morning of her love shou'd be,
    Her fading Beauties Night.

Then if to make your ruin more,
    You'll peevishly be coy,
Dye with the scandal of a Whore,
    And never know the joy. [*Poems* 36]

The speaker here knows something Phillis is supposed to learn: that love is not a high spiritual matter but a vulgar comedy. He attacks the romance of beauty with a "realism" of the ugly and gross.[19] Like the speaker of "The Golden Age," he claims to see love without its veils, but to him that also means without its beauty or seriousness— qualities Phillis feebly puts on to enhance her value. The poet's gambit here is more than mere literary iconoclasm. Goreau's excellent discussion of this genre of poem shows that it voices the prevailing attitude among Rochester's circle, representing the way real "gentlemen" treated demimondaines such as actresses, who would be punished with "the scandal of a Whore" whether they granted favors or withheld them (Goreau 161, 168-73, Woodcock 56).

If, as Goreau says, "Rochester's attitude toward women, sex, and love represented everything that [Behn] opposed," how could it also be true that "at the same time she genuinely admired him and found him attractive" (213)? Possibly she sensed, or imagined, behind the cynical persona an idealism in some ways like her own, turned into angry satire at the "cheat" of love's illusion. (I suspect she may also have fallen for Hoyle because she wrongly imagined his libertinism disguised similar depths of sensitivity.) Like Hoyle, Rochester was bisexual, and like Behn's poetic persona, his seems to have turned to his own sex out of disappointment with the other; hence his poem "Love a Woman! y'are an Ass," which ends, "There's a sweet soft Page, of mine,/ Does the trick worth Forty Wenches" (*Poems* 25). Women are the targets of Rochester's satire because they have proved to be all too unlike the goddesses of romance. Poems such as "To Phillis in foul linen" make women symbols of real physical love; the daring obscenity seems to be a cover for embarrassment and horror, like the jokes of early adolescent boys:

> Fair nasty Nymph, be clean and kind,
>   And all my joys restore;
> By using Paper still behind,
>   And Spunges for before. [*Poems* 45-46]

His page, presumably, bathed—and did not menstruate. Though we would seem to be a long way from Behn's Cupids, their absence is conspicuous; one can almost see them flying away, as they would later do, literally, in Swift's "Strephon and Chloe." The disgusted speaker is still hankering for his unfallen youth in the "Myrtle Groves"—or perhaps only for the days of the courtiers' exile in romantic France, land of the bidet.

Rochester's satires are like all the best works of the wits in striking faint overtones of romantic despair along with their Hobbesian cynicism. Wycherley's *The Country Wife,* for instance, ends with Horner trapped in his own too-successful cuckolding scheme, overrun with women clamoring for his "china." Sex ultimately destroys love, for mere physical pleasure creates an increasingly urgent need for new challenges, as Philander in *Love Letters* says (165), until in the end one would almost prefer celibacy. No wonder Horner would degenerate in a few years into Congreve's jaded Fainall, who plays villain to the more sentimental libertine Mirabell in *The Way of the World.* And no wonder the Restoration wits wore an air of world-weary boredom long before the age of thirty.

Some of Behn's female characters, such as Sylvia, take up this rakish pose in self-defense, conquering and despising lovers by dozens (*Love Letters* 134); but despite ubiquitous poetic complaints about women's fickleness and inconstancy during this period, Behn believed libertinism was not natural to women: "without all dispute, Women are by Nature more Constant and Just, than Men" (*The History of the Nun, Works* 5:263). The remark suggests that love is comic for men, who see lovers as interchangeable, and tragic for women, who totally devote themselves to only one; but the difference is moot, for her comment is part of a disquisition on inconstancy in both sexes. And more important, Behn did not believe that men were rakes at heart either, for in the Golden Age, men were as constant as women would like to be, "every Vow inviolably true" (6:141). They had simply become inconstant—and cynical—by "over consuming" in an age that had turned love into commerce. While Philander still loves Sylvia, he proves a devotion equal to hers by putting his life on the line for her twice; but when he tires of her he cheerfully tosses her away. By concluding, as the anti-romantic wits did, that what does not last forever is not real, they implied a respect for eternity similar to Behn's desire to turn love into baroque art. Ironically, then, they were driven to seduce and then revile women out of the same vulnerable idealism that made women seduceable. Men and women were enemies simply because the artificial polarization of the sexes prevented them from seeing that they shared a tragic loss of illusion.

Behn's pastoral declares that the wits' conclusion is not inescapable; one need not wallow in the stench of "reality." In asking for the preservation of the ideal, she was far from naive; she also knew that "Love, that almighty creator of something from nothing, forms a wit, a hero, or a beauty, virtue, good humour, honour, any excellence, when oftentimes there is neither in the object" (*Love Letters* 161). But love is a powerful, beautiful illusion, and in lending oneself to it one may escape both ugly comedy and tragic sacrifice and return, if only temporarily, to the innocent pleasures of the Golden Age and to Arcadian nymphs, infinitely preferable to Phillis and her dirty linen. Behn not only wrote but lived according to this principle; she belonged to a group of friends of both sexes, known in her poems as the "cabal" (named facetiously after the political conspiracies of the time), who tried to bring back the age of beauty and innocence by cavorting in the countryside in conscious imitation of the love games of *L'Astrée* (Duffy 125).

In Behn's poems it appears that men find this imaginative exercise difficult; Hoyle in the cabal was rather a wolf among sheep. In "A Farewel to Celladon, On his Going into Ireland," a woman's persuasion to love that alludes nostalgically to the hero of *L'Astrée*, Behn's speaker mourns the loss of a lover to "business," linked in the poem to the ambition that drove Adam out of Paradise. She wants him to come back to the beauty that unites the sexes as "business" divides them. "Business" is what her age would call reality, while love is the imagination; the poem makes a case for willingness to believe in ideal beauty. As Goreau notes, "business," or reality, in this poem is masculine, and love, or imagination, is feminine, because at this time women rarely had any "business" of their own.[20] But Behn herself sees no reason for this division by gender (Goreau 270, *Works* 6:144-45). Her defense of love, idealism, and imagination is also a plea for men, as our own jargon would express it, to "get in touch with their feminine side"; at the same time, she wishes to be allowed to release her "masculine part," which she calls "the Poet in me" (*The Lucky Chance, Works* 3:187).[21]

Despite Rochester's anti-feminist satire, Behn persisted in seeing him as a symbol of hope that men and women might not always be at cross-purposes. To her he had the "feminine" ability to love, and the sense to appreciate "masculine" intelligence in women. In *The Rover* she presents this idealized Rochester in the character of the hero, Willmore, and makes him voice her own well-known views on matrimony—a constant theme of hers ever since her first play, *The Forc'd Marriage*. Given the alienation of the sexes at the time, one might expect men and women to oppose each other on this issue; since extramarital affairs were acceptable for men but not for women, men would have less reason to dislike the conventional loveless marriage of convenience. But in Behn's view men and women can agree about marriage because they share an abhorrence of sex without "Inclination," which she describes in *Love Letters,* possibly from her own experience (Goreau 85-86, Duffy 48-51), as "a trick . . . to make the nauseated, tired-out pair drag on the careful business of life, drudge for the dull-got family with greater satisfaction, because they are taught to think marriage was made in heaven" (108-9). The antithesis of this conventional marriage is the love match, for which Willmore (though "trembling") willingly surrenders the rake's freedom and variety (1:105). His libertinism is not deeply cynical or antiromantic, but a modern, urban version of the shepherd's innocent joy in loving.

This portrait of Rochester is not at all like his twentieth-century image. If he ever wrote romantic verses—and, as Behn was in a position to know, he did—his excuse is familiar: "A song to Phillis, I perhaps might make,/But never Rhym'd, but for my Pintles sake" ("Satyr [Timon]," *Poems* 78). These lines suggest that he did not "mature," as his age is often said to have evolved, from romance to satire, but rather that he wrote in both modes simultaneously, or in turn, as expressions of his two faces.[22] He would not be the first or the last man to have a different voice for men than for women—without necessarily lying, exactly, to either. Rochester's romantic face helps explain why the differences we see between his poetry and Behn's were so invisible in their own time that after his death some of her lyrics were published as his by mistake.

It is this romantic face we see in Behn's elegy, in which the satirist appears as the ideal pastoral lover and love poet:

He was but lent this duller World t'improve
In all the charms of Poetry, and Love;
. . . .

Mourn, all ye Beauties, put your Cyprus on,
The truest Swain that e're Ador'd you's gone;
. . . .

Mourn, all ye little Gods of Love, whose Darts
Have lost their wonted power of piercing hearts;
. . . .

Bewail him then oh all ye little Loves,
For you the humblest Votary have lost
That ever your Divinities could boast;
Upon your hands your weeping Heads decline,
And let your wings encompass round his Shrine;
In stead of Flow'rs your broken Arrows strow,
And at his feet lay the neglected Bow.
   Mourn, all ye little Gods, your loss deplore,
   The soft, the Charming Strephon is no more. [6:369-70]

It may seem odd to think of Rochester as a Strephon, tragically destroyed by the ugly reality he so enjoyed describing, but the elegy has an ironic aptness. For thumbing his nose at life was for him a kind of joy—for which, like the innocent shepherds, he lost his life. Devoted to comedy, at the end he was surprised by tragedy, if one may believe Bishop Burnet's account of his last days (Duffy ch. 20). He died, at the age of thirty-three, of love—or, rather, of syphilis.

As Behn was writing *Oroonoko* in 1688, she knew that soon she too would succumb to this great leveling disease, very possibly given to her by the promiscuous Hoyle.[23] Reading *Oroonoko* with this fact in mind, one is all the more prepared to see truth in this novel in which innocent lovers are destroyed by masculine greed, the disease that wrecked the Golden Age.

   The setting of *Oroonoko* is as real as the countryside of Kent that inspired Behn's pastoral lyrics—with the added advantage of remoteness. As she says in her "epistle dedicatory," "If there be any thing that seems Romantick, I beseech your Lordship to consider, these Countries do, in all things, so far differ from ours, that they produce unconceivable Wonders; at least, they appear so to us, because new and strange" (*Oroonoko,* ed. Amore, 3). Romance thus intersects with travel literature to provide "wonder" consistent with truth.[24] Surinam in the 1660s (when Behn apparently was there) resembled the world of the Golden Age and Paradise before the fall. Behn's account combines imagery from these Greek and Christian traditions in a way that recalls *Paradise Lost:*[25] "'tis there eternal Spring . . . the Trees bearing at once all Degrees of Leaves, and Fruit, from blooming Buds to ripe Autumn: Groves of Oranges, Lemons, Citrons, Figs, Nutmegs, and noble Aromaticks, continually bearing their Fragrancies . . . bearing at the same Time ripe Fruit, and blooming young, or producing every Day new" (*Works* 5:178).

Against this perfect but fully realized background, swains and nymphs, or Adams and Eves—in the form of Indians—innocently frolic, without the veils and coquetry of corrupt Europeans:

> And tho' they are all thus naked, if one lives for ever among 'em, there [is] not to be seen an indecent Action, or Glance: and being continually us'd to see one another so unadorn'd, so like our first Parents before the Fall, it seems as if they had no Wishes, there being nothing to heighten Curiosity: but all you can see, you see at once, and every Moment see; and where there is no Novelty, there can be no Curiosity. . . . And these People represented to me an absolute Idea of the first State of Innocence, before Man knew how to sin. [5:131]

She does not hold the Christian note long, however: "[S]imple Nature is the most harmless, inoffensive and virtuous Mistress. 'Tis she alone, if she were permitted, that better instructs the World, than all the Inventions of Man: Religion would here but destroy that Tranquillity they possess by Ignorance" (5:131-32). Pagan and Christian thought agree well at the outset of the story, as in Milton's epic they agree about man before the fall; but as Oroonoko's fate unfolds, Christianity becomes allied with Europe, colonialism, the rape of the land, and tragedy.

Oroonoko transports "The Golden Age" to a real, though exotic, setting. To succeed, the novel must convince readers of its historic truth, or factuality, while also conveying the poetic truth of Behn's pastoral vision—a difficult if not impossible task. It was no easy matter, for example, to transform travel-literature oddity—such as Indians with their faces "painted in little Specks or Flowers here and there" (5:131)—into romantic beauty.

Behn rose to the challenge; her description retains the marvelous while bridging the cultural gap: "for they have all that is called Beauty, except the Colour, which is a reddish Yellow; or after a new Oiling, which they often use to themselves, they are of the Colour of a new Brick, but smooth, soft and sleek." The African hero and heroine, by virtue of their position, must be even more beautiful and even more odd than the Indians—and therefore they are even more artistically challenging. They too are decorated; Oroonoko has "a little Flower, or Bird, at the Sides of the Temples" and Imoinda has "fine Flowers and Birds all over her Body" (5:174). But their flowers are not painted on, but carved, or as it would appear, "japan'd." To get her readers to accept Oroonoko and Imoinda as Mars and his "black Venus," Behn must conveniently "forget" to mention the carvings until very late in the story, instead concentrating on the lovers' more European characteristics.

Both Oroonoko and Imoinda, we are assured, can blush, despite their color, so their faces can register the many changes of emotion necessary in romance (5:145). Imoinda is so universally beautiful that the narrator says, "I have seen a hundred White Men sighing after her, and making a thousand Vows at her Feet" (5:137). And Oroonoko, we are told, does not have negroid features: "His Face was not of that brown rusty Black which most of that Nation are, but a perfect Ebony, or polished Jet. . . . His Nose was rising and Roman, instead of African and flat: His Mouth the finest shaped that could be seen; far from those great turn'd Lips, which are so natural to the rest of the Negroes. The whole Proportion and Air of his Face was so nobly and exactly form'd, that bating his Colour, there could be nothing in Nature more beautiful, agreeable and handsome." He seems to accept what Behn calls "the Standard of true Beauty," making his appearance as caucasian as possible "by the Aids of Art": "His Hair came down to his Shoulders . . . by pulling it out with a Quill, and keeping it comb'd; of which he took particular Care" (5:136). Thanks to his natural gentility—and to his French tutor—he "in all points address'd himself as if his Education had been in some European Court" (5:135).

Behn does everything possible to allow Oroonoko and Imoinda to seduce the English reader's imagination; but as always with romance, there must first be a willingness to surrender. Within the story Oroonoko's own willingness to imagine makes him the ideal lover. Instead of exposing love's illusion, like the Restoration wits, he is content to see with love's eyes, and thus can pledge eternal constancy to Imoinda in a country where polygamy is customary: "no Age or Wrinkles shou'd encline him to change; for her Soul would be always fine, and always young; and he should look into his Heart for that Idea, when he could find it no longer in her Face" (5:139). Unlike Celladon, he needs no coaxing to give up the "business" of war for love. When he believes Imoinda is dead he cannot move a muscle to save his men. And unlike Shakespeare's and Dryden's characterizations of Antony, he is unambiguously shown to have his priorities in the proper order.

Oroonoko's imagination is not too sorely taxed, because as a romance hero he inhabits a world of symbols and of realized ideas; he can see in Imoinda's lovely face and form the beautiful soul that he loves. Just as Oroonoko proves his heroism by his uncommon monogamy, Imoinda transcends the "real" ladies of Coramantien—a place much like Behn's England—by her distaste for being treated as a commodity. When she receives the "honour" of the king's command to attend him, the narrator comments that "'twas a Glory that could well have been spared her, tho desired and aim'd at by all the young Females of that kingdom" (5:153). In Surinam, where she is literally sold into slavery, her nobility is recognized and respected even by her white master, who finds himself unable to rape her, explaining that "she disarms me with that Modesty and Weeping, so tender and so moving, that I retire, and thank my Stars she overcame me" (5:172).

Oroonoko also, we are told, appears in bondage with his soul stamped on his face and his heroism intact: "The Royal Youth appear'd in spight of the Slave, and People cou'd not help treating him after a different manner, without designing it" (5:168). But this statement proves overly optimistic. One of the more searing ironies in this story is that Oroonoko and the other slaves receive the names of Roman heroes like Caesar and Tuscan from the masters who strip them of all dignity. As romance figures in a pastoral landscape, Oroonoko and Imoinda can be seen as what they are: royalty. But with the intrusion of the evil white man, appearance is separated from reality, and symbols lose their meaning. The hero and heroine suffer the indignity of slaves, and refusing to submit, they die a horrible, tragic death.

The first of the white villains of the story is the captain who lures Oroonoko and his men onto his ship, gets them drunk, and locks them up, planning to sell them into bondage. The narrator remarks, "Some have commended this Act, as brave in the Captain; but I will spare my sense of it, and leave it to my Reader to judge as he pleases" (5:162). Oroonoko is easily tricked because for him words and appearances represent facts; he is too "generous" to believe the captain could lie. When Oroonoko starts a hunger strike, the captain is forced to release him and his men, exchanging promises that they will take no revenge and that he will return them to their country. The episode illustrates the contrast between what we would now call a Christian "guilt culture" and a pagan "shame culture," to the advantage of the latter. The captain fears to accept Oroonoko's word that, once free, he will "behave himself in all friendly Order and Manner," because he "could not resolve to trust a Heathen . . . upon his Parole, a Man that had no Sense or Notion of the God that he worshipp'd . . . for the captain had protested to him upon the Word of a Christian, and sworn in the Name of a great God; which if he should violate, he must expect eternal Torments in the World to come" (5:163-64). Oroonoko's reply shows that it is his own code that gives "parole" real meaning:

> Is that all the Obligations he has to be just to his Oath? . . . Let him know, I swear by my Honour; which to violate, would not only render me contemptible and despised by all brave and honest Men, and so give my self perpetual Pain, but it would be eternally offending and displeasing all Mankind; harming, betraying, circumventing, and outraging all Men. But Punishments hereafter are suffer'd by one's self; and the World takes no Cognizance whether this God has reveng'd 'em or not, 'tis done so secretly, and deferr'd so long; while the Man of no Honour suffers every Moment the Scorn and Contempt of the honester World, and dies every Day ignominiously in his Fame, which is more valuable than Life. [5:164]

The rest of Oroonoko's short life is a repetition of this pattern of trust and betrayal. The hero finally concludes that "there was no Faith in the White Men, or the Gods they ador'd; who instructed them in Principles so false, that honest Men could not live amongst them"; furthermore, "a Man ought to be eternally on his Guard, and never to eat and drink with Christians, without his Weapon of Defence in his Hand; and, for his own Security, never to credit one Word they spoke" (5:196). Yet even at the very last—on the verge of suicide after leading a failed slave rebellion and killing his pregnant wife—he is persuaded to trust a white man again, giving himself up on a false promise of leniency. As a result he is whipped almost to death, and then grotesquely and savagely executed:

> He had learn'd to take Tobacco; and when he was assur'd he should die, he desir'd they would give him a Pipe in his Mouth, ready lighted; which they did: And the Executioner came, and first cut off his Members, and threw them into the Fire; after that, with an ill-favour'd Knife, they cut off his Ears and his Nose, and burn'd them; he still smoak'd on, as if nothing had touch'd him; then they hack'd off one of his Arms, and still he bore up, and held his Pipe; but at the cutting off the other Arm, his Head sunk and his Pipe dropt and he gave up the Ghost, without a Groan, or a Reproach. [5:207-8]

Oroonoko's death is just strange enough to be true—as Behn insists it was, for "my Mother and Sister were by him all the While" (5:208). The presence of verifiable facts and recognizable names in the story serves the purpose of helping us believe the unbelievable; the story is so "Novel" it is hard to imagine anyone could have made it up.[26] This is certainly the case with incidents that do not advance the plot, but which seem to come straight from the traveler's diary: Oroonoko's experience with an electric eel, the killing of a tiger with seven bullets in its heart, and the visit to the Indian village seem all the more believable for the inclusion of "wonderful" detail. Though instruction was not Behn's primary aim, this combination of romance and realism did serve a didactic purpose. By hanging pieces of real life on the romantic framework of her pastoral verse, she was able to guide her readers to her own interpretation of the facts, much as Dryden had done in *Absalom and Achitophel*.[27] And as Delarivière Manley would later do in *The New Atalantis*, she used the beauty of romance to comment satirically on the ugliness of reality.

But the mixture of romance and realism in *Oroonoko* is also confusing. First, because the novel was a pastiche of several other literary forms, the tone was difficult for the author to control and for the reader to understand. The reader has no "prestructure" (Davis 12) to guide her interpretation of the story and must constantly shift orientation, sorting facts from nonfacts, recognizing real people's names, yet wondering whether perhaps "'tis all a lye." This disorientation, often identified today as the distinguishing feature of novels,[28] generated problems that the novelists who followed Behn's lead felt the need to resolve.

Instead of aiding the seduction of the imagination, realistic details sometimes bring the reader to the ground with a bump. Imoinda's angelic purity, for example, depends oddly on the technical impotence of the king who takes her to bed every night and fondles her right in front of Oroonoko.[29] Her death is meant to be romantic and tragic: "'tis not to be doubted, but the parting, the eternal Leave-taking of two such Lovers, so greatly born, so sensible, so beautiful, so young, and so fond, must be very moving, as the Relation of it was to me afterwards" (5:202). But Behn's own "Relation" borders on the nauseating: "the lovely, young and ador'd Victim lays herself down before the Sacrificer; while he, with a Hand resolved, and a Heart-breaking within, gave the fatal Stroke, first cutting her Throat, and then severing her yet smiling Face from that delicate Body, pregnant as it was with the Fruits of tenderest Love" (5:202-3). The combination of the romantic and the grisly makes her death only slightly less grotesquely surreal than the death of Oroonoko, which in our own time, if not in Behn's, strikes readers as darkly comic rather than tragic.

Second, the disorientation produced by the mixture of tones interferes with didactic clarity. One does not always know whether to see Oroonoko as a romance hero, above all other mortals, or as a real man whose lot is to be compared to that of other slaves. At times he seems to represent a whole nation of non-Christian and therefore superior human beings, especially in their treatment of women. Men may have as many women as they want in Coramantien, but they are obliged to take care of them; "the only Crime and Sin with Woman, is, to turn her off, to abandon her to want, shame and misery: such ill Morals are only practis'd in Christian Countries" (5:139). But the king's treatment of Imoinda shows that the hero and heroine are in fact exceptional, and that most of their nation are no better than Iron-Age Englishmen.

The issue of extraordinariness accounts for the dispute about whether this is an abolitionist novel. Montague Summers writes, "Certainly we may absolve Mrs. Behn from having directly written with a purpose such as animated Mrs. Harriet Beecher Stowe's *Uncle Tom's Cabin;* but none the less her sympathy with the oppressed blacks, her deep emotions of pity for outraged humanity, her anger at the cruelties of the slave-driver aye ready with knout or knife, are manifest in every line" (*Works* 5:127).[30] The question is whether all slaves receive the same sympathy, and—as many readers have pointed out—they do not. Most of the slaves in Surinam are presented as deserving their fate—first, by losing in battle to Oroonoko, who sold most of them in the first place, and second, by lacking the heroism to face tragic death. As their defeated leader says, "they wanted only but to be whipped into the knowledge of the Christian Gods, to be the vilest of all creeping Things" (5:196).

Behn herself seems to have been undecided about what her hero represents, as her presence in the story helps us to see.[31] Though she does not arrive on the scene until everyone is assembled in Surinam, on her first appearance she makes much of her position—both with Oroonoko, with whom she has "made a Friendship," and with the British settlers: "As soon as I came into the Country, the best House in it was presented me," because her father, who died in transit, was to have been Lieutenant Governor (5:174, 179). But soon she finds her loyalties divided. Whatever she might say as a narrator writing of the experience some twenty-five years after the fact, as a character she is a Christian who, with no pressure from anyone, tries to convert Oroonoko and Imoinda "to the Knowledge of the true God" (5:175).

Because she is the only one Oroonoko trusts, the narrator is sometimes able to restrain him and prevent a rebellion; he calls her his "Great Mistress; and indeed my Word would go a great Way with him" (5:176). She uses that trust in an ambiguous way. Having "assured them of Liberty as soon as the Governour arrived," she is in much the same position as the well-meaning Trefry, overseer of the governor's plantation, whose similar promise leads to Oroonoko's final betrayal. She does, in fact, come to see herself as a kind of spy: "After this, I neither thought it convenient to trust him much out of our View, nor did the Country, who fear'd him" (5:177).

As the story builds to the climax, Behn as character more and more clearly represents the party she opposes as narrator. When it is found that all the slaves have fled, she includes herself in the group of outraged slave owners (much in the same way Trefry later scolds Oroonoko for acting "to the Prejudice of his Lord and Master"): "*we* had by Noon about 600 Men, they call the Militia of the Country, that came to assist *us* in the pursuit of the Fugitives [my emphasis]" (5:195, 193). Yet in the same passage, as narrator she calls the army "comical" and notes that "the better sort wou'd not meddle in the matter." The worse the situation becomes for Oroonoko, the harder it is for the author to explain her apparent hypocrisy.

One obvious explanation is that Behn was not as powerful as she makes herself sound. Oroonoko is nearly beaten to death when "all the Females of us" have been sent away to be safe from the slave revolt, "for I suppose I had Authority and Interest enough there, had I suspected any such Thing, to have prevented it" (5:198).[32] At the time of his execution, she has become ill and has been sent away again, perhaps overcome by the strain. Or maybe the strain is only that of the narrator, who has no other way to excuse her acquiescence in his downfall. Her promise to Oroonoko may have been sincere, but it lay with others to make it come true.

The cause of the tonal and didactic inconsistencies in *Oroonoko,* then, is not simple artistic failure but the author's powerlessness to shape the events she was writing about. She was in much the same position as Oroonoko, with whom she identified: his defeat and death in the novel are paralleled by her own flight and illness (Spencer 50). Their enemies were the same, for those who destroyed ideal love and beauty made it impossible to write a believable romance—and very difficult for a woman to write anything at all.

Although as a character in *Oroonoko* Behn fled the battlefield, as an author she firmly stood her ground against the male writers who wished to keep her from trespassing on what they considered their private domain (Woodcock 73-76). It was common to attack "the ruin of her face" along with her wit, as Prior did in 1684,[33] and to impugn her modesty and virtue, as Wycherly did in a poem addressed "To the Sappho of the Age, Supposed to Lye-In of a Love-Distemper, or a Play" (Goreau 231-32). Nevertheless, she kept writing to the very end of her life, still demanding "the Privilege for my Masculine Part, the Poet in me . . . to tread in those successful Paths my Predecessors have so long thriv'd in" (*Works* 3:187). To call herself "masculine" in this way may seem a capitulation, an acceptance of the separation of genders. But her plea was not generally feminist any more than Oroonoko's oration is abolitionist; she was merely consenting to be a hermaphroditic freak if that was what it took to be left alone to do her job. Yet, as many readers were moved to abolitionism by Oroonoko's antislavery oration, ignoring the context that makes that speech ambiguous (Goreau 289), Behn's personal defiance set an example for other women writers from her own century to ours.[34]

Behn was more comfortable with her public voice—both in colloquial prose and in highly structured verse—than women would be again for a long time to come. Her ability to turn her supposed lack of education into an asset set her apart from Delarivière Manley, who insisted she knew as much as anybody, and Fanny Burney, who was afraid to seem to know anything. Of course, even for Behn the act of narrating was not to be done without humility and apology. She says it was her hero's "Misfortune . . . to fall in an obscure World, that afforded only a Female Pen to celebrate his Fame" and wishes him "a more sublime Wit than mine to write his Praise" (5:169, 208). But this is not her last word; the end of the novel changes the meaning of these professions: "Yet, I hope, the Reputation of my Pen is considerable enough to make his glorious Name to survive to all Ages, with that of the brave, the beautiful, and the constant Imoinda" (5:208). The sentence builds not to the hero but to the heroine; and the reputations of both are seen to depend on the reputation of another heroine, the author, who knew her "Female Pen" required no sincere apology.

Unfortunately, courage is no guarantee of a happy ending, in fiction or in life. Behn's intelligence and persistence earned her a measure of freedom—but the way she chose to use it may have cost her life. In the prologue to *The Forc'd Marriage* she had joked that woman's wit was just one more of her "Artilleries" for capturing men; her own wit captured John Hoyle (3:285). The possibility of making such a man constant when so many "Phillisses" before her had failed, thereby becoming the queen of her sex, was apparently a temptation worth the risk—or rather the near certainty—of dishonor, disease, and death.

Behn's artistic problems were nothing compared to this one; bringing real life into romance may have been difficult, but bringing romance into real life was fatal. In Behn's vision the wreck of the Golden Age, of Oroonoko and Imoinda, of all true lovers of both sexes was a tragedy. The disease that was eating away at her in 1688 was, in fact, the hallmark of a fallen world without "safe sex." Today's readers know all too well that this tragedy is real; yet its ugliness, vulgarity, and sheer senseless waste make it seem rather absurd—like the death of Oroonoko, a terrible, ironic joke. Not the least of the ironies is that in death by venereal disease, the sexes are reunited. In April 1689, nine years after Rochester, Aphra Behn claimed her equal right to die for love.

2

Delia and Rivella
Romantic Autobiography

The life of every Woman is a Romance!
—Fanny Burney

BY the turn of the eighteenth century, when Delarivière Manley[1] was at the height of her career, the cultural decline Behn had complained about had gone a few steps further. The baroque splendor of pastoral seemed increasingly ridiculous to the cultivated reader; to the less educated, mostly interested in "news and new things," it was wholly unknown. The romantic ideal was vanishing, and novelists were losing access to the exclusive, aristocratic places where its last rays might still be visible.

Manley was a gentlewoman—even, by a stretch, a low-ranking member of the nobility; but her actual status, like that of her writings, was "proletarian" (Frye, *Secular Scripture*, 23).[2] Like Behn, she was a poet who became famous for her plays, particularly heroic tragedies, and who ultimately found prose fiction a comparatively easy way to turn a profit. Her political romans à clef showed a talent for satire that prompted Swift to hire her to write for, and later to edit, the Tory *Examiner*. Thus, as Behn could consider Rochester and Buckingham her colleagues, Manley could hobnob with courtiers through the practice of her profession, assuming the high status of defender of Queen Anne and enemy of the Duke and Duchess of Marlborough. Personally, however, she was much less at home in the inner circles than Behn had been. She was the abused dependent rather than the friend of the Duchess of Cleveland, and now that Charles II was gone and actresses were no longer unofficial heads of state, her theatrical connections led only to association with the growing class of professional writers, and no further.[3]

Even for Behn, equality in the profession had not meant equality in private life. Rochester, who apparently knew how to conduct a love affair in the high style, was not her lover; the lawyer Hoyle was a cheap imitation, and her husband (though few facts are known about him) probably no imitation at all. Thus there was an important difference between the men she could take to bed and the gentlemen she wrote about. In Manley's time this gap was widening; the men available to her—and to the women readers of her class, destined for elderly merchants like Mr. Behn—were even less likely to be readers of Ovid who would know how to make the act of love an aesthetic experience. No orange flowers and jessamines and carved Cupids on the bedstead would mitigate the brutality and ugliness of sex in an age in which people thought bathing was dangerous.[4] There would be an end to pleasant dalliance, or foreplay; the invitation to love would be a command, such as "turn to thy known old man, and buss him soundly" (*Love Letters* 170). Beauty would marry Beast, and the gulf between imagination and reality, woman and man, would become a yawning chasm.

Romance, with its celebration of the erotic and elevation of the feminine, could liberate the sexual imaginations of women whose real-life marriages and affairs were likely to be unfulfilling. Manley sought this liberation, for herself and for her readers, in two main ways. First, by imitating the style of the French romance and its antecedents, Manley could create her own brand of erotic literature and express in words the sexuality her society forced women to suppress. Second, by using romance settings as utopias against which to measure and satirize her society, she could criticize the sexual double standards that caused her so much suffering.[5]

In two of Manley's novels romance serves a personal purpose: it provides a sympathetic structure for her autobiography, to make her reputed sins appear more like virtues. *The New Atalantis,* written in 1709, gives her account of a key event in her life, her invalid marriage to her already married cousin. The narrative frame consists of the goddess Intelligence telling stories about the inhabitants of the fictional kingdom of Atalantis to the goddesses Virtue and Astrea. The latter—who recalls the departed Behn along with d'Urfé, Spenser, and Ovid—questions Intelligence about famous people to aid her in the task of educating a prince on the moon.[6] As Intelligence replies, she exposes the private lives of contemporary Londoners—including Manley herself as Delia. The rest of Manley's story is narrated in the 1714 "autobiographical romance," as Gwendolyn Needham calls it, *The Adventures of Rivella* ("WB" 269). Here also, the narrative frame is elaborate, as Rivella's friend Sir Charles Lovemore (based on Manley's real-life friend Sir John Tidcomb) narrates her biography to the Chevalier d'Aumont, a French nobleman who has fallen in love with her by reputation.

Both works contain the facts as Manley saw them, but both use obvious fictions to make her view seem more believable than the common gossip about her. The title pages of both state that they were originally written in foreign languages by disinterested third parties—a ruse that was probably meant to be transparent, since in *Rivella,* at least, the title gives a strong hint of the author's true identity (*R* 6, *NAt* 1:ii–iii). A letter from Manley to her publisher indicates that she expected *Rivella* to be read as autobiography (Fidelis Morgan 155). Thus, like Behn in *Oroonoko,* Manley created a fictional frame that allowed her to present her romantic account of the events of her life as if it were objective truth.[7]

If the romance in Manley's novels were to liberate female sexuality—and vindicate the author's own sexual conduct—it would have to go beyond escape, to illustrate how women could be free in action as well as in imagination. Manley's success in this endeavor was mixed, for reasons that would also affect the women novelists who followed her. This chapter will illuminate Manley's difficulties in combining romance and realism by examining: first, her critical opinion of the romance; second, her adaptation of the language of romance in the two novels that contain her autobiography; and third, her use of romance settings and plots in these novels as a means of satirizing what was called reality.

Manley's critical statements resemble Congreve's in praising modern fiction over the romances of the previous century. In some respects her practice bears out these statements; her novels contain the kinds of realism that earn her the praise of today's readers—a realism, ironically, that had its source in the French romance.[8] Few of Manley's characters are extremely handsome or beautiful, and even the best have serious character flaws—such as the Marquis, "as ambitious of Glory as a true Hero, as Covetous as his Wife, as Self-interested as self-love could make him, yet shining in a thousand Virtues that obscur'd his Vices" (*NAt* 2:121). Manley followed Behn and anticipated Fanny Burney in her talent for imitating the speech patterns of the lower classes.[9] And she was sometimes given to Behn-like gruesome details; one bad-tempered woman nearly chokes her step-daughter: "by flying upon her, with her two Hands about her Throat, she had stopt her Wind-pipe, till the poor Girl's Tongue hung out of her Mouth, and her Face was grown black" (*NAt* 1:161).

In the manner of Cervantes—and of Behn, when she included a "novel" within her "history" of Oroonoko—Manley introduces romances into her novels to point up the superior realism of her own works. The violent woman described above, though a termagant to the husband who loves her, sends "Love-Verses and Dialogues of

Clarinda and Daphnis [to] a pitiful Lawyer's-Clerk . . . with rattling
Epithets, bumbast Descriptions, romantick Flights, and, in short,
nothing of Nature in 'em" (*NAt* 1:161). The contrast between this
woman's real and assumed character shows that to Manley romances
were not only absurd (especially when appropriated by the lower
middle class) but dangerous, encouraging those with ungoverned
natures to commit adultery. By this time romances were blamed for
arousing—even manufacturing—women's sexuality. They were also
held responsible—with some justice, as Behn's life shows—for the
destruction of young women who tried to live by them.

But romance in Manley's novels is not present only to be criticized; it provides the surrounding "realistic" narrative with both
style and plots. This apparent contradiction is, in fact, in keeping
with her definition of the novel. Perhaps because of her interest in
actual readers' responses rather than theoretical dichotomizing, she
did not follow Congreve in reducing romance vs. novel to "wonder" vs.
"delight." In her preface to *Queen Zarah* (1705), she explains why
realistic narrative now pleases more than "great adventures and
extraordinary accidents": "for we in some Manner put our selves in
the Room of those we see in Danger; the Part we take therein, and the
fear of falling into the like Misfortunes, causes us to interest our
selves more in their Adventures, because that those sort of Accidents
may happen to all the World; and it touches so much the more because
they are the common Effects of Nature" (*Zarah* 1:preface). Manley's
theory shows what Behn's practice had also pointed out: that realism
is only a means of giving the new reading public the "adventures" and
"accidents" romances had once given a less demanding, or more
imaginative, generation.

Manley's insistence on abiding by the rules of "nature" gives her
works a slightly different sort of believable wonder than Behn's—the
sort Hunter says distinguishes the novel from the romance: statistical
improbability and coincidence rather than travel-literature miracles
("Novels" 483-84). For Manley, "nature" was not the distillation of
man's essence, not the opposite of "civilization," but something ap-
proaching what we now call psychology. But when she wrote about
contemporary England, she did have Behn's work for an example: not
Oroonoko, which uses real names, but *Love Letters from a Nobleman
to His Sister,* a roman à clef so transparent that even today the "clef" is
hardly needed. By imitating Behn's combination of romance and
realism, Manley could do what contemporary male satirists such as
Dryden, Pope and Swift were doing: guide readers' perceptions of
actual people by placing them within a fictional allegorical frame. In
her day, she was one of the most famous practitioners of the type of

prose satire better known to our own time in later works such as *Gulliver's Travels.*

Manley's complex opinion of romance had a profound effect on her attempted self-vindication. Because romance was associated with dangerous female sexuality, its presence in her novels enabled her to broach the subject of her own alleged misconduct. Superficially accepting her age's condemnation of romances, she could blame them for her mistakes. These stories, which she was force-fed by her aunt, warped her perception: "[they] infected me, and made me fancy every Stranger that I saw, in what Habit soever, some disguis'd Prince or Lover" (*NAt* 2:183). Only their influence could lead her to accept the marriage proposal of the villain, her cousin. "I was no otherwise pleas'd with it, than as he answer'd something to the Character I had found in those Books, that had poyson'd and deluded my dawning Reason" (2:184). Manley thus conveys her innocence by suggesting that any shadowy notions about love she may have had at fourteen came entirely from an artificial source outside herself.

Throughout *The New Atalantis* scores of innocent women, too well protected from the world to be able to judge the unreality of what they read, are corrupted and seduced by means of romances. One lady falls for a heroic-looking soldier because her "curmudgonly" father "wou'd never let her go to Angela our chief City, nor wou'd he give her any of her Portion till he dy'd, or she marry'd to his liking; but yet he never look'd out for a Husband for her" (1:150). The illiterate and therefore uncorrupted countrywoman who tells her story remarks that if this lady had seen "fine Company" instead of reading romances and plays, "she wou'd not have thought a ranting Officer such a God-a-mighty" (1:150). Far more sensible is the peasant's view of these so-called heroes, and of the unromantic lives of their women: "for fall out what will, they must have a clean Shirt every day. Some of their beggarly Soldiers Trulls does nothing but Launder for 'em, they'r always at the Wash-Tub, and, I believe, seldom enough paid for what they do" (1:150).

Seducers in *The New Atalantis* sometimes deliberately encourage their unsuspecting victims to read romances, knowing that these books will do half their job for them, as in the story of the Duke and his ward, Charlot. Originally the Duke "banish'd far from her Conversation whatever would not edify, Airy Romances, Plays, dangerous Novels, loose and insinuating Poetry, artificial Introductions of Love, well-painted Landskips of that dangerous Poyson" (1:53). But when Charlot grows into a beauty and he decides to seduce her, he gives her the key to his library and tells her to "seek her Diversion, amongst those Authors he had formerly forbid her the use of" (1:62).

Such examples make Manley's duplicity clear, however, since her condemnation of these wicked stories enables her to exploit them. One sees how proud she was of her talent in this direction in the praise she has the Chevalier d'Aumont give her for it in *Rivella:* the story of "her Young and innocent Charlot, transported with the powerful Emotion of a just kindling Flame, sinking with delight and Shame upon the Bosom of her Lover in the Gallery of Books," is one of his favorites (4). Manley's ambivalence about romance translates into an ambivalence about sex. Her self-vindication finally depends on creating a milieu in which female sexuality—hence the romance which creates and expresses it—can be seen in a positive light. But first she had to find a language appropriate to the description of women's sexual experience—for despite Behn's efforts, such a language did not yet exist.

Dolores Palomo is undoubtedly correct to point out the ironic overtones of Manley's erotic writing (42-43); but though Manley might have meant to amuse her readers, she also meant to titillate them. Manley was as serious about eroticism as Ovid, whose example lent an air of classical grandeur to her popular poems and novels (*R* 43). Ovid was useful in another way as well; just as Behn used her free translation of a section of Ovid's *Epistles* as an opportunity to decry the sexual double standard (Goreau 254-55), Manley adapted Ovidian language and themes in order to point out that women have the same desires as men.[10]

This impression is reinforced by the doubling of erotic episodes in *The New Atalantis,* as a love scene is repeated using similar language but with sex roles reversed: in one seduction scene the woman inopportunely mentions marriage and the man suddenly cools, and in another the man mentions marriage and the woman cools.[11] Technical point of view also proves to be gender-reversible. Manley's erotic episodes recall the love scenes of Behn's prose fiction: less ornate than "The Golden Age," but still "baroque" and pastoral enough to preserve the resemblance between the sexes. The following passages suggest that Manley believed that, in the erotic imaginations of women, men look almost exactly like women look in the erotic fantasies of men.

> Tuberoses set in pretty Gilt and China Posts, were placed advantageously upon Stands, the Curtains of the Bed drawn back to the Canopy, made of yellow Velvet embroider'd with white Bugles, the Panels of the Chamber Looking-Glass [omission?], upon the Bed were strow'd with a lavish Pro-

fuseness, plenty of Orange and Lemon Flowers, and to compleat the Scene, the young Germanicus in a dress and posture not very decent to describe; it was he that was newly risen from the Bath, and in a loose Gown of Carnation Taffety, stain'd with Indian Figures, his beautiful long, flowing Hair, for then 'twas the Custom to wear their own tied back with a Ribbon of the same Colour, he had thrown himself upon the Bed, pretending to Sleep, with nothing on but his Shirt and Night-Gown, which he had so indecently dispos'd, that slumbring as he appear'd, his whole Person stood confess'd to the Eyes of the Amorous Dutchess, his Limbs were exactly form'd, his Skin shiningly white, and the Pleasure the Ladies graceful entrance gave him, diffus'd Joy and Desire throughout all his Form; his lovely Eyes seem'd to be closed, his Face turn'd on one side . . . was obscur'd by the Lace depending from the Pillows on which he rested. [1:33-34]

She had nothing on but her Night-Dress, one Petticoat, and a rich Silver stuff Night-Gown that hung carelessly about her. It was the Evening of an excessive hot Day, she got into a shade of Orange Flowers and Jessamine, the Blossoms that were fallen cover'd all beneath with a profusion of Sweets. A Canal run by, which made that retreat delightful as 'twas fragrant. Diana, full of the uneasiness of Mind that Love occasion'd, threw her self under the pleasing Canopy, apprehensive of no Acteon to invade with forbidden Curiosity, her as numerous perfect Beauties, as had the Goddess. Supinely laid on that repose of Sweets, the dazling Lustre of her Bosom stood reveal'd, her polish'd Limbs all careless and extended, show'd the Artful Work of Nature. [2:227-28]

Despite the parallels between the male- and female-centered scenes depicted above, role reversal is not really possible in some important ways. In the first scene, which takes place in a bedroom with a prominent "Looking-Glass," the self-conscious Germanicus deliberately makes himself attractive to tempt the Duchess, who thinks she is coming to the bed of Fortunatus, her lover. In the second scene, which takes place outdoors, the only "artist" is "nature"; Diana is unconscious of her beauty, which is in effect stolen by the scheming Rodriguez.[12] Although men's and women's sexual fantasies might be similar, Manley emphasized their practical differences in this antithesis: "Enjoyment (the death of Love in all Mankind) gives Birth to new Fondness, and doating Extasies in the Women; they begin later, withheld by Modesty, and by a very ill tim'd Oeconomy, take up their

Fondness exactly where their Lover leaves it" (1:229). This was already a cliché, as Behn had noted in her fiction and in her letters to Hoyle, and Manley follows her lead in deploring sexual polarity and in longing for sexual proximity (*Love Letters* 85). But whereas Behn had believed that such proximity was "natural" and sexual disharmony a perversion, to Manley the incompatibility of the sexes was as inexorable as the law of gravity.[13]

This sexual alienation affected not only the act of love but also the way men and women talked and wrote about it. Behn had blamed the problem on men's refusal to use their imagination—and hence, in Manley's view, their love language was impoverished, harsh, and totally inadequate to feminine experience. In *The New Atalantis* one sees this communication gap when male characters are surprised to find that female characters do not laugh at their dirty jokes. A doctor, treating a woman for "Vapours," tries to cure her by telling her "something which he thought very diverting, his own Amours, and the Favours that had been bestow'd upon him." Not recognizing that a woman must identify with the butt of these jokes, the doctor and the patient's husband are baffled by her lack of response: "he seriously advis'd her Husband to take care of her; she had the height of Vapours, which might degenerate into Lunacy" (1:110).

In contrast, Manley's female characters more usually express themselves in the loftier style of the seventeenth-century romance. Just as men's ribaldry is incomprehensible to women, the heroic tone of women's love language strikes the "real" men in these novels as exaggerated and false. In Behn's works, men used romantic language sincerely at the beginning of an affair, becoming hypocrites only when their interest waned; but in Manley's novels, men use this language only as part of an elaborate game which they believe their mistresses are also playing by feigning innocence. Mosco, for instance, having romanced Zara into believing that polygamy is perfectly acceptable in many countries and in the eyes of God, later admits not only that this is untrue, but that he never expected her to believe it: "I did not doubt but you knew this, and when I first gain'd the Pleasures of your Love, said the contrary, only to allow your Virtue that pretence for yielding" (1:240). Similarly, when Rodriguez first kisses Diana, he cries out, "Inchanting Sweetness, ineffable Rapture . . . who wou'd not dye upon the Bliss?" (2:225). But later, when Diana's husband approaches, he tells her while fleeing that "'twas time for 'em both to be Wiser," and "as to his own Part he must take care of his Life" (2:234-35). Both men assume that their women, like themselves, are playacting, but the women are in earnest. Diana answers Rodriguez that "to a Heart that was sincere and truly ingag'd like hers, Separation wou'd be worse than Death" (2:234). Zara proves these words by leaping into the river and drowning.

The challenge for Manley was to create a language that would communicate the emotional intensity of women's erotic experience to readers of both sexes. To do this she permitted herself a wide range of tones, sometimes descending to dirty jokes in the masculine manner—as in the story of "one of the handsomest Women in Atalantis, from the Chin downwards" who covers her face with a handkerchief during sex "lest something less charming than her Body, shou'd pall [her lovers'] Ardors, and abate of their Excess" (2:206). More usually, she opted for the style of the pastoral love lyric—the style that was satirized and dropped by male poets, and picked up by female poets, in the seventeenth century. But this adaptation had always presented a problem for the woman writer, who in imitating Ovid and Petrarch found herself speaking with a man's voice. Gender confusion was often the result: readers then and now have no clear idea of the relationships between the women who wrote each other love poems in this period, such as Aphra Behn and "Clarinda." Even in clearly heterosexual verses, a woman writing like a man unsexed herself by becoming the aggressive pursuer. *Rivella* gives an account of some verses in which Manley confessed her "flame" for a "dangerous Swain" (50). To her contemporaries, a woman's compliment to a man could not carry the same tone of gallantry as a man's to a woman, and the verses simply confirmed the general impression of her lasciviousness.

Gender also made a difference in the way Ovid himself was read. Ovid was a favorite with women, according to Dryden, because his "soft Admirers" lacked the critical judgment to see his inferiority to Virgil in originality and true wit.[14] But in *The New Atalantis,* it appears that female readers see in his poems something male readers miss: sympathy with the feminine condition. The particular "romance" the Duke uses to awaken Charlot's "flame" is Ovid's story of the love affair between Myrrha and her father. "He pretended to shew her, that there were Pleasures her Sex were born for, and which she might consequently long to taste!" (1:63). But Charlot's interest in the story is not quite what he expects: "The Young Charlot . . . had by a noble Inclination of Gratitude a strong propension of Affection for the Duke, whom she call'd and estem'd her Papa, being a Girl of wonderful reflection, and consequently Application, wrought her Imagination up to such a lively heighth at the Fathers Anger after the possession of his Daughter, which she judg'd highly unkind and unnatural, that she drop'd her Book, Tears fill'd her Eyes, Sobs rose to oppress her, and she pull'd out her Handkerchief to cover the Disorder" (1:64). The story of Myrrha does not directly arouse Charlot's desires; rather, it arouses her guilt over her own feelings for her "papa," her pity for the victim, with whom she identifies, and her horror over the injustice perpetrated by men. In the turmoil of her grief the Duke comforts her and thus succeeds in seducing her, but without any sign of understanding or participating in her true feelings.

Even Master Ovid, then, would have to be altered to serve Manley's purpose. In *Rivella,* Lovemore quotes a dedicatory poem to one of Manley's plays which describes her superiority to her "father":

> Quote Ovid now no more ye amorous Swains,
> Delia than Ovid has more moving Strains.
> Nature in Her alone exceeds all Art;
> And Nature sure does nearest touch the Heart. [43]

Putting her definition of the novel in practice, Manley added physical detail to make the romance more believable and more moving. The intended effect was to take supernatural ecstasy out of the realm of romantic escape literature and put it within the reach of every real-life man and woman. Lovemore compliments her for "inform[ing] us that we have in our Composition, wherewith to taste sublime and transporting Joys: After perusing her Inchanting Descriptions, which of us have not gone in Search of Raptures which she every where tells us, as happy Mortals, we are capable of tasting" (*R* 4).

By encouraging her readers to let their fantasies brighten reality, Manley especially appeals to women, who in this way can enjoy romance without youth or beauty (Manley/Rivella describes herself as too fat and scarred to be wholly attractive). As Lovemore comments: "I do not find but Love in the general is well natur'd and civil, willing to compound for some Defects, since he knows that 'tis very difficult and rare to find true Symmetry and all Perfections in one Person: Red Hair, Out-Mouth, thin and livid Lips, black broken Teeth, course ugly Hands, long Thumbs, ill form'd dirty Nails, flat, or very large Breasts, splay Feet; which together makes a frightful Composition, yet divided amongst several, prove no Allay to the strongest Passions" (9). In *Oroonoko,* a love that could overlook such defects belonged only to the exceptional hero and heroine; here, the reader is instructed how to make it a part of everyday experience.

The Charlot episode was popular, apparently, because it succeeded in making the romantic-erotic immediate:

> But the Duke's pursuing Kisses overcame the very Thoughts
> of any thing, but that new and lazy Poison stealing to her
> Heart, and spreading swiftly and imperceptibly thro' all her

Veins, she clos'd her Eyes with languishing Delight! deliver'd up the possession of her Lips and Breath [Breast?] to the amorous Invader; return'd his eagar grasps, and, in a word, gave her whole Person into his Arms, in meltings full of delight! The Duke by that lovely Extasie, carry'd beyond himself, sunk over the expiring Fair, in Raptures too powerful for description! calling her his admirable Charlot! his charming Angel! his adorable Goddess! but all was so far modest, that he attempted not beyond her Lips and Breast. [1:64-65]

The "raptures," "extasies" and "delights" of romance are given physical location in the veins, thus mitigating the vagueness of euphemism. And, like Behn writing about Imoinda and the king, Manley has a woman's pragmatic sense of the line between "heavy petting" and "going all the way." Though far from the crude masculine cynicism of Rochester, Manley's language is romantic without the stereotypically feminine coyness about the sex act.

The combination could backfire, however; instead of elevating the physical, romantic language could seem to be a silly, pretentious covering for vulgarity. *The Female Wits,* a 1704 anonymous satiric comedy—in which Marsilia/Manley is made to boast, "I am the first that made Heroick natural" (31)—exposes this possibility by parodying her erotic style. In one of Marsilia's plays, the young wife of the hero's father is described as "the bright Partner of your Fathers Bed, too sweet a Blossome, alass, to hang on such a wither'd Tree, whose sapless Trunck affords no Nourishment to keep her Fresh and Fair!" (35). Another stylistic problem results from the originality of Manley's attempt: because she had to create her own frame of reference as she went along, her blend of romance and realism could be as disorienting as the tonal shifts in *Oroonoko.* Different episodes of *The New Atalantis* are to be read with different assumptions. In one story we are told a couple "pass'd the guilty Night" together and must imagine the rest; in another, though the couple has spent many nights together we are mistaken in jumping to conclusions (1:228, 2:66). Even when details are supplied, the level of euphemism may be unclear. When Diana's lover faints with ecstasy, she "fix'd her Mouth to his, and . . . press'd 'em with that Eagerness! that warmth of Love! as darted new Rays into the dying Lover!" (2:225). At its most figurative, this description tells of a man brought back to life by the power of love, and since this is Manley, there is the more physical suggestion of sexual arousal. But because we do not know the precise metaphorical meaning of the "rays," it would be possible to read the passage as a very poetic description of first aid.

Manley's erotic writing is easy to laugh at if one approaches it with detachment, as critics such as John J. Richetti have done; Palomo's interpretation reminds us that Manley was probably aware of this response, and that she had a sense of humor about herself. But Manley's ideal male reader was her own creation, Lovemore, a man looking for a thrill and willing to lend his imagination to her romantic-realistic love language; and within her novels, such readers are rare. Her typical male characters' failure to see that romantic language can ever be sincere is a sign of their unfitness to be heroes, of their inadequacy as lovers—of their inferiority to women. After Rodriguez has gone, Diana addresses him: "Ingrateful Rodriguez, thy Coward-Heart was never design'd a Lover, unworthy the meanest Lady's Favour," and says of him to her husband, "The ungratful Object of my Crime has prov'd as base as Cowardice wou'd make him. . . . I shall never again throw away the minutest Thought upon such a Wretch, but to detest him as the Author of my Folly!" (2:237). Ironically, by misapprehending and abusing romantic language, these men make love into the heroic tragedy they themselves do not believe in. As a result, Petrarchan metaphors of Love's artillery take on a peculiar realism for women that Petrarch himself could not have foreseen; when women like Charlot are "invaded," love really is assault with a deadly weapon.

A few women in Atalantis, disappointed with the brutality and banality of men, have established a "Cabal"—something like Behn's in its devotion to romantic love, but with this difference: no men are allowed. The cabal is like a sorority, complete with rules and rituals, which provides each member with the only partner worthy of her love, another woman. Though the heads of the organization recognize that it is "almost indispensible . . . for all Ladies once to Marry," they reserve the right to approve or disapprove any proposed match, and to insist that their members "reserve their Heart, their tender Amity for their Fair [female] Friend: An Article in this well-bred wilfully undistinguishing Age, which the Husband seems to be rarely sollicitous of" (2:47).

Ultimately, Manley rejects the cabal as a viable subculture, however, because like the dominant culture it either forces women to deny their sexuality—to "be rendred insensible on the side of Nature"—or encourages them to behave as lewdly as men, despite romantic words such as "Amity" and "Tenderness."[15] The Marchioness of Sandomire and her "female Favourite Ianthe," for example, dress as men and pick up prostitutes, who "fail'd not to find their Account, in obliging the Marchioness's and Ianthe's peculiar Taste, by all the Liberties

that belong'd to Women of their loose Character and Indigence"
(2:49). Oddly, we are told that the Marchioness has no "Adventures
. . . that could in reality wound her Chastity" (2:49), presumably
because her lovers lack what Faderman calls the "proper tool." But in
Manley's view, if the "Mysteries of the Cabal" make everyone behave
like the Marchioness and Ianthe, the organization does not provide
the romantic alternative it claims. Even if these women do manage to
combine sex and love, Manley does not approve, for this is not "what
Nature design'd." She does not finally wish to see normal marriage
subverted: "if they . . . fortifie themselves by these new-form'd
Amities against the Hymenial Union, or give their Husbands but a
second place in their Affections and Cares; 'tis wrong and to be
blam'd" (2:57-58).[16]

By rejecting the cabal, Manley in effect denies that women have
any alternative to heterosexual love and its attendant pain. Her own
experience taught her the folly of forgetting for a moment that love is
the particular enemy of women—of imagining that in love women
can be equal to men. Lovemore, she says, warned her against listening to "the Casuists [who] told her a Woman of her Wit had the
Privilege of the other Sex, since all Things were pardonable to a Lady
who could so well give Laws to others, yet was not obliged to keep
them her self" (R 44). But even when Rivella is actually innocent, she
further damages her bad reputation merely by courting the attention
of such men, and later admits that Lovemore was right (45). Developing a new erotic language might have helped Manley express her
feelings about this inequity, but only satire could help her combat it.

For this satire, Manley turned once again to the romance. Frustrated women had long been reading and trying to act out romance,
hoping "by the Charms of their Beauty, and their sweet and insinuating way of Conversation, [to] assume that native Empire over Mankind, which seems to be politically deny'd them because the way to
Authority and Glory is stop'd up" (NAt 1:55). In writing romantic
novels Manley was also motivated by a frustrated will to power,
choosing this mode only after years of mudslinging—including an
arrest for libel—had taught her that "Politicks is not the Business of a
Woman, especially of one that can so well delight and entertain her
Readers with more gentle pleasing Theams" (R 117).[17] But romance
was kinder to her than to the average woman. There was no longer
any real "Empire" to be gained by love; the days of powerful royal
mistresses were already passing in the time of Scudéry (Aronson
116-17), and women who tried to live romance merely "risque their
Virtue to gain a little contemptible Dominion over a Heart that at
the same time it surrenders it self a Slave; refuses to bestow esteem

upon the Victor" (*NAt* 1:55). A woman who wrote romance, on the other hand, could gain a sort of "Empire" by creating her own reality. By placing real people and events in romantic settings and situations, Manley could force her readers to interpret those events according to an ideal value system that gives women—especially herself—their due.

The New Atalantis provides two utopian worlds, Atalantis and the moon, which attack sexual injustice in different—seemingly opposite—ways: in Atalantis, women are as sexually active as actual men, but on the moon of the future under the rule of Astrea's prince, men are to be as modest and pure as ideal women. The utopia of the moon does not yet exist; its sketchiness shows the difficulty of even imagining how the world would be different if a woman had the running of it. In contrast, Atalantis is fully realized; it is exactly like England, except that here the woman's point of view seems normal, and so occasionally women can embarrass men with a boudoir version of male "locker-room" humor.[18]

When the fortune hunter Antonio is unexpectedly introduced into the bed of a widow he hopes to marry, and who "resolved not to be disappointed in a Husband, and would therefore try him beforehand," he finds himself unable to perform and hence an object of feminine ridicule (2:75). "Lettice, says she, bring some Cordial Water: Poor Don Antonio is not well: I fear a Lethargy has seized him! We had best then, Madam, answer'd Madamoisel Pert, send for a Surgeon to bleed him. I'm not certain, reply'd the Lady, that any thing can restore him; in my Opinion, his loss of Spirits are irrecoverable" (2:74). The humor here derives in part from Antonio's inability, as narrator of his own story, to see what was so funny or to conceal his resentment, and from his feeble attempt to regain his dignity by condemning the women's looseness. He is ludicrously unable to impose his view of the situation on a reality that is here defined by women.

Such feminine revenge is rare, however, because in most respects Atalantis is not a utopia at all, but a thinly disguised realistic rendering of Manley's England, which Astrea is studying in the hopes of avoiding similar errors on the moon. Astrea has observed that the Atalantan system for encouraging chastity and discouraging adultery is to give the criminal the power of both judge and executioner over the victim. Because men misunderstand women's love-language, they can excuse their own conduct by reasoning that women want to be lied to and abused. Even rape can be defended as a compliment to a lady, for it "give[s] her Virtue [the] Pretence for granting" (2:105; see also 2:131). As an Atalantan man explains:

There's something unaccountable, 'tis one of the Arcana's of Nature, not yet found out, why our Sex cool and neglect yours, after possession, and never, if we can avoid it (and have our Senses about us) chuse our selves Wives from those who have most obliged us; 'tis, I confess, the grand Specifick of Ingratitude, but it seems so in-born in all, that I wonder there are still found Women that confide in our false Oaths and Promises, and that Mothers do not early, as they ought, warn their Virgin Daughters from Love and Flattery, the Rocks upon which the most deserving are generally lost. [1:144-45]

Astrea's lunar solution is not to excuse inchastity in women, but to punish men for it as well—to raise men to the spiritual standard Atalantis demands only of its women: "I will have my Prince renown'd for his Chastity; I will have him introduce the fashion amongst the Men; let the Reformation begin but there, and the World will be modest" (2:192-93). On the moon, men's "false Oaths and Promises" will become true as they learn remorse for their "invasion" of women and become the heroes they now only pretend to be: "My Prince shall adore, and serve the Fair, by Methods truly advantageous! truly to their Glory! not by false-deluding-Praise, Heartbreaking Sacrifice, or fond Complaints of Cruelty and Charms; but in being their Champion against all unlawful Invaders" (2:192-93).

Like Atalantan women, lunar men who lose their reputations will have lost their means of livelihood as well: "Never shall [the Prince] cast a glance of Favour, or reward with Riches or Employment, an Adulterer or Debauchee" (2:192). The submerged political message in Manley's novel appears in the methods the Prince will employ to bring about this equality. "Since sense of Shame and Reputation can't with-hold 'em! since Conscience, Honour, and what the World calls Principles, can't deter those Betrayers; the Laws must, and those shall be Sanguinary." To be specific, "Death to those who can be prov'd to have seduc'd a Virgin. . . . [T]hey shall die without the hope of Mercy! branded and unlamented" (2:192-93).

The difference between the two worlds, one chaste and the other freely sexual, reveals Manley's ambivalence about sex and chastity. But the moon and Atalantis are not completely opposite, for even the moon is not free from lust. Both lunar and Atalantan women—unlike Behn's innocently sexy nymphs—are warned to struggle against their sexual nature; the only difference is that in Atalantis, women usually lose the struggle, whereas on the moon they are to be given the chance to win it. Only evil male characters, usually attempting to justify incest or polygamy, recommend surrender to nature (2:22,

1:219-20); the author recommends the opposite course when educating children: "to watch the Ascendency of their Temper and perpetually to ply 'em with the Antithesis." If a young girl shows amorous tendencies, her parents are advised to "stem the Tide of Nature" by keeping her away from "Opera's, Romances, Books of Love"—including, presumably, Manley's own. The most effective solutions: "early Marriages," hunting, and—oddly enough—cards, which ordinarily she abhorred: "let 'em even exceed Diversion, and make a Business of their Play: So it employ their Thoughts" (2:36).[19]

This advice, inconsistent as it is with Manley's eroticism, is actually less contradictory—at once both less realistic and less idealistic—than the more ordinary worldly view of her time. On one hand, the common view was based on a myth of innate female purity that persisted despite well-documented evidence of its untruth and despite the counter-myth of woman as "seething cauldron of lust" (Prior 123); on the other, it ignored women's subjective experience and focused only on externals: technical virginity, or the reputation for it. Thus the world rewarded women for becoming either frigid, heartless coquettes—"Coquettry may make the Fair ridiculous, but Love can only make her wretched"; or hypocrites—for the world "never look'd after what was really Good, but only after what appear'd so" (2:219, 2:21).

In contrast, Manley's seeming ambivalence about chastity is given some consistency by her romantic glorification of love. The first requirement of a Manley heroine is that she have strong passions, which she must try to resist. Given the world, she who resists is bound to be happier; but by this code a fallen woman is more truly innocent than one who preserves her chastity through coldness or shrewdness. The novels recommend chastity before the fact and defend lapses afterwards. Martyrdom gives the fallen heroine a sort of halo, as she has been made a victim by her belief that "it was a Merit in me to love what seem'd so meritorious," for "I know nothing so base and guilty as dissimulation" (1:234).

According to this romantic morality, the fallen Manley can be the romance heroine of her own life story—despite the fact that traditionally such heroines were virgins. In both the Delia episode of *The New Atalantis* and the entire *Adventures of Rivella,* Manley creates a fictional context that not only vindicates but sanctifies the actions that led to her ruin. The innocent Delia, as we have seen, has been made susceptible to the advances of her cousin Don Marcus by the romances her aunt forced on her. After the cousins are married, Don Marcus confesses that his first wife is not dead. The world assumes (as was usual in such cases) that "either I was never Married, or else could be no Stranger to his Ladies being alive" (2:186). Manley takes this opportunity to assert publicly that she was completely in the dark. Her evidence is, first, the role-reversed dirty joke: "Those that know his Person will easily believe that I was not in love with him" (2:185). Second, disclaiming the usual unromantic motives for marriage in Atalantis, she notes that she could have had nothing to gain financially, because he had married his fortune, and "unless his Wife were Dead, I must find him a Beggar" (2:186). Most important, the crime she has been blamed for could never have taken place if she had not been so thoroughly innocent and unsuspecting: "I was then wanting of Fourteen, without any Deceit or Guess of it in others. . . . Oh unexperienc'd Youth!" (2:188). In short, she was too good for the world, not too bad for it.

The world's judgment is wrong in every respect. Even those who blame Don Marcus do so for the wrong reason, citing his prior marriage as his greatest crime; whereas Astrea comments, "I can't tell whether his Marriage may not be the most excusable part." By lying about his marital status, he deceived his victim, and "whilst innocent of her undoing, the deluded Maid is blameless as to Honour." If he had merely seduced her, "made her a conscious Party to her Ruin," his villainy would "sink him, with eternal Infamy into the black Waters of Cocytus" (2:193-94). But of course so fair and ingenious an assessment of the case is possible only for God, or goddess, and the author; the world is too crude and stupid to imagine and weigh the motives of the bigamist and the victim.

In *Rivella* Manley continues her depiction of herself as above rather than below worldly morality by filtering the narration through the ears of Lovemore's friend, the Count d'Aumont. Within the story, Rivella speaks of France as a distant utopia where she "had a very great Inclination to pass her Days" (41). Since she cannot go there, she must settle for having Lovemore and d'Aumont interpret her life according to the morality of France—or of France as she imagines it from its fiction, a land that worships love. In *Rivella,* as in *L'Astrée,* love excuses all crimes by robbing the lover of "Freewill, or the Benefit of Reflection" (20). In d'Urfé's romance, Céladon apologizes to his foster father for disobeying him: "It is love which forces me to displease you. . . . I have no free will" (112). In the same way, Lovemore excuses the young Rivella for stealing from her father to pay the debts of the object of her first crush. "Being perfectly Just by Nature, Principle, and Education, nothing but Love, and that in a high degree could have made her otherwise" (22-23).

Following this code, Manley establishes her innocence not by denying passion but by frankly narrating the extremity of her first love, which the young Rivella is too naive to conceal or control. Everyone recognizes what is wrong with her but herself, and to preserve her innocence her father "forbore saying any Thing to the Girl which might acquaint her with her own Distemper" (21). When the object of her affection, a young soldier, is transferred and takes his leave, "poor Rivella fell from one Fainting into another without the least immodest Expression, Glance or Discovery of what had occasion'd her Fright" (25). The honest display of her feelings and their intensity enhance rather than detract from the narrator's sense of her goodness and purity.

Of course, such unconsciousness cannot last into adulthood—but sincerity can. The author notes bitterly that if she had been less honest and true to her own principles of love, she would have kept the world's esteem; but she has refused hypocrisy as firmly as she eschewed frigidity. Lovemore proposes marriage, and later at least the protection of cohabitation, but she turns him down because "she must first be in Love with a Man before she thought fit to reside with him" (41). Conversely, because she is in love with Cleander, her affair with him is justified; his wife is the "Termagant" who threatens to spoil it all. In fact, according to Manley's romantic code, the married Cleander is a sort of virgin who "as yet knew not what it was to Love" (68)— "so awkward, and so unfashion'd as to love; that if he did bear her any great good Will, she was sure he neither durst, nor knew how to tell it her" (71).

The world, of course, views the matter differently; respectable women cease to visit Rivella, among them the prude Calista (Manley's fellow playwright Catherine Trotter). Rivella, with her usual inconsistency denying any actual unchastity, declares herself superior to this worldly villainess: Rivella only "hazarded Appearances by indulging her natural Vanity . . . tho' perhaps with more Innocency than Discretion" (52), whereas Calista "allow[s] Freedoms with the Air of Restraint" (66). When at length it comes out that Calista has been guiltier than Rivella herself, "Rivella laugh'd in her Turn, because Calista had given her self Airs of not visiting Rivella now she was made the Town Talk by her scandalous Intriegue with Cleander" (102).

Rivella can have the last laugh here because her narrative gives her the power Manley could only wish for in life. In the story of Delia in *The New Atalantis* Manley ridiculed the delusions of grandeur women may get from romance: "I had the Honour and Cruelty of a true Heroin, and would not permit my Adorer so much as a Kiss from my Hand, without ten thousand times more Intreaty than any thing of that nature cou'd be worth" (2:184). But Rivella's grandeur is no delusion; in this novel Manley depicts herself as rejecting rather than rejected, the recipient of Lovemore's undying and unrewarded devotion, as he says: "such was the Effect of that early Disappointment, as has for ever hinder'd me from knowing the true Pleasures of Passion, because I have never felt a Concern for any other Woman, comparable to what I felt for Rivella" (27). Manley puts in the mouths of Lovemore and d'Aumont the opinion of herself she would have liked men to have—for men of her own creation can have their imaginations intact. Thus, though she wrote in *The New Atalantis* that the world had grown to care only for beauty and that "their whole Care is outward, and transferr'd to the Person . . . Love resides not in the Heart, but in the Face" (1:3), in *Rivella* a connoisseur of women tells us that beauty is unnecessary. Here, Manley can finally get even with the "two Sisters perfectly Handsom" whom she obviously envied by having Lovemore quote as public opinion that "they had less Power over Mankind than had Rivella" (15).

With the help of her sympathetic narrator and his lovestruck listener, Manley revises the romance heroine to make beauty less important than other more solid qualifications. First, she must have experience—and so the older woman who is "entirely Mistress of the Art of Love" is more appealing than "a Lady perfectly Beautiful, of the Age of Sixteen." Second, she must have "Wit and Sense," which (as Behn more jokingly said in her first play) are "so powerful a Charm" that "a Woman without either Youth or Beauty" who has these qualities may yet "make a Thousand Conquests, and preserve them too" (2). By these rules Rivella/Manley is the perfect heroine, not only possessing amatory experience and wit, but combining them to become the age's best writer about love.[20] D'Aumont has said she makes "Raptures" available to all Mortals; but Lovemore replies, "For my Part, I believe they are to be met with no where else but in her own Embraces." And d'Aumont adds, "That is what I would experience . . . if she have but half so much of the Practic, as the Theory, in the Way of Love, she must certainly be a most accomplish'd Person" (4-5). Though she claims to be now fat, unattractive, and ineligible (in fact she had at least one more affair ahead of her), at the end she is depicted, in the imagination of Lovemore, as the heroine of one of her own typical love scenes:

> I should have . . . carried you (in the Heat of Summer after Dinner) within the Nymphs Alcove, to a Bed nicely sheeted and strow'd with Roses, Jessamins or Orange-Flowers, suited to the variety of the Season; her Pillows neatly trim'd with Lace or Muslin, stuck round with Junquils, or other natural

Garden Sweets, for she uses no Perfumes, and there have
given you leave to fancy your self the happy Man, with whom
she chose to repose her self, during the Heat of the Day, in a
State of Sweetness and Tranquility. [119-20]

The romance in these two novels is kind to Manley, kinder than the
real world was to her—yet it does not finally provide the solution to
the problem of being a woman of passion and sexuality in the eighteenth century, for herself or for her readers. For romance to liberate,
it must provide a consistent vantage point for seeing and evaluating
life so that its insights can be acted upon. Unfortunately, as long as
critics, novelists, and readers defined romance as the opposite of truth
and of realistic fiction, it did not lend itself to such practical purposes.
Manley's personae and the worlds that contain them struggle against
their romantic framework, preventing romance and realism from
blending, and ultimately obstructing the satire.

Theoretically, Manley's life should have made good satire, for her
personal motives for writing were completely consistent with—or
bound up in—her more general satiric motives.[21] Readers from Manley's time to ours have cited her personal attacks on individuals—
reminiscent of Scudéry's "naughty" practice (Aronson 89)—as reasons to dismiss her satire as mere gossip. But most notable satire of
the period—from Boileau to Pope—was personal as well as political;
the concepts were inseparable in an age that was only beginning to
accept the notion that good people could have honest differences of
opinion on serious subjects.[22] Knowing that others would say—had
said in the *Tatler,* in fact—that a serious satirist rises above "particular Reflection," Manley again went back to the classics and invoked
for her justification "our Great Fore-fathers in Satire, who not only
flew against the general reigning Vices, but pointed at individual
Persons, as may be seen in Ennius, Varro, Lucian, Horace, Juvenal,
Persius" (*NAt* 2:dedication). By their authority, she asserts that personal motives and specific portraits are appropriate to satire if they
provide a center for general truths. As she could have said herself, the
details she included about the private lives of famous people might
have seemed like satire rather than gossip if they had been written by
a man—as the *Inferno, Mac Flecknoe,* and the *Dunciad* might have
been read as gossip if they had been written by a woman.[23]

Manley saw her suffering as part of the general corruption of the
world in the Iron Age.[24] Her marriage and ruin are shown to have a
basis in the unjust laws and mores of her society, which provide no
recourse against a bigamous husband (*NAt* 2:193).[25] She blames her
bad reputation on the sexual double standard that discriminates

against all women, as Lovemore remarks: "I have often heard her say, If she had been a Man, she had been without Fault: But the Charter of that Sex being much more confin'd than ours, what is not a Crime in Men is scandalous and unpardonable in Woman" (*R* 7). She also depicts her ruin as political in a more specific sense—as a Whig plot to discredit her as a Tory satirist. Rivella reports that a "wit" of her acquaintance—her former friend Sir Richard Steele—"in Print has very lately told the World, 'twas his own Fault he was not Happy [i.e. that he had rejected her advances], for which Omission he has pub-lickly and gravely ask'd her Pardon."[26] She blames the insult on "[t]he Prejudice of Party," which "runs so high in England, that the best natured Persons, and those of the greatest Integrity, scruple not to say False and Malicious Things of those who differ from them in Principles." Though, she claims, the world knows enough in most cases to discount insults from political opponents, the public appetite for sex scandal makes them credulous: "who is there besides myself, that thinks it an impossible Thing a Tory Lady should prove frail, especially when a Person (tho' never so much a Whig) reports her to be so, upon his own Knowledge?" (*R* 119).

In combining the personal and political, Manley merely followed the practice of her attackers, and therefore she felt no need to conceal her "rancor" against them (Needham, "TD," 259), or her desire for revenge: "she did no more by others, than others had done by her: i.e. Tattle of Frailties" (*R* 110). Her private and public indignation were one and the same; Lovemore calls her "a perfect Timon, or Man-Hater; all the World was out of Humour with her, and she with all the World, more particularly a faction who were busy to enslave their Sovereign, and overturn the Constitution" (*R* 109). She had no use for objectivity in the personal or the political realm, seeing her task as creating reality out of subjective vision. She was therefore annoyed with her own party when they criticized her work "with as much Severity as they would an Enemy's, and at the same Time value themselves upon their being impartial, tho' against their Friends" (110-11).[27]

Personal motives and subjectivity, then, do not in themselves impede Manley's satire. The problems come from her attempt to use romance both to justify herself and to make general statements on the condition of women. One difficulty, which we have already seen in the discussion of *Oroonoko,* is that romance deals with the exceptional rather than the typical. Manley's erotic language is intended to make all men and women heroes and heroines, but the plots of romance are not so democratic. If Delia and Rivella are convincing as romance heroines, they must be above the ordinary reader; by becoming a heroine, Manley vindicates herself at other women's expense.[28] Because she is "the *only* Person of Her Sex that knows how to Live," according to d'Aumont, "it would have been a Fault in *her,* not to have been Faulty [my emphasis]" (120)—but not, presumably, in anyone else.

Other women within these novels are the heroines' competitors rather than sisters in the same cause. One story in *The New Atalantis,* we're told, has as one of its morals "That no Woman ought to introduce another to the Man by whom she is belov'd" (1:83). Mothers bear an equal part with husbands in the bullying of heroines; Corinna, for example, is like a shuttlecock tossed back and forth between an abusive mother, who had her imprisoned for lunacy, and an abusive husband, whom she married in an attempt to escape (2:169-79). And of course besides mothers there are the "termagant" wives, usually represented as having married for worldly and therefore wrong reasons, who uphold the status quo by excluding "other women" such as Manley from respectable society.

As long as Manley is fighting only for herself, she can complain of unfair treatment of women without attacking the general assumptions that cause her suffering. For example, she does not question that wit harms the character of women—in general. In *The New Atalantis* the Duke "wisely" warns Charlot to stifle "a desire of being applauded for her Wit," and to avoid all "Embellishments of the Mind not connected with Duty," because "the possession of 'em was attended with Self-Love, Vanity and Coquettry" (1:53-54). Wit in women is elsewhere associated with violence and bad temper as well as egotism; it is a witty woman who almost strangles her stepdaughter (1:159). Any attractive female wit, besides her own, is peevishly labeled "superficial": "an agreeable manner of telling a Story, no matter whether the Story be good or bad . . . incessant Flattery . . . are their Letters of Mart, and pass better in Love's-Exchange, than fine Understanding" (1:109). Manley's own true wit, on the other hand, finds fit audience though few. Lovemore says of Rivella "that one might discourse Seven Years together with [her], and never find out from her self, that she was a Wit, or an Author" (11). Thus the average woman, Manley's reader, is told to keep quiet and leave wit to heroines such as Manley, not to join with her in opposing the world's prejudice.

Romance thus fails as satire when Manley succeeds in becoming a heroine; it also fails when she fails. Her revision of the traditional heroine does not go far enough to include herself. For example, in the preface to *Queen Zarah,* she accepts the notion that chastity is the source of the heroine's attractiveness and therefore of her power. She does speak up for realism, referring to the "extraordinary virtues [of] their heroines" as "a Fault which Authors of Romances commit in every Page." "It wou'd in no wise be probable," she argues, "that a Young Woman fondly beloved by a Man of great Merit, and for whom she had a Reciprocal Tenderness, finding her self at all times alone with him in Places which favour'd their Loves, cou'd always resist his Addresses; there are too Nice Occasions, and an Author wou'd not enough observe good Sense, if he therein exposed his Heroins." But the alternative to foisting this "miracle" on the reading public is to omit the "nice occasions" that strain belief—not to allow the heroines to succumb (*Zarah* 1:preface).

These remarks suggest that Manley herself did not fully believe in the heroinehood of her abundant fallen women, including herself. Certainly the angelic figure she describes here could hardly get down in the dirt with her enemies, as she felt the need to do in her autobiographical romances. In her flashes of "rancor" she comes across most convincingly and appealingly, but hardly romantically; and so her belligerence interferes with the strategy she has chosen to vindicate her life and character. In *Rivella* she nearly manages a ladylike, ironic reply to Steele's insult that would have put him gently and firmly in the wrong. She has the courtly Lovemore speak for her: "since the charitable Custom of the World gives the Lie to that Person, whosoever he be, that boasts of having receiv'd a Lady's Favour, because it is an Action unworthy of Credit, and of a Man of Honour; may not he by the same Rule be disbeliev'd, who says he might and would not receive Favours . . . ?" (*R* 118). But as the passage continues, the tone changes, and we no longer hear Lovemore: "especially from a Sweet, Clean, Witty, Friendly, Serviceable and young Woman, as Rivella was, when this Gentleman pretends to have been Cruel; considering that in the Choice of his other Amours, he has given no such Proof of his Delicacy, or the Niceness of his Taste" (118). The satire degenerates into a cat-fight in which an undisguised and inelegant Manley lashes out not only at the man who claimed to have rejected her, but also at any other women he may have had in her place.

Manley's persona often shifts abruptly from chaste dignity to feisty bawdry, thus confusing the reader about who she "really" is. She seems to have one foot on the moon and one on Atalantis, even asserting her purity and impugning a man's sexual potency at the same time, as when she attempts to prove that she did not have or even want to have an affair with Sir Peter Vainlove (Sir Thomas Skipwith), who boasted publicly that Rivella gave him syphilis: "Rivella was much to his Taste . . . but because he found she was a Woman of Fire, more than perhaps he could answer, he was resolved to destroy any

Hopes she might have of a nearer Correspondence than would conveniently suit with his present Circumstances, by telling her his Heart was already prepossess'd" (46-47). The mistress, she claims, is just a cover-up: "for upon Report of a fair young Lady whom he brought to tread the Stage, that he had pass'd three Days and Nights successively in Bed with her without any Consequence, he was thought rather dangerous to a Woman's Reputation than her Vertue" (51).

In these passages Manley's projected character is not the only source of inconsistency and disorientation. The world that reacts to her conduct is sometimes the real world that misunderstands her, sometimes the ideal, fictional world that sees her as she wishes to be seen. Manley's reply to Steele begins with the graceful assumption that the world is too "Charitable" and "Chevalier" to believe Steele's remarks; but the angry ending betrays her lack of confidence in it. As for the Sir Peter incident, Rivella claims that "the World found out the Cheat, detesting his Vanity and Rivella's Folly; that cou'd suffer the Conversation of a Wretch so insignificant to her Pleasures, and yet so dangerous to her Reputation" (52). Yet who makes reputations if not "the World"?

Because Manley does not distinguish those of her experiences that generalize from those that do not, she does not hesitate to create a new fictional world for every new occasion without regard to internal or external consistency. Her almost pathetic lack of restraint in aiming all her cannons at the most insignificant targets weakens her credibility. Whenever anyone she dislikes, such as the Duchess of Cleveland, appears in her novels, she bends the entire satiric framework to make that dislike seem universal and therefore objective and fair: "she was hated not only by all the World, but by her own Children and Family; not one of her Servants, but what would have laugh'd to see her lie dead amongst them, how affecting soever such Objects are in any other Case" (*R* 34-35).[29] But no matter how many others are invented to confirm the truth of Manley's opinion, the angry tone reminds the reader that this woman would not be in Manley's novels at all if the world had really taken the author's side against her.

This constant shifting between worlds—the real and the ideal—harms more than the satire; it makes the lives of Manley's heroines, including herself, unlivable, and therefore as tragic as Oroonoko's, Imoinda's, and Behn's. For each of Manley's worlds judges women according to its own code, and the codes conflict, even when both pay lip service to the same virtue. Chastity, for instance, in theory is no more a virtue in women than in men; in practice, only women are punished for its loss. Theoretically, a heroine who is innocent according to the romantic code should be able to ignore what the real world thinks of her: "the real Worthy, the truly Virtuous . . . know themselves Innocent" (*NAt* 2:15). But practically, "Care ought to be taken by others . . . to prevent the ill-nature'd World's refining upon their mysterious Innocence" (2:46). A humane author could hardly recommend ignoring a world that had so much will and power to punish women. Therefore, her heroines must satisfy both codes—and therefore, they cannot survive.[30]

The story of Urania and Polydore stands out as a disturbing example of the martyrdom Manley's heroines undergo. Sincerity ennobles these twins, who represent Golden Age innocence and sincerity, believing in "the divine Precepts of Truth and openness in Manners . . . since Hypocrisie is certainly the very worst Ingredient in the Character of any Woman of Quality or pretended Honour" (*NAt* 2:21-22). Their more worldly cousin Harriet speaks for Iron Age corruption, using Behn's metaphor of the veil to link inhibition and coquetry: "Oh how necessary was Dissimulation! how it bought Opinion! 'Twas like a Veil to the Face, conceal'd all that one wou'dn't have disclos'd to vulgar Eyes, and intirely at ones own pleasure and discretion, when to wear or when to lay aside" (2:21).

Subsequent events test these competing opinions and finally show that "Dissimulation" would not be necessary if the world were not made up of Harriets. Urania and Polydore commit incest, a sin even Manley cannot condone, though she does almost excuse it by blaming it on the superficial education they have received from their guardian, Harriet's mother. Like Adam and Eve, they fall in love because they have not been told that it is wrong; their likeness to each other recalls the days of innocence in which all men and women were (in a sense) each other's twins. Despite their crime they are far superior to the self-righteous Harriet, who discovers Urania's pregnancy and—in the name of "her Duty! her Honour! her Religion! her Glory! her adored Virtue!"—betrays the secret (2:29).

During her lying-in, Urania grows to understand her sin, and she is much harder on herself than the reader—harder even than God: "Her guilty Passion gave place to a serene Horror, and fixt Despair . . . unavailing Repentance! unavailing, because united Waters cou'd not wash away her Stain! no Mortification! no Amendment, restore her to the World's Opinion" (2:33-34). Her unwillingness to defy the World—her goodness above and beyond strict justice—is what makes Urania a heroine. She destroys herself because she has internalized the voice of her unjust society. In a scene even more gruesome than the death of Oroonoko—for despite the exclamation points it is horrifically plausible, given the commonness of infanticide—Urania forces herself to die in childbirth: "when the Mother-Pains came upon her, [she] forbore to call! she forbore to groan! she trembled for fear of being assisted! she dreaded to be relieved, since Life was her greatest Pain, Death must be her greatest Ease! her throws redoubled! so did her Resolution! she drank her Tears, supprest her Cries, groan'd inwardly with strongest Woe." She hesitates momentarily when she realizes she is about to "Murder the Innocent, the unborn hapless Infant. . . . But when by a Revolution of Thought, she remembered it was the Offspring of Incestuous Joy; that it must come branded into the World for ever unfortunate to its self, by its Parent's Crime: She wish'd not to disclose to Light a Wretch so miserable! Then fortifying her Resolution with conscious Pride, Honour, and the World's Opinion, she gave her self new Fortitude to meet her Fate" (2:34-35). Somehow Manley wishes the reader to feel that Urania has died because she is too good for this world, although she has committed incest, suicide, and murder.

When Manley tells her own story she is also (if less dramatically) hampered by the rule that forbids heroines to appear to know their true worth. Delia's self-blame makes her hesitate to tell her story to Beaumond, because "Where I should be so fond of Esteem, I am entring upon Methods to destroy it." But the story, as we have seen, makes villains of her aunt, Don Marcus—everyone but herself. She was only "unwary" because of her "extreme Youth and Innocence"— like Urania, a sinner only because of her extreme goodness (2:181). As Rivella, Manley covers her self-congratulation by letting a fictional other tell her story. Her behavior as heroine follows the same pattern of martyrdom and unnecessary guilt when she selflessly rejects her just romantic reward to placate an unjust world. After the death of Cleander's wife, she refuses his offer of marriage in order to leave him free to marry a rich widow, for although in romance it is evil to marry for money, she cannot endure the anticipated reproach, however unfounded, of "having preferr'd the Reparation of her own Honour, to the Preservation of his" (106).[31]

Romance could not free Manley, her heroines, or her readers as long as she balked at defying reality. But as with Behn in *Oroonoko*, one must look beyond the author for the real causes of her authorial inconsistencies. The problem of balancing the ideal and the real, the theoretically and the practically just, haunted most early novels, by men as well as by women. This problem made Behn loyal to her hero as his narrator, but not as his friend; and it would make Richardson, in the coming decades, reward his best characters with the world's admiration for being above wanting that reward. Furthermore, it would not have seemed hypocritical to Manley's readers, as it might to those of our own time, to point out a sexual double standard without trying to start a revolution, for in the eighteenth century the Juvenalian satirist could complain, like Job, without expecting to do away with evil. Manley seems to have recognized that women could gain a measure of freedom by avoiding offense; one of her favorite satiric techniques, as Needham points out, was to insult by pretending to praise ("TD" 276-77). In the same way she could write pornography while condemning it. The famous irony of later women writers, such as Jane Austen, has its source in Manley's talent for working subversively within the system.

Inconsistency is especially noticeable in Manley's novels because on the topic of love—Manley's constant "Theam"—the ideal and the real were polar opposites, especially with respect to female conduct. Furthermore, Manley's contrasts are unusually sharp: her romance is truly fantastic, and her realism is, in many respects, real. To appreciate her place in the development of the novel, it is important to note that neither romance nor realism alone would have been able to depict the injustice of life from a woman's point of view. Manley was more radical than Eliza Haywood, Charlotte Lennox, and Fanny Burney in even attempting to imagine a world with no gender barrier—even if that world existed only in a France that never was, or in a distant future on the moon.

3

Betsy Thoughtless & Harriot Stuart
Unacknowledged Sisters

Au fond peu vicieuse elle aime à coqueter.
(Basically not very wicked, she loves to flirt.)
—Boileau

IN 1751, two very similar novels with very similar heroines appeared: *The History of Miss Betsy Thoughtless,* by Eliza Haywood, and *The Life of Harriot Stuart,* by Charlotte Lennox.[1] There was no question of direct mutual influence: the two novelists did not know each other and expressed little respect for each other's work.[2] But the resemblance was no coincidence: Betsy and Harriot, who have much in common with many other heroines of the 1740s and 1750s, were in a sense engendered by current ideas about women and fiction.[3] One of their more insistent traits is extreme chastity, carried almost to the point of frigidity. By this time the Manleyesque heroine who gave all for love—a stock figure of many a tragic novella and heroic drama—had grown tiresome, an unappealing love object for male readers, and a dispiriting model for females. Manley's novels suggested that the only way a woman could avoid tragedy was to avoid love—and so, as she believed, to be an inferior person. The heroines of the newer fiction, in their resistance to passion, were part descendants—nieces, perhaps—of Manley's realistic, unromantic, calculating coquettes; but to the new generation of readers, they seemed both more believable and more admirable than the passionate heroines they replaced.

The shift in taste away from passion and tragedy was dramatic and comparatively sudden, taking place during the writing career of Eliza Haywood and dividing it into two phases. From 1719 through 1730, Haywood was renowned for popular novels and novellas of many types, especially racy love stories and romans à clef, most of which, like Manley's, ended tragically.[4] After 1740—and especially after the appearance in 1742 of Richardson's *Pamela,* which also reflected the new taste—Haywood made her heroines virgins who seemed to deserve a happy ending, prompting Clara Reeve to write in 1785, "I would be the last to vindicate her faults, but the first to celebrate her return to virtue, and her atonement for them" (*Progress* 1:122). Like most eighteenth-century dichotomies, however, the distinction between Haywood's two phases seems far less sharp now than it seemed at the time. In her later works, and in the novels of the 1740s and 1750s in general, romance characteristics by no means disappeared or gave way either to realism or to morality. The new taste simply meant a reshuffling of the deck, a new blend of romance and realism with a clear didactic purpose—and a new set of paradoxes and problems for the novelist.

This chapter will examine these complications as they appear in *Betsy Thoughtless* and *Harriot Stuart*. We must begin, however, with the atmosphere of ideas about women and about fiction that helped create these heroines and their sisters.

Why had the combination of romance and realism seen in Behn's and Manley's romans à clef ceased to please readers? An answer may be found in Henry Fielding's *Joseph Andrews* (1742), in which he writes that such books "contain, as I apprehend, very little Instruction or Entertainment" (4). The roman à clef allowed Manley to surround what was called reality with a romance world, but the critique that resulted does not seem to Fielding to point to a higher morality. Furthermore, he doubts that the roman à clef contains reality at its core, especially the versions by "modern novel and Atalantis writers"—that is, the early works of Eliza Haywood (Elwood 186-87).

Fielding barely allows a distinction between these novels and Scudéry's "immense Romances," which most English readers did not know were also about real people. Both, he claims, "without any Assistance from Nature or History, record Persons who never were, or will be, and Facts which never did nor possibly can happen" (187). Because "secret histories" pretend to be true, Fielding here implies that Haywood is not only a bad writer but a liar. And in a way her practice merits the accusation, for instead of actual people with romance names, Haywood gave her readers romance characters with romance names, apparently placing the phrase "secret history" on the title page only to encourage suspension of disbelief.[5]

Instead of Manley's and Haywood's tragedy, Fielding prefers comedy, which he believes has greater possibilities for realism and didacticism. The preface to *Joseph Andrews* defines that novel as a "comic Epic-Poem in Prose," in part to sever its connections with the female "moderns," the classically uneducated granddaughters of the précieuses who had offended Boileau (4); and also to justify by "ancient" Aristotelian precedent the introduction of "Persons of inferiour Rank, and consequently, of inferiour Manners," or "natural," common folk rather than sublime heroes (4).[6] Such characters, he says, are a source of the ridiculous and are therefore entertaining. Because he derives the ridiculous from the moral flaw of affectation, he also considers these characters instructive (7-10).

Haywood also insisted that her purpose was to instruct as well as to entertain; her early, tragically fallen heroines, she claimed, were meant not to titillate readers but to warn them (Whicher 12, 19). But when her early works are read this way, instruction conflicts with delight by discouraging the reader's attraction to or identification with the fallen woman. Comedy, on the other hand, is wonderfully suited to the more challenging moral purpose of showing the reader what to do rather than what to avoid. And in a general way, comedy was far more compatible with dominant modes of thought in the eighteenth century, which, as Margaret Doody remarks, had almost entirely lost its tragic vision (*A Natural Passion* 245). Tragedy celebrates "Dionysian" qualities that are not consistent with social morality. Furthermore, it depends on a belief in a fate beyond human control. Men, especially, who liked to envision themselves as in command of their destinies, found little to pity in sufferings that they believed must necessarily be the hero's or heroine's own fault—hence the constant tinkering with Shakespeare. In contrast, comedy confirms social morality, because comic heroes and heroines ultimately achieve personal fulfillment by finding their place in relation to God and their fellow creatures.

In the interest of realism and didacticism, then, comedy became the mode of choice—especially for male novelists and critics. In 1750—one year before the publication of *Betsy Thoughtless* and *Harriot Stuart*—Samuel Johnson in his *Rambler 4* followed Fielding in connecting realism and didacticism with comedy, praising the modern "comedy of romance" in contrast to the "heroic romance" of writers such as Scudéry. But the realism Johnson prefers in modern fiction is not of character but of plot; "natural" plot development, he says, has more instructive possibilities than the "machines and expedients" of the older romances, because in modern fiction characters are forced to deal with the consequences of their actions (19). To borrow Frye's terms, Johnson praises the "hence" type of narrative (which one finds in Richardson) over the "and then" style of the old romances (Frye, *Secular Scripture*, 47-48).

Johnson's essay indirectly criticizes Fielding, particularly the "and then" plot of *Tom Jones*. But despite the essay's praise of realism, the more serious indictment of Fielding here is not that his plots are too romantic, but that his characters are not romantic enough. Johnson warns novelists against too much "nature" in their characterizations; one must not "so mingle good and bad qualities in their principal personages that they are both equally conspicuous," for then "we lose the abhorrence of their faults because they do not hinder our pleasure, or perhaps regard them with some kindness for being united with so much merit. . . . For while men consider good and evil as springing from the same root, they will spare the one for the sake of the other, and in judging, if not of others at least of themselves, will be apt to estimate their virtues by their vices" (23-24).

Johnson acknowledges what Manley also saw: that realism in itself is not didactic. (It is worth noting that when Johnson wrote fiction he used the Oriental tale, a form not very different from Manley's utopian allegorical romances.) In fact, in Manley's time, realistic fiction often took the form of the criminal biography or scandal novel and was therefore the opposite of "improving"; highly moral writers such as Penelope Aubin deliberately avoided it (Whicher 65-66). A didactic purpose requires some frame of reference for judging reality, whether it be the implicit religious allegory Richetti has seen in criminal stories or the explicit romantic allegories of *Atalantis* and *Rivella* (Richetti 13, 31, 53). Although Johnson's chapter in Lennox's *The Female Quixote* shows agreement with Fielding's estimation of seventeenth-century French romance, in a broader sense the polarization of good and evil he recommends is "romantic."[7]

Neither Haywood nor Lennox heeded Johnson's warning about "mixed" characters, for in theory both considered realistic characterization more instructive than models of perfection. In 1752 Lennox would devote her entire second novel to the subject, and in 1748 Haywood had called herself "an enemy to all romances, novels, and whatever carries the air of them, tho' disguised under different appellations," thus condemning two decades of her own fiction. Her statement goes on to support Fielding's preference for "natural" characters, balancing what Johnson was soon to write in the *Rambler* by pointing out the dangers of polarization: "[I]f the pattern laid down before us, is so altogether angelic, as to render it impossible to be copied, emulation will be in danger of being swallowed up in an unprofitable admiration; and, on the other hand, if it appears so monstrously hideous as to take away all apprehensions of ever resembling it, we might be too apt to indulge ourselves in errors which would seem small in comparison with those presented to us" (*Life's Progress* 1-2).[8]

Haywood and Lennox put their theories in practice by creating "mixed" heroines, thus confusing and offending the many readers who shared Johnson's opinion. The *Monthly Review* disliked in Betsy

Thoughtless the very realism today's readers are most likely to admire, complaining that she does not elicit a single clear response: "Tho' such an example may afford lessons of prudence, yet how can we greatly interest ourselves in the fortune of one, whose character and conduct are neither amiable nor infamous, and which we can neither admire, nor love, nor pity, nor be diverted with?" (Whicher 162-63). Female characters in particular were expected to be exemplary, and readers were especially unhappy when they were not; Lady Mary Wortley Montagu commented that Harriot Stuart, "being intended for an example of wit and virtue, is a jilt and a fool in every page" (Séjourné 151). By using "mixed" heroines despite readers' sense that they were poor vehicles for instruction, Haywood and Lennox asserted a fairly revolutionary moral principle: that young women, as well as young men such as Tom Jones, learn virtue through experience. They thus opposed the commonly held idea that goodness in women is a kind of blankness, as chastity is merely an absence of sexual contact.

Of course the authors, as real women, were "mixed" in this way; like Manley, they demanded for their heroines only what they wanted for themselves. In fact both authors whetted their readers' appetites for true "secret histories" by matching their heroines with their own public personae. Haywood could expect her readers to recognize her as the reformed Betsy Thoughtless from her self-portrait in the opening number of her periodical, *The Female Spectator* (1744): "I have run through as many scenes of vanity and folly as the greatest coquet of them all. . . . I should have thought that day lost which did not present me with some new opportunity of showing myself. My life, for some years, was a continued round of what I then called pleasure, and my whole time engrossed by a hurry of promiscuous diversions." But she goes on to treat these mistakes as her qualifications as a writer:

> The company I kept was not, indeed, always so well chosen as it ought to have been, for the sake of my own interest or education; but then it was general, and by consequence furnished me, not only with a knowledge of many occurrences, which otherwise I had been ignorant of, but also enabled me, when the too great vivacity of my nature became tempered with reflection, to see into the secret springs which gave rise to the actions I had either heard or been witness of, to judge of the various passions of the human mind and distinguish those imperceptible degrees by which they become masters of the heart, and attain the dominion over reason. [1-2]

Barred by her sex from assuming a voice of detached moral authority, as Fielding and Johnson had done, Haywood found a different kind of authority by identifying with her heroine in a reformed state.

By narrating her first novel in the retrospective first person, Charlotte Lennox achieved a similar identification and authority.[9] Though new to fiction and much younger than Haywood, Lennox had already established a public persona in a series of poems, one of which, "The Art of Coquetry," was much read and talked about when it was reprinted in the *Gentlemen's Magazine* in 1750.[10] The narrator of that poem is an experienced flirt who gives advice on how various types of women may conquer various types of men in the battle of love—as long as they themselves beware the Petrarchan weapons Manley had described and "guard against the soft invader love." A year later, Lennox introduced a flirtatious heroine who is also a poet (like Lennox, and every other female poet, known as Sappho), who also claims to be impervious, and whose verses are also taken to suggest that she is not.[11] "The Art of Coquetry" was disliked in Bluestocking circles, where it was nicknamed the "Art of Tormenting" (Small 8-9, 86). These readers were prepared to see *Harriot Stuart* as a barely fictionalized autobiography of an improper woman—especially after Lady Mary Wortley Montagu discovered a "clef": the insulting portrait of her friend Lady Isabella Finch, Lennox's former patron, as Lady Cecilia (Small 6, 49, Séjourné 18).[12] Eventually other Bluestockings would approve Lennox's writing, once Johnson had taken her up—though according to Fanny Burney and Hester Thrale, "nobody likes her" (Small 49, Séjourné 24).

This reaction—together with the reviews of Haywood's and Lennox's 1751 novels—suggests how easily a woman novelist's attempt to establish moral authority through experience could backfire, working against the heroine rather than in favor of the author. Because of the special nature of female experience and the special standards by which women were judged, Haywood's and Lennox's commitment to realism and instruction led them back to romance and kept their later comic works surprisingly close in theme and form to the tragic novels of the first half of the century. As these authors knew too well, experience for women was likely to make their stories tragic, for according to both social and romantic morality only the chaste woman could be rewarded with a happy ending. Although they described themselves, like their heroines, as coquettes rather than whores, no one believed them. After Pope's salacious attack on Haywood in *The Dunciad,* it was late in the day for her to set up as a pattern for her sex, like Jane Barker or Penelope Aubin.[13] She was known to have left her husband, as Lennox was rumored to have done

(Séjourné 20). Both women had had brief stage careers, thereby revealing a desire for attention and applause far less redeemable than Betsy's and Harriot's flirting. If the authors themselves had been characters in a novel, they would have been warnings to the reader, like Haywood's early tragic heroines. Only the comic heroine could provide a positive as well as a negative example—could be the reader's friend instead of the outcast she was expected to shun. Therefore, Haywood and Lennox stopped their alter egos short of their own gravest mistakes and gave them the traditional romance heroine's chastity. Still, the comic endings do not quite dissipate the cloud that hovers over Betsy and Harriot during most of their adventures.

The heroines' chastity may qualify them for comedy, but it is also largely responsible for these novels' tragic overtones. Chaste heroines avoid experience as a source of corruption, so that their "adventures" literally "come *to* them" from an external source rather than emanating *from* their own characters.[14] When Harriot says to herself, "Ah! let me profit by these accidents, and for the future, spare myself such vexatious adventures!" she unwittingly reminds the reader that the whole novel up to that point—and the word "accidents" itself—has made this admonition pointless (2:163). And although Betsy's novel looks less like an old romance than Harriot's—without *Harriot Stuart*'s pirates, shipwrecks, and Indians (most of which Lennox probably had actually seen)—she too lacks control over her life. Whether a woman is nearly raped by a ship's crew on the Atlantic or by two young students at Oxford, men are "at the helm." These novels do not follow the "hence" pattern Johnson identified as realistic, nor the comic pattern he and Fielding considered instructive; the "and then" plotting of romance affirms the validity of the tragic view of life by contradicting the notion that all suffering is deserved. Furthermore, because Haywood and Lennox insist that their heroines develop consciousness of the fate they are helpless to change, their condition is almost Sophoclean.[15]

Chastity also increases the tragic tone of the novels because of the ever-present danger of its loss—a danger that does not seem real in comic novels by men, in which the fallen woman is merely an object of bawdy humor.[16] The tragic, ruined heroines of Manley's and Haywood's earlier novels have been reduced to minor status and sprinkled liberally throughout *Betsy Thoughtless* and *Harriot Stuart,* reminding the reader that women who escape disaster are not ordinary women but lucky exceptions—figures from romance rather than reality. Eroticism is thus as much a mainstay of the new comic novels as it had been of the older tragic ones.[17] Whereas earlier heroines such as Haywood's Idalia are raped and die, Betsy and Harriot narrowly escape rape and live; and both phases of Haywood's fiction express discontent with this state of affairs.[18] Mary Anne Schofield suggests that the passionate villainesses of the early novellas release the author's own rage (*Eliza Haywood* 21); the same sublimated rebelliousness is seen in *Betsy Thoughtless*'s nightmare sequence, just before Betsy's marriage to the villain Munden (*Quiet Rebellion* 109). The new novels do not show a new or more positive view of the sex war, but merely a transfer of interest from the tragic axiom that a woman who loves is doomed, to its comic corollary: that a woman who does not love may live happily, and freely, ever after.

This corollary is not truly comic, however; traditional comedies end with marriage for love—as do *L'Astrée, Clelia,* and most novels of the mid-eighteenth century. Nor is it realistic, for real-life women did feel that marriage—with or without love—was the "end" for most of them. The only real escape from tragedy for Betsy and Harriot, then, is not virginity, as they believe at first, but its opposite. In the end Betsy cashes in her chastity for a Manleyesque love scene; seated in "an arbour . . . overspread with jessamines and honey-suckles," "in the most negligent night-dress that could be," she is accosted by Trueworth, who "threw his arms about her waist, not regarding the efforts she made to hinder him, and clasp'd her to his breast with a vehemence, which in all his days of courtship to her he never durst attempt" (567, 569, 571).

But how does a heroine impervious to passion come to want this comic reward? How are we to believe in the cold heroine's potential for warmth—to understand Harriot's claim, for instance, to be both hard and sentimental, or in Lady Mary's phrase, "a jilt and a fool"? (1:4-5, 8). The difficulty had not appeared in older romances in which the woman was a symbolic object, the beloved; but when the woman becomes the subject, the central consciousness of a psychologically realistic novel, the combination of cold and warm complicates the problem of seeing the "mixed" heroine clearly. Betsy and Harriot are "mixed" in more than the moral sense; each is a sometimes confusing combination of real and romantic, ordinary and extraordinary.[19] Even their chastity serves several contradictory purposes: to make them more respectable and therefore more "normal" and believable than their tragic predecessors; to invoke the old romance archetype of the angel, which even Manley had seen as traditional; and to show how real women can use spiritual excellence to inspire a romantic love that will outlast the loss of youth and beauty.[20]

The moral value of chastity in these novels is especially difficult to pinpoint. For both Betsy and Harriot, chastity is connected to a flaw: vanity. This failing explains their coquetry while preserving

their innocence, for they are completely without the "vicious inclination," or lustfulness, that is commonly supposed to turn women into
flirts (Haywood 3; see also Lennox 1:23-24). In a sense their vanity
even prevents viciousness: the moving toyshops of their hearts are
incapable of receiving deep impressions. But as they perfect themselves they must be cured of their vanity by love; and love, ironically,
makes them as susceptible to "vicious inclination" as Manley's or
Haywood's tragic heroines. This moral paradox makes the novels
appear to be moving in opposite directions at once. Betsy and Harriot
must learn to stop flirting, and to fall in love: in a sense, to discourage
men's attention just as they are developing a true taste for it. As their
hearts become freer, their actions become more circumscribed. And as
they move toward a comic ending, they skirt the edges of tragedy; for
although they do not die of love, they spend most of their time in the
Iron Age world in which love itself is dead.[21]

The rest of this chapter will trace the simultaneous opening and
closing of the heroines in these two very similar works.

The forward movement of *Betsy Thoughtless* and *Harriot Stuart* consists of the heroines' progress from cold to warm, described in the
language of French romance. Although Haywood claimed to dislike
romances, she did once write that her degenerate age had much to
learn from writers such as Scudéry (whom she believed to be a man),
who she says merely used romance "to cloath Instruction with delight" and thus to trick readers into reform (*The Tea-Table,* quoted in
Schofield, *Eliza Haywood,* 105).[22] *Betsy Thoughtless* and *Harriot
Stuart* approach the same goal in a different way. The "Instruction" is
the "cloathing"; the didactic names for the characters (less pervasive
in Lennox's novel than in Haywood's) replace the pastoral names of
French romance, and the "delight" is found—consistent with Congreve's definition of the novel—in the realistic details that locate the
allegory within the actual times and places of the readers' lives. This
inversion enables the authors to spell out how abstract allegories
such as Scudéry's Map of Tender apply to the experiences of young
English women readers struggling to maintain identity under the
pressures of a patriarchal courtship system.[23]

Both novels open with the heroines' early adolescence and the
beginning of their awareness of the opposite sex. This time frame
underlines their importance as subjects rather than as mere mar-
riageable objects and allows the authors to observe and comment on
the young women's feelings as they develop, before others' decisions
on their behalf make those feelings insignificant.

Before describing the process that we might call the heroines' psychosexual development, I would like to address the problem of using modern psychological terms in place of older romantic ones. Although "Tenderness" and "Inclination" may seem vague and unscientific, even euphemistic and evasive, any words we replace them with may lead to the distortion women writers were trying to avoid by continuing to use them despite the prevalence of male anti-romantic satire. One of Freud's legacies is a tendency to talk about sex in isolation rather than as one small part of a complex emotion—and women still complain that this language does not describe their experience. Because eighteenth-century women *were* often evasive, I will sometimes need to isolate sexuality as a corrective in this discussion. But I do so without implying that modern language is necessarily any more descriptive or clear than the language of Scudéry.[24]

At the outset of their stories, Betsy and Harriot believe they have no "inclination"—that is, no positive desire or will for sex, though Harriot is not always consistent on this point. Their emotional immaturity is presented as a function of their undeveloped intellect: both are more or less "thoughtless," resistant to "lasting impressions," and therefore able to learn only after many repetitions of the same mistakes (Lennox 1:38-41, Haywood 519). Harriot starts out slightly ahead of Betsy in feeling and consciousness because she is a writer. Her native "enthusiastic tenderness" cries out for expression in romantic letters to a female friend, and the letters feed the tenderness—"I became in love . . . at eleven years old . . . and to that inspiring passion my muse first owed its existence" (1:4-5). But despite this literary emotion, Harriot continually denies ever being "deeply in love" and is surprised when everyone who reads her poetry senses that she is smoldering with desire (1:24).

Betsy, in contrast, does not write; in the early stages of the novel it would be surprising even to see her read, for she suffers from the attention and memory deficits child psychologists now expect to find in teenagers diagnosed as hyperactive. Unlike the readers of her history, she lacks curiosity about other people and thus misses many opportunities to hear their exciting stories—though characters such as Lady Mellasin seem almost eager for an audience (68-69). Because she does not concentrate, traumatic events such as the death of her father and the loss of her school friends fail to produce "more than a momentary regret" (10).

Although Betsy and Harriot are "too volatile for reflection" (Haywood 8), they are as fond of mirrors as any character in Aphra Behn's *Love Letters*. At age eleven the one thing they know about themselves is that they are desired, if not desiring; they define themselves as objects to be looked at, and their sense of worth derives from the power they imagine they exercise over their admirers. Their suitors and their mirrors are often interchangeable, for both merely serve to confirm their identity. When Betsy is bored with "her own resemblance in the great glass," she looks for company that will fill the same purpose in a more entertaining way (246). And we are once shown Harriot dressing for dinner on board a ship, fantasizing in the mirror about the "conquests" she is about to make among the sailors, and then going down to her table and receiving their compliments while "casting my eyes at the same time on the glass" (Lennox 1:175, 179).

The heroines' emotional and intellectual growth—and their arrival at the happy ending—requires that they become more than mere objects. They must learn to look at themselves in a different way, allowing "some part of that time, which is wasted at the toilet, in consulting what dress is most becoming to the face, [to be] employed in examining the heart, and what actions are most becoming of the character" (Haywood 3). Both girls are clearly capable of this maturity from the start: in her first volume Betsy already sees in Flora Mellasin "as in a mirror, her own late follies," and by the second volume she is asking Lady Trusty "to shew me to myself" (21, 184). In a sense, the heroines' preoccupation with mirrors is proof of their potential for intellectual and sexual maturity, because self-consciousness is a prelude to self-awareness, and autoeroticism precedes heterosexual love.[25] *Harriot Stuart* is an especially good study of the way self-love leads to love of men—through the medium of other women. As Faderman notes, tender friendship between women was encouraged in the eighteenth century as preparation for marriage (75)—a real-life practice strangely reminiscent of the gender transformations of *L'Astrée*.[26] Harriot's love letters to her female friend prepare her to love a boy, though at first only an androgynous one (like d'Urfé's Céladon) whose "beauty . . . had something too sweet and delicate in it for one of his sex" (1:5).

Although Betsy and Harriot are clearly capable of thought and feeling, they are surrounded by conditions that discourage their development. For one thing, most of the men they meet do not have a woman's sweetness and delicacy, and therefore the heroines' "narcissism"—an eighteenth-century as well as a Freudian term—does not lead naturally to heterosexual love. When Betsy and Harriot gaze at their reflections—like any woman today who watches television, goes to movies, or reads magazines—they assume an imagined male point of view toward what they see. Men are to look, not to be looked at. To the heroines, the "modern Narcissus" types who, like themselves, live to be admired are merely ludicrous competitors: as Harriot says of the male coquet Repoli, "I very soon had the pleasure of making this Narcissus admire another face besides his own" (Haywood, *Female Spectator,* 90-93; Lennox 2:23).

Some female characters in these novels do desire men, but Betsy and Harriot do not understand why. The authors themselves treat women who enjoy sex merely as a physical act—who, to paraphrase Manley, "enjoy the lover for the sake of the pleasure, not the pleasure for the sake of the lover"—as aliens, from either a foreign country (America in *Harriot Stuart,* France in *Betsy Thoughtless*) or a foreign class (the aristocracy). Women who fall for love rather than simple lust are more pitiable but no less puzzling. The only motive Betsy can suggest for the misbehavior of her comrade Miss Forward—who, incidentally, is a great reader of romances—is "curiosity": "People . . . have naturally an inclination to do what they are most forbid" (93). Even if such women were comprehensible, they are certainly not admirable; the "wantonness of [their] inclinations" is sure to lead to the most dreadful crimes (Haywood 547). Adultresses are forced to become dangerous outlaws because "it is in the interest of a mistress to sell her favours as dear as she can, and to make the best provision she can for herself, because her subsistence is precarious, and depends wholly on the will of him who supports her" (Haywood 306). Even when innocent women are seduced to their ruin, their surrender to "inordinate desires" makes them a prey to other "poisonous" feelings: "envy, malice, [and] revenge" (429, 419).

The suffering of passionate women would in itself be enough to discourage imitation. Their small tragedies confirm the "moral" of Manley's novels and Haywood's early novellas: that even good men will take advantage of any sign of "inclination" in a woman to use and then discard her. Haywood was once fond of exploring this theme in fairly graphic sexual detail, as in *The British Recluse,* in which Cleomira's slight hesitation before struggling out of Lysander's grasp becomes his justification for assaulting her (Schofield, *Quiet Rebellion,* 58). The decorousness of *Betsy Thoughtless* in making the same point makes the danger to women all the more threatening: it takes so little to give men license to "proceed to force, to give your fantastic virtue an excuse for yielding" (Lennox 1:201). The downfall of Miss Forward occurs when she and her schoolgirl friends, led by the governess, Mlle. Grenouille (a Gallic stereotype), follow the sound of a band playing and come a little too close to the gate of a neighboring lord's park, where they are seized by several men, who cry out, "Nay ladies . . . you must not think to avoid paying the piper, after having heard his music" (77).

When men in these novels are not frightening women into coldness, they are embarrassing them into it. The cynical view of love that had made the Restoration wits libertines was still being called reality in 1751; male characters in both novels call the heroines' desire for respect and equality "romantic" (Haywood 101; Lennox 1:194).[27] Female sexuality could easily wither in the bud under the sneering gaze of the father whose job it was to find her a husband; such scenes are frequent in fiction of the period. Thus the old libertine Sir Thomas Grandison in Richardson's last novel (in progress in 1751) humiliates his daughter Caroline by calling her "amorous"—to him a dirty word—because she has dared to return the love of a perfectly deserving man (1:338-43). Only a "humble" and "creeping" woman (as Miss Belville in *Harriot Stuart* refers to her sister)—a woman with no proper pride—would be able to tolerate being thought "amorous" (2:118). To avoid this accusation—to prove that their rejection of one proffered suitor does not proceed from "inclination" for another— Betsy and Harriot renounce love altogether before they have ever felt it.

The heroines believe that coldness will save them from these various forms of male bullying; as Harriot declaims, "I glory in that insensibility which preserves my freedom" (1:190). They mean to ensure that as many men as possible "wear their chains" while they themselves remain unfettered (Haywood 250, Lennox 1:215). They keep several lovers in play at once because they hope never "to be cooped up like a tame dove, only to coo,—and bill,—and breed"—that is, to be married (Haywood 196). Betsy's adept juggling prompts her guardian to remark that "it was a pity she was not a man—she would have made a rare minister of state" (108), a remark that suggests that she, like Harriot, is prolonging courtship indefinitely in order to make the most of her only opportunity to exercise her political or "Machiavellian" talents (103). By coldly manipulating their lovers, Betsy and Harriot believe that they can reverse the "she-tragedy" of love, as described in the lines from Congreve (*Works* 4:93) used as epigraph to Haywood's *The Rash Resolve:*

> Woman is soft, and of a tender Heart,
> Apt to receive, and to retain Love's Dart:
> Man has a Breast robust, and more secure;
> It wounds him not so deep, nor hits so sure.

Betsy sees herself as the wielder of the Petrarchan darts, the "destroying-angel" who glides blithely along as quarrels and duels follow in her wake (146). Harriot justifies her desire to wound: "Sure . . you cannot blame me, if, filled with resentment for the injuries many of my sex have received from men, I embrace any opportunity that is offered me, to revenge their wrongs, and retaliate the pain they have given" (1:185). The heroines use their wit to arm themselves against love's darts—and, ironically, to enable them safely to encourage the enemy's "fire." They return satiric answers to their suitors' flattery, as Harriot says, not to silence them, but to "defend me against all the impertinence of gallantry, without being obliged to suppress the natural sprightliness of my disposition" (Lennox 1:176).[28]

If coldness really could make women free and powerful, then Betsy and Harriot would have no incentive to grow warm, or to grow up. But the advantages they expect to enjoy turn out to be illusory; for women "pay the piper"—in one way or another—not for desiring, but for being desired. One especially dramatic form of payment is rape, which constantly threatens the incautious heroines. Harriot foolishly brags of her "insensibility" and "freedom" while on board a ship full of men in the middle of the Atlantic, trusting to her own lack of interest to keep the amorous captain at bay: "He has certainly most reason to be uneasy; since, whatever inclinations he may have for me, I feel nothing for him but indifference or dislike" (1:182). She is shocked to discover that her inclinations are of no concern to him, that her disdain only makes him feel "obliged" to rape her—as another of her lovers expresses it—and that when she stabs him in self-defence, the crew members are ready to punish her, the victim: "What, our captain murdered by a girl, for such a paultry trifle as a rape, and not committed neither! Hang law, and a court of justice, as she talks of; deliver her up to us, noble lieutenant; let us punish her our own way" (2:162, 1:204). After several repetitions of this scene, on land and on sea, each heroine comes to fear the man who is "prostrate at her feet," because in reality she is "in his power, and . . . [uncertain] how far he might exert that power" (Haywood 512).

It is not "insensibility" but luck that saves Betsy and Harriot from rape; and nothing can save them from marriage, the legal and socially sanctioned form of piper-payment shown on the Map of Tender as Recognizance. Betsy once naively insists that since men offer to worship her without consulting her preference, she has a right to take their attention as a gift and to plague them as she pleases (138). But she and Harriot find that they can be forced to reward their suitors' devotion. By not choosing one of the crowd they convince their families that they have in fact chosen a "career of coquetry"—a bad career choice that seems to entitle their guardians to give them away to their most persistent admirers: Betsy to Munden, and Harriot to Maynard (Lennox 1:29). Harriot escapes only when carried off by Belmein (from whom, it later turns out, she will also need to escape);

appeals to reason and humanity accomplish nothing. When Dumont returns from an unsuccessful attempt to persuade Maynard to release Harriot from her forced engagement, he reports, "Your chains, miss . . . are not so easily broken; . . . Maynard seems resolved to continue your slave" (1:34). His irony reveals what romantic diction ordinarily tries to hide: that the real prisoner of love is the beloved.[29]

The suitor's humble vows, like the jargon of Manley's seducers, are "but words of course." As Haywood would write shortly before her death, "The tables, after marriage, are revers'd, the goddess now stripped of all her divinity;—it is no more her province to impose laws, but to receive them" (*The Wife,* quoted in Schofield, *Eliza Haywood,* 114). After enduring the "divine object's" repartee during courtship, a husband has the last laugh for the rest of her life. Even Betsy's ideal man, Trueworth, pretends more submission before marriage than he intends to show after; the difficulty of keeping up the pretense is one reason he and Betsy quarrel and part (200-1).

Marriage in these novels is every woman's ship on the Atlantic. Once on board, she cannot leave without her captain's consent unless she is an amazingly strong swimmer. A wife must receive justice gratefully from her husband as if it were mercy, just as Harriot must thank the lieutenant for stopping his men from "punishing" her (Lennox 1:206). Sometimes the husband even looks forward to marriage as his chance for revenge and takes a perverse pleasure in the legal rape of his wife's will. Mr. Munden—whose name implies that he is typical, and who closely resembles Lennox's Maynard—puts up with Betsy's trifling because he knows that "it would one day be his turn to impose laws" (266). Once married, he tries to defraud her of her settlement, smashes her pet squirrel, takes her house guest Mlle. de Roquelair as his mistress, and when Betsy leaves him, threatens to have her brought back and imprisoned in the house. Betsy is shown to have no recourse, escaping Munden first through the contrivances of her friends, and then through his miraculous death.

Life with such a tyrant, rather than freedom, is the most likely result of each heroine's persistent refusal to choose a husband for herself. The turning point for Betsy and Harriot occurs when they understand that their only freedom is the choice of masters—and even that is regarded as a privilege rather than a right. By failing to recognize Trueworth as her best option, Betsy (as her guardian unromantically says) "outstand[s] her market" (107). Her main foil and rival in the novel, Harriot Loveit, has at least as much virgin pride as Betsy; when Trueworth proposes to her (through her older sister), her first reaction is, "I have no inclination to marry." But she is sensible enough to be persuaded that "that was childish talking; that she would, doubtless, marry some time or other; that she might, perhaps, never have so good an offer, and could not possibly have a better; therefore [should] not . . . slip the present opportunity" (340). Only the death of the exemplary Harriot—and, coincidentally, of Munden—saves Betsy from the fatal error caused by her prolonged, "childish" resistance to reality.

Harriot Stuart makes the same point through the introduction of two eligible heroes: Campbel (whose name recalls a hero of *The Faerie Queene*), a worthy man whom Harriot does not love, and Dumont, whom she does love but who appears at times to be unworthy. She is not rewarded with Dumont until she has brought herself to a true appreciation of Campbel, following her governess' suggestion to "suffer" his merit "to make some impression on you" (1:224). After Harriot's engagement to Campbel, she learns that Dumont has not betrayed her, the generous Campbel releases her, Dumont saves his life, and all three remain good friends.

Harriot and Betsy have extraordinary luck: Harriot gets Dumont after all, and Betsy does not have to marry Trueworth until she is good and ready. But both novels strongly warn the ordinary woman against holding out for a miracle. If marriage is like Sisyphus' rock, then freedom, as Camus said, is a matter of attitude. It was a cliché that women are irrational and hypocritical about marriage—that, as Sir Bazil Loveit in *Betsy Thoughtless* says, "All young women are apt to talk" against it, "but when once the favourite man comes into view, away at once with resolution and virginity" (328).[30] Yet this supposed inconsistency does not exist from the woman's point of view, for both the words and the deed show that the worst of all evils is marriage to a man who is *not* the "favourite," whom someone else has chosen. If one can "look to like" the right man, one can marry with at least a semblance of inclination, or free will.[31]

But who is the right man? Betsy and Harriot are too busy deflecting love's darts to recognize him, to notice the difference between his sincere compliments and the phonies' empty "bombast" (Lennox 2:25). Betsy fails to see that Munden is any worse than most of her suitors until she has married him; Harriot fails to see through the aptly-named Belmein until he has her surrounded by Indians on a canoe in the American wilderness. Betsy and Harriot are too kind to villains and too cruel to good men. They indulge their "fantastic desire of giving pain" because, rather like the men in Manley's novels, they do not believe in love or the suffering it is supposed to cause: Betsy "triumphed in the pains she gave, if it can be supposed that she, who was altogether ignorant of them in herself, could look upon them as sincere in others" (Lennox 1:38, Haywood 114).

Until Betsy and Harriot know what love is, they have no guide for eliminating the suitors who are merely going through the motions. Though it would be infinitely safer to pick out the right man and then somehow make oneself love him, they have no choice but to take a blind leap, as it were, into the River of Inclination and wait to see what Unknown Lands it will take them to—even if they turn out to be the wilds of America. The "insensibility" that was their "glory" must be redefined as "false delicacy" and then discarded (Haywood 520). Learning to love is a long and difficult process through which each heroine comes to feel for her lover what she wishes her lover to feel for her—that is, she transforms herself into the likeness of her imagined ideal mate. When she has done so, she can pick out the right man by looking for the one who resembles herself.

Fortunately for Betsy, among her suitors is one who is not only truly worthy himself, but also an infallible judge of true worth in others—the best possible mirror her heart can have as it struggles to mature. It is Trueworth who first induces the "thoughtless" Betsy to "reflect." She makes his acquaintance at Oxford, where he is lost among the crowd, and "not seeing him afterwards, nor hearing any mention made of him, at least that she took notice of," she would no doubt have forgotten him, as she forgets everyone, in the "hurry of promiscuous diversions" that is her social life (67). But when her brother describes him to her as an admirer, "she called to her mind the idea of those persons who were present at the entertainments he mentioned, and easily recollected which was most likely to be the lover, though she remembered not the name: she very well now remembered there was one that seemed both times to regard her with glances, which had somewhat peculiar in them" (67). Trueworth continues to improve Betsy's attention span and memory by judging her unworthy of him as long as it appears that she will never be sufficiently thoughtful to settle down to a quiet life in the country, which "seemed to her little better than being buried alive" (32). When she ridicules his plan for pastoral wedded bliss, he withdraws the offer and tries it out instead on Harriot Loveit—who finds it charming.

Eventually, as expected, Betsy learns to regret this mistake. Near the end of her story, she rises in a "contemplative humor" to enjoy the garden at the country house where she is hiding from her husband; taking note of her new maturity, she immediately begins to "wonder . . . what Mr. Trueworth would say if he knew the change that a little time has wrought in me! he would certainly find me now more deserving of his friendship than ever he could think me of his love" (568). Now that her mind is awake, so is her heart; soon she will be admitting both "tenderness" and "inclination" for him (572, 588). And now that she can accurately see both herself and him—for as Lady Trusty remarks, in the country "every one is known for what he really is" (589)—she notices the likeness between them that makes them compatible as friends. Friendship is possible because she has gradually become able to imagine what it would be like to *be* Trueworth: "if I were in his place, I would not take such treatment from any woman in the world" (246). Near the end of her own story, Harriot Stuart gives herself a similar scolding; once she feels for Dumont what Campbel feels for her, she understands how wrong she has been to trifle with Campbel's "honest sincerity" and agrees to consider his addresses (1:185, 2:202-3).

Of course, in a society that does all it can to widen the gender gap, the man must also do his part to foster resemblance and friendship between the sexes. The right man must be as femininely "sweet" and "delicate" in character as Harriot's first love was in appearance. Like Aronces in *Clelia,* he must be unusually sensitive to the feelings of his beloved and respectful of her will. In the harsh worlds of these novels, chivalry is dead; the heroes can bring it back only by foregoing their male prerogatives. Their efforts in this direction are not always successful. Trueworth cannot help oppressing Betsy with his attentions because he cannot singlehandedly change the rule that forbids a woman to get to know a man until she has promised to marry him; the pressure of his courtship is removed only when he marries someone else. As long as Trueworth is moving toward her, he is a blur; Betsy, like the Princesse de Clèves before her and Elizabeth Bennet after, sees her lover more clearly when looking at his portrait than when staring him in the face (452-53). Campbel also nearly fails the hero's test when he accepts Harriot's hand without her heart, surrendering to the conventional, one-sided marriage of Recognizance.

But for the most part these men transcend their time, championing the heroines' right to choose freely—even to choose their rivals. Campbel finally does give Harriot up to her beloved Dumont, who first won her heart with the statement, "A man who seeks the possession of you by the arbitrary commands of a parent, is unworthy so great a blessing" (1:31).[32] Trueworth will not take Betsy as a prize either from a rival he has defeated in a duel—"It is by Miss Betsy herself our fate is to be judged" (160)—or from her overbearing brother. By their actions as suitors, these men encourage the heroines to trust them as future husbands; their tender respect is in effect a promise not to take undue advantage of their "mundane" legal rights.

The heroes, like the heroines, want something better than the conventional marriage, in which the man is a "slave" (Trueworth's word) before the ceremony and a tyrant after; they want equality (216). One way to achieve this is through "tender friendship," which implies mutual compassion and respect. This is what Trueworth offers Betsy, and what she finally comes to feel she deserves from him (179). And it is what Campbel offers Harriot: "My affection for you, tender and passionate as it is, takes in all the calmer qualities of friendship; and while I view your lovely person with the raptured eyes of a lover, as a friend your honour, your interest, and happiness, are dear to me as my own" (2:2). But tenderness in itself is not enough for the perfect marriage of romance; tenderness in a man is chiefly valuable in giving the woman's inclination room to grow, and Harriot has no inclination to spare for Campbel. Full equality requires both parts of love, tenderness and inclination, on both sides; and so Campbel must give way to Dumont, who, like Trueworth, is the full mirror image of his beloved.

The heroes' and heroines' reflexive emotions enable them to act out the metaphysics of French romance, in which "the Lover is transformed into the Beloved, and the Beloved into the Lover, and thus two become one, and each being at once Lover and Beloved is therefore two" (d'Urfé 165).[33] The climactic (or in one sense anticlimactic) love scene between Betsy and Trueworth demonstrates this mutual "transformation." When Trueworth overhears Betsy in her arbor of jessamines, talking passionately to his portrait, his inclination is aroused by hers, and he makes a Manleyesque pass at her. When she commands him to "forbear," he lets her go, moved to tenderness by her restraint: "you are all angel—be all angel still! Far be it from me to tempt you from the glorious height you stand in" (571). In turn, Betsy's tenderness is awakened by the fact that "merely for her sake, and not through the weak resistance she had made, his own honour had nobly triumphed over wild desire in a heart so young and amorous as his" (574). For Betsy and Trueworth, as for Harriot and Dumont, reciprocal tenderness and inclination form a perfect circle, to be symbolized by their wedding rings.

If *Betsy Thoughtless* and *Harriot Stuart* consisted solely of the forward movement described above, they would be perfect mixtures of realism and romance—practical demonstrations of how good, ordinary women can attain true love. But the progress toward the comic denouement is neither as steady nor as systematic as the discussion up to now has suggested; for there is a retrograde movement in these novels as well, working against the heroines' growth, against the plausibility of their happy endings, and against their friendship with their readers.

While the heroines open themselves up to receive true love, they also learn to close themselves off. They learn inhibition, as they also learn feeling, through "reflection" and self-awareness. The ability to see themselves accurately brings with it the ability to see themselves as others see them—as they are "reflected" in the eyes of their various suitors. At first, these "mirrors" give the heroines back the image of themselves they wish to see; but only a fool, like Miss Belville's sister in *Harriot Stuart,* would fail to see that this image is false (2:113-14). As Harriot Loveit astutely remarks, "As [love] is generally allowed rather to be the child of fancy, than of real merit in the object loved, I should think it would be sufficient for any man in his addresses to a lady, to tell her, that she happens to hit his taste—that she is what he likes; without dressing her up in qualities, which, perhaps, have no existence but in his own imagination" (343). Betsy and Harriot Stuart also have the wit to deflate romantic, hyperbolic compliments; yet their enjoyment of them shows that in a way they believe them.

Men in these novels are usually aware themselves that their compliments are insincere; but their actual impressions are also distorted, because it appears that most of them cannot see women clearly. Only Trueworth and Dumont are interested in the "heaven within" the beloved (Haywood 344). To most men, women are flat surfaces, not complete human beings like themselves; therefore, they judge the "opposite sex" without empathy, and far too harshly, according to the degree of annoyance women cause them. They interpret the heroines' vanity, for example, as "petty pride" (the seventh definition in Johnson's *Dictionary*), a sin deserving punishment.[34] But these women experience their vanity rather as a "desire of pleasing"—a phrase that reminds us of their insecurity, their continuing need to test their power and confirm their identity (Lennox 1:41).

Haywood's opening sentences announce, and Harriot's and Betsy's adventures confirm, that for a woman vanity is rather a self-punishing "mistake"—in Johnson's definition, a "fruitless endeavour"—that gives people who do not understand her feelings the power to define her personality. Betsy's narrator laments that she should "for the sake of indulging the wanton vanity of attracting universal admiration, forfeit, in reality, those just pretensions to [it,] which otherwise she had been entitled to from the deserving and discerning few!" (325).[35] And Harriot comes to see her "vanity" as the "fatal source of all my misfortunes": "How despicable . . . have I since thought this vice, for which coquettry is too soft a name, that could make me take pleasure in appearing lovely to the eyes of a man whom I detested!" (1:175; 127-28).

Betsy and Harriot are particularly shocked to discover these "detested" men's opinion of their sexuality, for here their suitors' image of them is directly opposite to their view of themselves. Since they flirt because they feel nothing for the men they flirt with, they can hardly believe it when their coquetry is wrongly interpreted as an expression of lust. It seems logical to the captain that Harriot, so often at her glass, "cannot be ignorant of her own charms," that she must intend to arouse men, and that therefore she wants to be raped (1:181); a whole string of men say the same to Betsy. But the sexuality these men correctly perceive is autoerotic and has nothing to do with them.

These men mistake the heroines' sexuality, it appears, because they do not clearly understand their own. They make women "projections" of their own ambivalence about sex, so that when they look at women they are really seeing, but failing to recognize, their own reflections. They are so uncomfortable with their own feelings that they can love only women who reject them—and "weak resistance" is not enough. Men in these novels constantly test women with attempted rape, as if hoping they will fall, and then admire them for risking their lives to save their honor. Harriot's willingness to die moves the sailors to refrain from revenge; and the captain, whom she nearly kills, "always preserved a very tender esteem for me" (1:206, 2:207). Betsy passes her test and earns Sir Bazil Loveit's admiration by threatening to throw herself out of the coach in which he has abducted her (210). And as we have seen, in their garden love scene, Trueworth is as much affected by Betsy's suppression of her desire for him as he is by the desire itself.

Oddly, the heroines pride themselves on these confirmations of their worth from unworthy, "detested" men—for men's opinions are considered reality. The libertine's cynicism at first made Betsy and Harriot afraid to love; ultimately it makes them hide love away. Literally, Betsy hides her love for Trueworth in the country, which no longer seems like a prison once she realizes that her admirers are her real jailers. And both heroines hide their love for the "favourite man" in the most conventional way: by agreeing to marry another. Betsy's "mundane" marriage is referred to at one point as "business" (444)—in Behn's vocabulary the antithesis of romance.

Lady Trusty can advocate the match because she believes it is too risky for women to feel love for their husbands: "for if you should find yourself deceived in that of the man, your own would only serve to render you the more unhappy" (590). At any rate, she says, a man does not want his wife to be too fond, for then she will be too intent on her own desires to satisfy his (457). Marriage even deprives women of the narcissistic sexuality they began with. Autoeroticism for the unmarried Betsy and Harriot meant fantasizing in front of the mirror about absent adoring males; for a married woman, this would be a form of adultery. After marrying Munden, when Betsy realizes she must quit flirting, or even thinking about flirting, her sex life appears to be over for good.

So thoroughly inhibiting is the typical marriage that it nearly returns Betsy to her original "thoughtless" state. During her engagement to Munden—just as she has begun to cherish solitude, inner "reflection," and her love for the now married Trueworth—her "friends" conspire to ply her with the same distractions they once disapproved. Knowing she is likely to regret her decision, they "keep her in good humour with her fate" by seeing to it that "her mind [is] continually employed" (456). And they succeed, for "she imagined, while in their presence, that her inclination had dictated the consent her lips had uttered" (451). Haywood nearly endorses these proceedings, for she refers to Betsy's private unhappy thoughts about Munden as "splenetic fancies" (451), refusing to acknowledge that the heroine's inner life is more "real" than the chillingly false version imposed on her by consensus.

Despite all Betsy and Harriot learn about themselves, their situation in an unromantic world makes a degree of self-deception necessary up to the very end. Believing that Dumont has deserted her, Harriot suppresses her love for him and convinces herself of her indifference: "I often attributed the emotions which agitated my breast, when he rose to my remembrance, to scorn and rage, which, in reality, were the effects of a too tender and lasting passion for this lovely deceiver" (2:195). Betsy becomes so duty-conscious at the end of her novel that fifty short pages from the happy denouement she is still "ignorant of her own heart, in relation to what it felt on Mr. Trueworth's account" (564). When they do know their own hearts, Betsy and Harriot must accept the likelihood that the information will be useless. As Harriot finally proves her worth by her willingness to give up Dumont, Betsy's maturity is not complete until she has at the same time felt all her love for Trueworth and learned not to express it: "Till this dangerous instance, she had never had an opportunity of shewing the command she had over herself" (572). And so the heroines' "insensibility" at the beginning of their novels is replaced by heroic self-denial at the end.

Once Betsy commands herself, once Harriot says she will marry Campbel, their authors can give them what they desire. The heroines are rescued at the last moment by the same romantic principle that gives Astrée to Céladon seconds before his suicide. This sudden turn of events splits each heroine into two people, "unmixing" her romantic and realistic elements, and projects a separate ending for each half. Campbel would be good enough for the ordinary Harriot, the nearest approach to comedy she could hope for in a world that chokes out women's inclinations; only romance heroines get Dumonts. The ordinary Betsy is left in an even worse plight: married to Munden, who in real life could not be expected to die so conveniently, and with her true love happily married to someone in every way better than herself. The ordinary reader—who has been the heroine's loyal companion in suffering through hundreds of pages—is left in the dust, looking on in "unprofitable admiration" at her former friend's luck, betrayed by the promise of realistic romance and a comic ending for everyone.

The abandoned reader is in much the same position as the "tender [female] friend" with whom Harriot once plans to end her days in a country retreat, reading Pope's Homer and "Plato's sacred page / Uncommon to our sex and age" (2:199-200). These lines are part of a poem, addressed to her friend, that celebrates love between women:

> O sing its tender chaste desires,
> Its equal, pure, and lasting fires;
> Such as in thy bosom burns,
> Such as my fond soul returns.
> Friendship is but love refin'd. [2:200]

The poem presents an imagined third, "lesbian" ending to the novel that makes moderate happiness seem possible for the ordinary woman; eventually, it would be the real ending of Lennox's later novel, *Euphemia,* as it had been the ending of Haywood's earlier *The British Recluse.*[36] But in *Harriot Stuart* it is not treated as a serious alternative; as Harriot writes this poem she is moments away from marrying Dumont. Though her entire story takes the form of a letter to a female friend, she writes in that letter, "Is there anything more frail than female friendships?" (1:79). The "tender friend" of one moment—Harriot's Mrs. Villars, for example, or Betsy's Mlle. de Roquelair—goes after one's lover or husband the next (Lennox 1:11).

Women in these novels abandon each other in search of romance—which in the end is not about moderate happiness or female friendship. The shepherdesses in *L'Astrée* love each other loyally and sincerely—but in the end, the "female" friend with whom Astrée thinks she is retiring turns out to be Céladon.[37] As Manley's novels demonstrate, the woman who sees herself as a romance heroine is not a good sister. Harriot (like Rivella) steals her literal sister's lovers and receives compliments at her expense (1:17, 1:43-44). Betsy's and Harriot's "sisters" in the broader sense, their so-called friends, are constantly trying to "blast [their] reputation[s]" and steal their crowns (Haywood 31).

Betsy is actually driven from her narrative for chapters at a time when Trueworth courts and then marries Harriot Loveit, who more closely fits Johnsonian readers' idea of the model heroine. Harriot Stuart's position is less precarious, but minor characters in her novel struggle pathetically to be the heroines of their own sub-plots. Harriot once tries to assume a supporting role in a companion's love affair; but when the man appears he turns out to be one of her own long-lost suitors, who re-declares his love for her on the spot and returns her to her natural place of ascendancy (2:33-35). In their different ways, both novels suggest that the average woman is always in danger of becoming a secondary character in the romance of her own life, one of a crowd of ordinary women tragically sacrificed to make the one true heroine happy.

Although *Betsy Thoughtless* and *Harriot Stuart* finally do not mix romance and realism comically, as they seem to promise, in another way they do celebrate the heroinehood—that is, the Manleyesque martyrdom—of the ordinary woman. In trying, and failing, to teach women what they can do to avoid disaster, these novels poignantly reveal the various ways in which women of the time were held responsible for problems beyond their control, not least of which is their inevitable failure to befriend one another. The opening sentences of *Betsy Thoughtless* suggest that self-knowledge should make women more charitable: "it is not above one, in a greater number than I will presume to mention, who, while she passes the severest censure on the conduct of her friend, will be at the trouble of taking a retrospect on her own. There are some who behold, with indignation and contempt, those errors in others, which, unhappily, they are every day falling into themselves" (3). "Want of a due consideration" prevents them from seeing other women as their own reflections—from recognizing their sisters. But the events of both novels show that women cannot solve this problem by reflection alone, because the causes lie outside themselves.

One cause of the rivalry between sisters, for example, is mother. Harriot's war with her sister begins when Mrs. Stuart, the Clytemnestra of the piece, grows jealous of her husband's love for Harriot and puts her other daughter forward (1:3-4). During most of the novel (until a miraculous reformation near the end), Mrs. Stuart delights in torturing and punishing Harriot (1:37)—much like the mother superior who presides over the convent where Harriot is later imprisoned. The viciousness of these mothers shows that, in Lennox's view, women with power behave no better than men. The convent episode is almost exactly parallel to the ocean voyage, except that here the "sailors" are nuns; Harriot placates the prioress with the same strategy she used on the captain: "I did not fail . . . to thank the prioress, with much submission, for granting me this favour, as she called it: tho', in reality, it was no more than a piece of justice she owed both me and herself" (2:151).

Apparently mothers had not improved since Manley's *Atalantis*—as *Betsy Thoughtless* also suggests. Betsy is luckier than Harriot: an orphan of independent means, she is comparatively safe from the evil machinations of her guardian's wife. Although Betsy often wants a mother, she mistrusts those who try to fill the role: unjustly in the case of her governess—"what she said seemed to Miss Betsy as spoke out of envy, or to shew her authority, rather than the real dictates of truth" (7)—but correctly in the case of Lady Mellasin, who "would rather turn her complaints into ridicule, than afford her that cordial and friendly advice she stood in need of" (18).

Jealous mothers create jealousy between sisters; but where does maternal jealousy originate? The answer lies farther up the totem pole. The prioress imprisons Harriot by order of Dumont's father, and Mrs. Stuart tortures her only with the permission of Mr. Stuart. Haywood and Lennox both show—and not, I think, in an unconscious or hidden, "subtextual" way—that behind every act of woman against woman lurks a man.[38] Yet they do not advocate revolution or reform; they do not even suggest the possibility of change, but rather treat male authority as so basic and unassailable that to oppose it would be absurd.

Hovering over these novels, and ultimately explaining what seems like a gap between text and subtext, or conformity and criticism, is the unmistakably paternal presence of God. As Betsy learns how much men can do to her if they choose, she does not forget to thank the "Author of all mercies" when she is spared any suffering, as she thanks the "generous" Sir Bazil for not raping her when he could (244, 211). The even more devout Harriot thanks God for her escape from gang rape with "tears of gratitude" still on her face from her earlier prayer of thanks to the lieutenant who spared her (1:208, 206).

Women in these novels act on male—and divine—authority when they destroy their sisters' reputations. A "cabal" in *Betsy Thoughtless* is not an organization of women against men, as in *The New Atalantis* (or *The Way of the World*), but rather a gossip session of women against women, much like Sheridan's Scandal Club (Haywood 165). But the scandal-mongers would have no weapons—and no motive—if it were not for men's insistence on female purity, supported by God's commandment. Both novels (as well as Sheridan's play) make clear that reputation has no absolute moral value; Haywood even suggests, like Manley, that a spotless reputation should be regarded with suspicion, for Betsy "said and did many things, which the actually criminal would be more cautious to avoid" (31).

One of Betsy's worst scrapes, being accused of having an illegitimate child, is even caused by "the unsuspecting goodness of her heart" that makes her show charitable concern for a foundling, rather than by "her vanity, or that inadvertency which had occasioned her former mistakes" (387). Betsy correctly observes that "as she meant no ill, those who censured her were most in fault" (146)—and in theory, her guardian agrees. But in a speech reminiscent of Peachum's lecture to Polly in *The Beggar's Opera,* Betsy's brother explains that a woman's reputation has an artificial meaning attached to it that makes it more important than her true character: "The forfeiture of what is called virtue . . . is more a folly than a baseness; . . . your reputation is of more consequence to your family; the loss of the one might be concealed, but a blemish on the other brings certain infamy and disgrace on yourself, and all belonging to you" (352).

Men, as we have seen, had the power to enforce their preferences, to make the appearance of virtue in a woman somehow more "real" than the reality. As Mrs. Dormer in *Harriot Stuart* learns after much suffering, a wife is no better than a mistress, even in her own eyes, if no one believes she is legally married (2:62-66).[39] If a woman knows that she will be judged by her reputation, then she must be morally flawed indeed to be careless or "thoughtless" about it. By the same principle, the prudent woman (Mabel in *Betsy Thoughtless,* for example), whom Manley had seen as hard and calculating, deserves unqualified praise for her wisdom and self-control (334).[40] Betsy is finally forced to admit (though "vexed") that "it is not enough to be good without behaving in such a manner as to make others acknowledge us to be so" (146).

In this way a woman becomes liable for any "stories" of which she is the subject; and thus it is up to her to deprive the gossips, or would-be romancers, of suitable material. In other words, she must avoid "adventures"—a word that in 1751 had wholly lost the positive connotation it had had for Aphra Behn. Lennox uses "adventure" as a synonym for "misfortune" (Lennox 2:8), both words implying that life is governed by chance; yet both Harriot and Betsy in their reformed state speak of their lives, or plots, as if they were "hence" rather than "and then," as if their faults had caused their suffering. They accept the judgment that they have been punished for wanting to be heroines by having their wish come true—even though for a woman to avoid adventure, according to Lady Trusty, is "half a miracle," almost a romantic impossibility (178).

These novels provide evidence that ordinary eighteenth-century women were required to live lives of extraordinary merit—of matter-of-fact heroinehood. As Doody has observed, every man felt entitled to play Jehovah, and every woman was expected to suffer, like Christ, for the sins of the world (*A Natural Passion* 271).[41] Every wife was taught to show her superiority to her husband by refusing to leave him even if "his Perjury and Inconstancy seem'd to deserve no less" (Haywood, *Memoirs of a Certain Island,* 240). Mrs. Dormer glories in the "too rigid virtue" that makes her honor her vow to the man who has betrayed her (Lennox 2:69). Betsy, pushed to the extreme limits of tolerance, still wonders whether "a breach of that solemn covenant was to be justified by any provocations," or "whether the worst usage on the part of the husband could authorize resentment in that of a wife" (562).

Romance heroes give back this gift of self-sacrifice: Betsy's "command over herself" in the garden inspires Trueworth's self-command; Harriot's generous offer to marry Campbel despite Dumont's reappearance prompts Campbel to return the favor by releasing her. But ordinary men—Mundens and Maynards—simply accept women's sacrifices as if they were burnt offerings. And ordinary women—the Mrs. Dormers of the world—perform one masochistic act after another in a vain attempt to win male approval (2:77-78).

Fictional heroines do get a reward for their self-sacrifice: fame.[42] When Lady Cecilia threatens to ruin Harriot's reputation with lies, Harriot counterthreatens: "I will not be content with the private testimony of an unblameable life and a clear conscience; I will, for once, affect ostentation, to make that virtue remarkable, which you will endeavour, in vain, to blemish" (2:49). But if she were anyone but a heroine, the speech would have a hollow ring, for in life only disreputable women were "remarkable." For real-life women, living romance simply meant embracing an anonymous sainthood—sacrificing praise to avoid blame. *Betsy Thoughtless* and *Harriot Stuart* both label the desire for applause as vanity; in a sense, their heroines are brought on stage only to tell their readers to get off.

Their authors too, one must remember, had been told to leave the stage—literally, as actresses, and figuratively, as much-calumniated public figures. Betsy and Harriot are so much luckier than their creators were—not to mention their readers—that at times both Haywood and Lennox seem to take a jealous delight in punishing them. Yet the authors chose these "vain" women as subjects over the vapid perfections many of their readers seemed to want because, ironically, they have a greater potential for befriending the reader. The vain woman may think herself extraordinary, and she may wish to drive all other stars out of her universe; yet no desire could be more ordinary, or—when viewed in the right spirit—more human and engaging. Harriot Stuart has more than one sister; unlike her older sister/enemy, her younger sister rejoices that "Harriot is an extraordinary girl, and everything that concerns her must be out of the common way" (2:230). Apparently, the good sister recognizes that there is room in the world for more than one "extraordinary" woman—just as there is room for more than one woman author.

All women were "extraordinary" in the sense that they were not, like the extremely average, storyless Harriot Loveit, free of all tension and conflict. Such bland, pure fictions were the best illustrations of Pope's famous dictum, "Most Women have no Characters at all."[43] Haywood and Lennox had all too much "character" to suit their time, and they bestowed some of it on their fictional creations. By creating female "characters" who were at least a little like themselves—as Lennox continued to do in her next and most popular novel—they helped to work out in imagination the problem all women were facing in life: the problem of having a personality. And so they turned out to be good sisters after all.

4

The Female Quixote
A Realistic Fairy Tale

We are handsome, my dear Charlotte, very handsome and the greatest of our Perfections is, that we are entirely insensible of them ourselves.

—Jane Austen

CHARLOTTE LENNOX's second novel, *The Female Quixote* (1752), delighted Fielding, Johnson, and even the Bluestockings and signaled the author's acceptance into the London literary scene. As she earned respect as a serious scholar and translator, she came in contact with reigning authorities on fiction and acquired a knack for predicting what a wide range of readers would like. Learned yet light, traditional yet original, *The Female Quixote* is a deft mixture of elements designed to satisfy her readers' varied tastes. But in addition to a talent for sharp "market analysis," this novel reveals the author's mature understanding of current literary theories and her serious interest in the relation between philosophy and narrative form.[1]

The Female Quixote is in a sense a realist manifesto; it exemplifies the principles set forth in *Joseph Andrews* and *Rambler 4* by satirizing the French romance as the antithesis of both realism (as historicity and as verisimilitude) and morality. The novel's antiromantic philosophy—unlike, for example, that of *Candide*—is essentially optimistic. Real life, it asserts, is free of adventure and therefore safe, secure, and happy. This was, broadly speaking, Tory philosophy; in 1752, it was a difficult philosophy for a woman, however much a Tory, to expound.[2] Although Lennox's second novel far more insistently affirms the status quo than her first, it retains much of *Harriot Stuart*'s potentially subversive message that, for women, whatever is, is *not* right. This contradiction had not been a serious problem for Delarivière Manley, because in her time Toryism was revolutionary. Nor did it much trouble Johnson, who revered order but did not expect happiness in this life—and who therefore did not write comic novels. But because Lennox did try to fit real life into a comic narrative pattern, she was pulled in opposite directions by principle and fact.

The Female Quixote treats philosophical issues in terms of a formal literary (anti-romantic) thesis; therefore, philosophical complications are most clearly seen here as formal complications. As a narrative form anti-romance is in itself complicated, or double-edged; like the mock-epics of the Augustan satirists, it points out the ironic gap between high style and real life, and both style and life can be targets of satire. Lennox could not wholeheartedly assert that women's real lives were complete, that romantic dreams were unnecessary; and so she did not unequivocally condemn the romance. Of course, in practice romance found its way into the most realistic fiction.

Despite the neat dichotomies of early criticism of the novel, realism was neither new to the eighteenth century nor absolute in its meaning. As we have seen, romance writers centuries before Cervantes set off the realism of their own works by including in them references to the more fantastic romances of earlier generations.[3] And realistic "modern" novels had a way of becoming romantic after a few years; in 1803, in *Northanger Abbey,* Jane Austen referred to Richardson's *Sir Charles Grandison* as the antithesis of "horrid" Gothic; but in an 1808 variation on Lennox's theme entitled *Female Quixotism, Grandison* is the romance that turns the heroine's brain (Small 112). Though romance characteristics were not always recognizable at the time of publication, romance was inevitable—for moralists, who wanted to help young readers perceive their "mixed" real lives with the sharpness and clarity of a fairy tale, and for some realists, who found the plot patterns and themes of French romance strangely relevant to the actual lives of women.

Lennox was both a moralist and a realist; and therefore, despite its anti-romantic premise, *The Female Quixote* is a romance, and Arabella, the quixote, is a romance heroine. She achieves that status, rather inconsistently, in two main ways: when Lennox uses her to satirize the real world, she gives her the heroine's power and perfection; and when the author punishes her for her egocentric delusions, or "vanity," she subjects her to the heroine's tragic martyrdom. The many facets of Arabella's character gave a variety of readers something to like about this novel, but her ambiguity, like that of Betsy Thoughtless and Harriot Stuart, must have frustrated those who were trying to gain from it what it seemed to promise: advice on how to live right and be happy. Although Lennox does not resolve the issues she raises here, her formal approach does help to crystallize them, and to point to the real sources of women's frustration and conflict.

The remainder of this chapter will examine the anti-romantic premise of *The Female Quixote* and the way the novel's romance elements complicate that premise and undermine the didactic purpose.

In an important way, *The Female Quixote* had to combine romance and anti-romance in one, for it was an imitation of Cervantes, an author well known (in our own time, at least) for his transcendence of categories.[4] The message about romance in *Don Quixote* is characteristically complex. Although the hero clearly reads romances the wrong way, all the sympathetic, educated characters in the novel do read them, and only the unsympathetic characters are against them. Cervantes allows the romance plot to support the hero, even as each new adventure makes him more ridiculous, by letting him become in Part II the renowned hero he planned to be in Part I. Lennox has great fun developing the comic possibilities of this paradox. The hero, Arabella's cousin Glanville, is "violent and hasty" enough to be the romantic lover he pretends to be to humor Arabella in volume two; he recalls Dorothea in *Don Quixote,* who is little less romantic than the Princess Micomicona she counterfeits (*FQ* 36). Like Cervantes, Lennox enjoys piling up layers of fiction; at one point she has an actress disguised as a princess recite the romance of her life, in which she meets a prince who recites the romance of his life. Lennox also comically exploits the many obstacles to the movement of the romance plot. So modest are the typical hero and heroine that their coming together can be difficult to arrange. First the hero must "struggle with the violence of his passion, till it has cast him into a fever. . . . Thus he must suffer, rejoicing at the approach of death, which will free him from all his torments, without violating the respect he owes to the divine object of his flame. At length, when he has but a few hours to live, his mistress . . . conjures him to tell her the cause of his despair. . . . [H]e acknowledges his passion with the utmost contrition for having offended her. . . . The lady is touched at his condition, commands him to live, and if necessary, permits him to hope" (319).[5] Lennox's own hero wins Arabella in much the same way—and Arabella herself must become conveniently ill before she can reform.

In a deeper sense, however, Cervantes was not Lennox's master. Romance may have been fun to play with, but the reigning philosophy of her novel presupposes commitment to a single truth; one must take sides, and here romance is definitely the wrong side.[6] When Don Quixote loses his delusion, the spell is broken and he dies. When Arabella loses hers, she is cured and can get married and—ironically—live happily ever after. To the narrator of *The Female Quixote,* the romances Arabella reads lack even the aesthetic merit that in Cervantes saves *Amadis of Gaul* from the flames; Glanville would rather clean the Augean stables than read—or even lift—Arabella's favorite books (53). The clergyman who ultimately converts Arabella (in a chapter probably written by Johnson) argues that "the only excellence of falsehood . . . is its resemblance to truth" (418).[7] By this rule of verisimilitude, Arabella's books are not even good lies. But more important, *romances are lies,* falsifications of history, and hence morally dangerous as well as aesthetically flawed. "Young people especially," Clara Reeve would later comment, "imbibed such absurd ideas of historical facts and persons [from French romances], as were very difficult to be rectified" (*Progress* 1:64-65).

The Johnsonian clergyman admits that books need not be literally true; in fact, they "ought to supply an antidote to example" (420).[8] But romances lie for no good reason; Arabella may consider them "books from which all useful knowledge may be drawn" (52), but the narrator informs the reader rather that this "study" has prevented the heroine from acquiring "a great proficiency in all useful knowledge" (6-7). In fact, romances are worse than useless, for as the clergyman says, they give "new fire to the passions of revenge and love" instead of helping "reason and piety to suppress" those passions; and we must suppress them, "if we hope to be approved in the sight of the only Being, whose approbation can make us happy" (420). An eighteenth-century Englishman would be hanged for many deeds romances present as heroic, as Glanville's sister Charlotte fears (Langbauer 39). And so the biggest cause of Arabella's remorse at the end of the novel is that she incited Glanville, she believes, to kill a rival for her love.[9]

The clergyman does not know—though Lennox no doubt did—that romances are dangerous to Arabella because, in a sense, they are all too true. His most serious objection is that they employ "and then" rather than the supposedly more realistic "hence" narration, and thus "teach young minds to expect strange adventures and sudden vicissitudes, and therefore encourage them often to trust to chance" (419). "Chance," for most women, was often all they could trust; it would be a romantic delusion indeed if they believed they could control their own destinies. Nevertheless, the plot—or rather the deliberate plotlessness—of *The Female Quixote* supports the clergyman's contention that life is orderly and consequential because civilization has effectively eliminated the "accidents" of romance. Whereas Betsy Thoughtless and Harriot Stuart were falsely secure, Arabella is falsely apprehensive, even paranoid; she constantly expects rape from the most unlikely quarters and refuses even her cousin a "private conversation" (34). And her delusion sometimes leads her to take the offensive—in effect, to commit crimes—as when she orders her servants to attack her suitor Hervey as an intended "ravisher," though he has been guilty of no more than ordinary silliness (22).

The only unimaginary dangers Arabella encounters appear to be the direct result of her willful carelessness. Fearing an assault by Edward, a gardener who she believes is a nobleman in disguise, she runs out of her house in the middle of the night and throws herself upon the first man who passes, asking this "generous stranger" for assistance. This "gentleman," who is "extremely glad at having so beautiful a creature in his power" and anxious "to have her at his own house," is a serious threat (110). Charlotte Glanville points out the foolishness of Arabella's flight, for "sure nobody would be so mad to attempt such an action" as rape in a woman's own well-guarded house (108), but as Betsy and Harriot could have told Arabella, no one would blame a gentleman for molesting a reckless woman. Thus the heroine illustrates the old crooked axiom that only a woman who wants adventures will have them, and also the corollary: that she somehow deserves them.

Romances have caused Arabella to undervalue not only her personal safety, but also the social hierarchy on which, according to Tory ideology, her safety depends. The fear of being raped in her own home by her gardener is absurd because of the class distance, symbolized by the stairs he would have to climb to get to her—stairs she abandons when she runs from the house and from the protection of her rank. The romance may once have been the literature of aristocracy (McKeon 21, 268), and therefore of political conservatism, but separated from its historical roots it becomes democratic—for it makes everyone an aristocrat. As Don Quixote explains to Sancho, romance subverts the existing order so that it can re-establish the divine distinctions that have been lost to the fallen world; that is why a large part of romance is finding out who one really is.[10] But in the Tory view, one can still see vestiges of God's plan in man's class system, and rank is still a meaningful clue to character, though by no means an infallible one. Edward may seem genteel for a gardener, but only because "he had contracted . . . a great deal of *second-hand* politeness" when he worked as a servant in London (24). Anyone more clear-sighted than Arabella, we are to believe, would know that Edward is only a servant when he is caught trying to steal carp from her fish pond. The heroine reasons thus: no gentleman would steal, Edward is a gentleman, therefore Edward would not steal. The reader is expected to accept the first premise but to know that the second premise is false: Edward has been caught red-handed. Thus the novel forces the conclusion that Edward is no gentleman.

In supporting the notion of hierarchy, the anti-romantic premise of *The Female Quixote* also endorses patriarchy; it asserts—despite everything Lennox and her readers knew to the contrary—that father knows best and that the clearest path to personal happiness is obedience to just authority. To illustrate this principle, which a too realistic rendering of female experience would surely expose as false, Lennox resorts to trickery, or romantic coincidence: she makes the man of the heroine's inclination the very man her father wants her to marry.[11] At first sight, Arabella is impressed by Glanville's handsome face and figure, intelligence, good nature, and charm (30, 33). But according to her inverted values, cooperation with her father would be "impropriety," as the narrator ironically notes: "What lady in romance ever married the man that was chose for her? In those cases the remonstrances of a parent are called persecutions; obstinate resistance, constancy and courage; and an aptitude to dislike the person proposed to them, a noble freedom of mind which disdains to love or hate by the caprice of others" (29). Her "repugnance" (30) arises merely from having to see Glanville as an approved suitor.[12] Her "heroic disobedience" (30) is made to seem especially foolish because her father is less overtly bullying than Juliet Capulet's or Clarissa Harlowe's (34). He simply expresses the wish that his daughter marry the man of his choice and hopes that her filial affection will incline her to accept. Arabella persists in seeing him as the tyrant of romance, however, and thus she nearly loses her Prince Charming.

The foil to the disobedient heroine—this novel's equivalent of Harriot Loveit in *Betsy Thoughtless*—is the "celebrated Countess of ———." When Arabella, after being introduced, asks the Countess to tell of her "adventures," her new friend is shocked, she explains, because "the word adventures carries in it so free and licentious a sound in the apprehensions of people at this period of time." Her own life has been adventureless: "I was born and christen'd, had a useful and proper education, receiv'd the addresses of my Lord ———, through the recommendation of my parents, and marry'd him with their consents and my own inclination, and . . . since we have lived in great harmony together" (365). The Countess has no inclination to interfere with her parents' will—and neither, she says, do most "other women of the same rank, who have a moderate share of sense, prudence and virtue" (365-66). Her message is that good girls should appreciate how lucky they are to be able to live without adventure— that is, without conflict. If Arabella could see that life is no more than it appears to be, she would have nothing to fear—and nothing to wish for—for she would discover that life is too good for romance to be necessary.[13] The Countess asks the young female reader to look kindly on her oppressors, to reexamine the causes of her discontent, to decide that rebellion is quixotic: in other words, absurd, unnecessary, and unchristian.

If the Countess is correct, then why does Lennox remove her from the story before she has had the chance to cure Arabella? The obvious answer is that once Arabella comes to her senses and marries Glanville, "all her adventures are at an end for the future"—and so is the book (152). In fact, it is difficult to imagine who, exactly, would derive profit or pleasure from seeing Arabella settle down into the safe but plotless existence the Countess describes. Chapter headings such as "Contains a turn at court, neither new or surprising" (5), "A mistake, which produces no great consequences" (14), and "an extraordinary comment upon a behaviour natural enough" (14) make clear that all the adventure, or interest, of this novel is owing entirely to Arabella's, or to Lennox's, imagination.[14] Despite the anti-romantic premise of *The Female Quixote,* Lennox could not write an "anti-book"; to satirize romance one must also write a romance. And to insult something while making such extensive use of it can begin to seem ungrateful and unmannerly—that is, the values of the satirized form can begin to take over. Romance does take over this novel thoroughly enough to introduce a sour note into its closing major chord—the final chapter in which Arabella is cured and, one supposes, happy.

By making Arabella the center of the narrative, Lennox "heroinizes" her and indirectly endorses her romantic delusions; on some occasions it suits her to endorse them more directly as well. As Don Quixote becomes the hero he believes he is, the Female Quixote entering the ballroom at Bath finds all eyes fixed on her in admiration and envy—unlike Austen's anti-romantic Catherine Morland, whom no one notices until the rooms are nearly empty. Charlotte Glanville, the typical woman of fashion, hopes everyone will laugh at her cousin, dressed outlandishly as Princess Julia. But this spitefulness must be punished, and so Arabella wins the day with her "noble air, the native dignity in her looks, the inexpressible grace which accompanied all her motions, and the consummate loveliness of her form" (305).[15] One wonders in scenes such as these whether Arabella really is deluded; she knows that she is not Princess Julia, but merely someone like her—a perception that is confirmed by consensus. And why cure her if she is not sick?

To satirize the world of fashion, Lennox makes Arabella more than a beautiful object; she also wins applause for her intellect.

Though she may read the wrong books, she is better informed than most inhabitants of London and Bath, who do not read at all and who sneer at women who do. The Countess, for example, is said to know "too much for a lady" (374). The greatest ignoramuses in the fashionable world, significantly, are male. Lennox adapts the old fop and the pedant, familiar since the days of Jacobean drama, to a feminist purpose by enlisting them on the losing side of the battle of the sexes. Arabella innocently exposes their folly, and they bitterly resent being "posed by a girl."[16] In such scenes the heroine gives her readers, and her author, the chance to live vicariously the fantasy of winning in intellectual competition with men.

Arabella's triumphs suggest that, for Lennox, romance had its occasional uses, its areas of superiority to the real world, or at least the world of fashion; they introduce into *The Female Quixote* an almost Cervantean complexity and enhance its appeal for twentieth-century readers while still permitting the anti-romantic premise, or "reality," to prevail in the end. But even when Arabella is finally humbled—or humiliated—according to plan, Lennox encourages the reader to sympathize with her in ways that not only complicate but subvert that premise.

Arabella is drawn with a completeness that may well be autobiographical: if Reeve was correct in her opinion that French romances were no longer fashionable when Lennox was writing *The Female Quixote* (*Progress* 2:6-7), then the unfashionable young women who read them anyway may well have been the "lunatic fringe" who went on to become women authors.[17] Lennox must have expected her readers to be similarly behind the times—at least passingly familiar with these romances—since she provided no gloss for her many allusions. Of course neither Lennox nor her readers were likely to be literally as eccentric as her creation; but in her triumphs Arabella does seem to win a victory for the would-be heroine in every woman. And so in her defeats, though ostensibly deserved, Lennox makes it possible for the reader to feel regret by treating Arabella's chief error with sympathetic understanding as well as criticism; after all, even the Countess was once a romance enthusiast. The result, as Johnson warned in *Rambler 4,* is moral ambiguity; the reader begins to "lose the abhorrence of [Arabella's] faults"—if they are faults, and if they are really hers.

By officially labeling Arabella as "faulty," Lennox leaves herself free to give her realistic traits that, ironically, encourage the reader's sympathy and identification. Among those traits is sexuality—which also conveniently helps to make an anti-romantic point. Like Betsy and Harriot, Arabella is at once both cold and warm—a paradox that here helps to expose the inconsistent morality of French romances, passionate love stories about unnaturally chaste heroines. Arabella's behavior toward men is both too strict (so that Charlotte's "liberties" shock her) and not strict enough (so that Charlotte is shocked in her turn) (99, 203). Romances exacerbate the normal female dilemma by giving Arabella even more inclination and less freedom to admit it than worldly convention allows; hence she is forced to be even more than conventionally wily and manipulative. After sternly forbidding her maid to accept any love-letters from Hervey, Arabella is "not without an apprehension of being too well obeyed" (12); and when Lucy does deliver a letter, "in reality, she was not displeased; yet, being a strict observer of romantic forms, she chid her woman severely for taking it" (14). Hervey interprets Lucy's warning not to give her a letter—"I . . . beg you will not offer to bribe me"—as what it is in fact: an invitation (13).[18]

This forwardness, we are told, is not the result of sexual desire, or as Lennox would be compelled to call it, "vicious inclination." Because Arabella is sometimes used as a paragon rather than as a target, she must be chaste and her sin must be venial, a form of Betsy's and Harriot's vanity. Yet Lennox provides strong hints of the heroine's sexuality in symbols of considerable subliminal power and moral subtlety. The Marquis's house is a sanctuary of order and safety because, literally and symbolically, it preserves the heroine's virginity—as Arabella is well aware: her euphemism for rape is "[to] be carried away by force from my own house" (102).[19] Thus, even according to her own symbolic vocabulary, her "escape" from the house the night of Edward's imaginary attack is also a quest for sexual adventure. The rooms in which the "rape" takes place—Arabella's antechamber, bedchamber, and closet—further develop this symbolism. The scene opens with Lucy and Arabella conferring in the closet, which represents the heroine's most private self. There is a knock at the door of the antechamber (the most public room), and Arabella commands Lucy to go talk to the supposed attackers. As the terrified maid shouts through the locked antechamber door, Arabella "advanced as far as the bed-chamber, longing to know what sort of conference Lucy was holding with her intended ravisher" (104). Her sexual curiosity thus leads her to the bedroom, which lies appropriately between her most private chamber and the outside world.

This scene proves that Arabella does have inclination to suppress, thus silently refuting the Countess's optimistic argument. Because Arabella is by far the more believable character, the novel implies that real women are like heroines, and their lives are like romances—however unromantic the world they live in may be. In fact, that world is the source of the persecutions that make up their "plots." Arabella's father is a tyrant not only in her disordered fancy, but in "fact," or deed; perhaps because Lennox's own words were her life, she made him, literally, a "dictator." When Arabella has indignantly dismissed Glanville from the house, the Marquis orders her to write an apologetic letter inviting him to return. Although the apology clearly is called for, it hurts to watch her father "leading her to *his* writing-desk [my emphasis]," commanding her to write, and finally telling the "sobbing" heroine what she must say. One is glad to see from the letter that the Marquis finally cannot rob her of her voice, deranged though it may be: "It is not by the power I have over you, that I command you to return, for I disclaim any empire over so unworthy a subject; but since it is my father's pleasure I should invite you back, I must let you know that I repeal your banishment" (43).[20]

The Marquis's wrath is kindled by what he sees as his daughter's "rudeness" (43). Arabella often violates etiquette because her reading has failed to teach her to suppress her feelings. Conversely, her only complaint against Glanville is his self-command. He is reasonably distraught when Arabella flees and cannot be found; but she expects him to "strike his bosom with the vehemence of his grief; and cast his accusing and despairing eyes to heaven, which had permitted such a misfortune to befal" (120). She likes Glanville best when, "a little elevated with wine," he ignores what Fielding might have called her "violent modesty" and throws himself at her feet, venting his feelings in romantic but sincere hyperbole (*FQ* 138). The message is supposed to be that real feeling is all around Arabella, if only she could recognize it through the calm expressions of conventional good manners. Yet the novel also conveys the sad fact that, though Glanville may express real love, Arabella can never have that freedom. Emotional intensity and honesty for her are, at best, rudeness—at worst, vice.

Arabella does find true love at the end, but only through self-abasement. After her conversion she not only stops exacting Herculean labors from Glanville but almost begs him to marry her, promising to "endeavour to make myself as worthy as I am able to such a favourable distinction" (423). According to the satiric premise this is no more than justice; the correction of her supposed error should increase her dignity by making her no longer ridiculous. And of course she was ridiculous when she considered "the reputation of her charms sufficient to bring a crowd of adorers to demand her of her father" (7), or required "signs of contrition" and "true repentance" from her admirers (51), or commanded her despairing suitors to live (as Astrée commanded hers to die). Yet somehow Arabella never seems less dignified than at the moment when she first awakens to a sense of her own folly.

For if Arabella's former errors were also her readers' dreams, then her "cure" may be more like the lobotomies that were once routinely performed to improve mental patients' "adjustment" to hospital routine. The analogy suggests an answer to the question raised earlier: who *does* derive profit or pleasure from the heroine's final awakening? Comparing her favorite books with so-called reality, Arabella tells the clergyman, "I am afraid, sir, . . . that the difference is not in favour of the present world"; if she is really happy at the end, she must have had this particular observation removed with a scalpel, since neither the clergyman's sermon nor the novel as a whole completely disproves it (420).

Instead of a "crowd," the isolated heroine is lucky to have even one decent suitor; her father permits her grand style of speech because he rarely listens to her. Her uncle tries to tell her that actual women are not mystic healers: "Why, madam, . . . you want to carry your power farther than ever any beauty did before you; since you pretend to make people sick and well whenever you please" (161). She does not believe him, for her romances are full of precedents; they are a sort of feminist revision of history in which women are behind every great event—not only as love objects, but as leaders of armies (139-40, 404). But he is right: the "present world" is no place for heroines. Arabella's attempt to swim the Thames as Clelia swam the Tiber nearly leads to her death.

Romance may have set Arabella up for a fall, but it is reality that bruises her, teaching her the old lesson that adventure means suffering. If this is comedy, it is very dark indeed, striking familiar overtones of tragedy. Depending on the degree of the reader's sympathy, the agent of Arabella's deflation may seem less like one of George Meredith's comic imps than like a nemesis; and what is called her vanity may seem more like hubris.

What, then, has happened to the thesis that romance does nothing for young readers but cultivate bad taste in literature, bad manners, and bad morality? The clergyman's objections are serious, yet few of those objections can stand against the impression of Arabella's martyrdom. However positively today's readers may view this ambiguity, it represents failure according to the novel's own expressed moral and critical standards. If a book cannot resolve issues, it cannot advise—and then it is not "useful."

Like the novels discussed in previous chapters, *The Female Quixote* criticizes the morality of the real world without permitting women to set up their own ideal code to take its place. The resulting hopelessness is apparent in the sad history of Miss Groves, a fallen woman who as a child was "a great romp," enjoying "masculine exercises," in sharp contrast to her "serious, reserved, and pious" foster sisters (80). Her lack of restraint brought the usual punishment for secondary female characters: she was seduced and became pregnant (or as her maid says, "ill"). The child died. When she became pregnant a second time, she was betrayed by her servants and abandoned by her lover, who took the child and spread the word that she was "too easy a conquest" (83-85). When Arabella and the reader meet Miss Groves, she seems to have no choice but to go her high-spirited way along the road to ruin. (She is finally married off to a relative of one of her servants.) Arabella misses the point of this harrowing story, because her romantic delusions make her believe Miss Groves is chaste but misunderstood, like the "unfortunate Cleopatra" of La Calprenède (86). But the female reader learns to fear the consequences of free behavior without forfeiting her awareness that if Miss Groves is bad, her cold, hypocritical lover is much worse.

This story—along with the turbulence of the heroine's own life—contradicts the Countess's claim that women have no real cause for frustration. Therefore, the Countess is not much use as an "antidote" to the various "examples" of women in this novel, including Arabella, who handle their frustration badly. But Miss Groves's experiences do support the Countess's recommendation of conformity, for although it may not be as painless as the Countess says, it is at least preferable to the loss of one's reputation and of one's child. There is a didactic message in this, but hardly a "moral": conformity is not "right," but prudent; rebellion is not "wrong," but insane, or pointlessly self-destructive. This message is not only amoral but inconsistent with the novel's stated optimistic philosophy, and with the implications of its comic form, both of which promise that a woman with her eyes open will be not merely resigned, but happy.

The morality of *The Female Quixote* is contradictory because the novel contains two worlds: one drawn from romance, and one from reality. Ironically, the morality propounded by the novel's realist philosophy operates only in the world of romance. The novel asks the reader to wake up, to surrender her dreams like Arabella, but once she has done so, she can hardly expect that her father will reward her with a Glanville. Like Betsy Thoughtless and Harriot Stuart, Arabella is ultimately "unmixed" as her romance self floats away to happiness, leaving her realistic self behind with her delusions. Meanwhile, the reader is left on the ground, contemplating her own choice between bad and worse. Even before the romantic denouement, Arabella can be a didactically confusing "mixture," a romance heroine presented as if she were real. Of course, as we have seen, she is "mixed" in the Johnsonian sense, a sometimes disorienting blend of good and bad qualities. But more damaging to the novel's didactic purpose is the nature of some of the qualities most clearly marked as "good," for they are the symbolic virtues of traditional heroines of romance and are therefore unavailable to real women.

Lennox knew very well that romance heroines did not make very "useful" moral models; in fact, this is one of the more astute and entertaining satiric points of *The Female Quixote*. Arabella's desire to *be* Clelia is doomed to failure by its inherent logical absurdity, because Scudéry's paragons are supposed to be natural and artless, qualities that no amount of deliberate effort can purchase (*Clelia* 1:32). Arabella can only *act* Clelia, thus falling into the comic Cervantean paradox of planned spontaneity. So, as Sancho Panza boasts of his charming simplicity, Arabella carefully contrives her "natural look": "Her fine black hair hung upon her neck in curls, which had so much the appearance of being artless, that all but her maid, whose employment it was to give them that form, imagined they were so" (9).[21]

Lennox further shows that this absurdity has serious moral implications. Scudéry's heroine, brave as she is, and well aware of her beauty and merit, nevertheless has a face full of "timerous [*sic*] modesty" (*Clelia* 1:19, 33, 35). In a real woman, which Arabella is supposed to be, this modesty would have to be put on; one either knows one's worth or one does not. Arabella can no more pretend ignorance of her beauty and abilities than Don Quixote can will himself mad like Orlando Furioso (though for both quixotes the willed act is ridiculously unnecessary: she is self-ignorant, and he is mad). On one occasion, she orders her maid, Lucy, to narrate the story of her mistress' life; this romance game is supposed to give the heroine a chance to reveal her modesty by asking Lucy "to soften those parts of my history where you have greatest room to flatter, and to conceal, if possible, some of those disorders my beauty has occasioned" (135). But since Lucy does not know her part, Arabella must prompt her "not only to recount all my words and actions . . . but also all my thoughts, however instantaneous" (135). What she reveals, comically, is not natural modesty but natural egoism.

It seems, then, that one cannot be a romance heroine by working at it. Yet, despite Lennox's awareness of the problem, at important points in the novel she gives Arabella the romance heroine's unconsciousness, making her as "useless" as Clelia. Though ridiculously careful of her hair and clothes in some scenes, Arabella is more usually the antithesis of her vain cousin Charlotte—in much the same way that Clelia contrasts with the worldly Betsys and Harriots who "have such a fancy to look on themselves, that they not only look on themselves with earnestness in all the glasses they find, but in the Rivers and Fountains, and even in the eyes of those which speak to them" (*Clelia* 1:32). One day Charlotte spends four hours getting dressed "in order, if possible, to eclipse her lovely Cousin." When she goes to Arabella's chamber shortly before they are to go out, she finds the heroine still undressed. She prepares with "haste and negligence," but "notwithstanding her indifference, nothing could appear more lovely and genteel" (93). Charlotte is understandably frustrated. What can she do? She might imitate her cousin by becoming careless of her appearance, but would she then be as adorable as Arabella?

The romance heroine's artless beauty is simply the visible manifestation of her soul's innocence. When she contrasts with Charlotte, Arabella is as natural within as without. Her preoccupation with love makes her ridiculous at times, but it does not make her unchaste because, like Clelia (not to mention Pamela and her "daughters"), she does not know what love is or recognize that she has felt it;[22] until just before the denouement, Glanville's faithfulness is "of more consequence to her happiness than she was yet aware of" (143). And she preserves her innocence, or ignorance, for as long as possible through willful self-deception: "As she was unwilling to acknowledge, even to herself, that the grief she felt at this discovery [of Glanville's supposed indifference] proceeded from any affection for her cousin, she imputed it to the shame of seeing herself so basely forsaken and neglected" (189). Like Jane Austen's Emma, she does not discover "the true state of her heart" until a rival appears to stir up "all the passions which attend disappointed love" (*FQ* 391).

The less-than-innocent reader, of course, has been told all about it; and thus she is in much the same relation to Arabella as Arabella is to Clelia. If she tries to learn about life from *The Female Quixote*, she *becomes* a Female Quixote, reading a romance as if it were a true or possible history. For this novel is, in essence, merely a version of the fairy tale Snow White subjected to realistic "displacement"—or in Reeve's phrase, "moderated to probability" (Progress 1:14). Like Charlotte Glanville, the wicked queen in the fairy tale is a slave to her mirror, yet she fails to be as beautiful as Snow White, the "unreflecting" heroine. Charlotte and the queen are punished for their vanity; Arabella and Snow White marry handsome princes. The fairy tale might teach a child not to be vain—but not, as Bruno Bettelheim explains, by offering Snow White as a model and the queen as a warning. The child would rather identify with both the heroine and the villainess, working out her inner struggles through the conflict in the story, coming to terms with her "dark side" (7). In contrast, didactic novels such as *The Female Quixote,* in which fairy-tale polarization of values is covered over with a layer of realism (a type Bettelheim disapproves), are meant to keep the young reader from wanting to be like any but the best characters. The goal of Johnsonian didacticism is to help the reader to suppress the "dark side." And if innocence is ideal, then the self-conscious reader has already fallen irredeemably.[23]

Any didactic intent assumes that learning is possible; the real-life cure for romantic delusion, as Reeve would later say, is "knowledge of the world, and . . . experience in it" (*Progress* 1:79-80). But by inviting the reader to learn from Arabella's mistakes, to look into her own heart and acquire self-knowledge superior to the heroine's, Lennox automatically deprives her of the innocence that makes the heroine perfectible; in contrast she may even look like "a monster in [her] own eyes" (Bettelheim 7). Like Charlotte, the reader must regard Arabella at her most perfect in much the same way the children in Saki's "The Story-Teller" regard the "horribly good" Bertha: as the perfect dinner for the big bad wolf.[24] For her part, Arabella eagerly befriends other women and praises Charlotte's beauty like the high-minded shepherdesses in *L'Astrée,* who "knew not what envy or emulation meant" (*FQ* 89; see d'Urfé 61). But heroines have no need to compete; by definition, they have already won. Charlotte gets her man in the end only because Arabella does not want him; Sir George is practically forced to marry her, and we are told that the marriage will be "common"—that is, loveless and probably unhappy (423). Arabella's uncommon, romantic marriage to Glanville, like Betsy's to Trueworth and Harriot's to Dumont, leaves the ordinary woman, her former friend, jealously looking on.

Nor is Arabella a loyal friend to the author, for in her guise as the innocent heroine of romance she is as far as possible from an autobiographical projection. She even indirectly insults Lennox by asserting that satire is unmannerly (301-2). When Arabella "poses" the fop and the pedant, she does it by accident, naively turning their own affectations against them. The author, however, is obviously "guilty" of a satiric purpose. As in her first novel, Lennox has given Arabella an innocence she could no longer claim for herself; but in this case she is separated from her heroine not only by her sexual experience but by the conscious intellectual designs on which her profession depended. The novel thus suggests an ambivalence about that profession not uncommon among women writers. (Jane Barker, Madame de Genlis, and Hannah More all published the sentiment that women should not write, and especially should not publish.)[25] Fanny Burney's heroines, as the next chapter will show, have a similar wistful naïveté—leading to similar didactic problems.

The "unreflecting" Arabella is someone no real woman can identify with; but the self-conscious, egotistical Arabella is "useful"—and not necessarily as a negative example. Apart from her delusions—or, rather, along with them—she also has wit and intelligence; though we are often forced to take those qualities for granted, her uncle does once brag that "if she had been a man, she would have made a great figure in parliament" (348). The remark does not have the same meaning as Mr. Trusty's similar compliment to Betsy Thoughtless; for politicians in this Tory novel are to be respected, not scorned as "Machiavels," and Arabella's talent is oratory, not intrigue. In this way *The Female Quixote* suggests that there is an arena in which women can exercise their powers—besides the game of love, which they generally lose. If that arena does not yet exist—Arabella, after all, has no career, though her author does—at least her powers find expression in her delusions: that is, in romance.

Lennox and Cervantes were right to point out the danger of mistaking reality for romance; after all, women of today can still feel the effects of being treated like symbolic objects during the Renaissance. But in a sense reality includes romance, in the same way that it includes imagination; and therefore eighteenth-century readers, as well as fiction writers—including Johnson, as we have seen—found romance difficult to avoid, though they believed they ought to try. By preserving romance—even against their own stated intention—women writers such as Lennox provided an important underground service for their readers and for the novelists who would follow them: for if today's realistic novels are tomorrow's romances, it is also true that tomorrow's reality will be shaped in part by today's dreams. Twenty-five years after Lennox wrote *The Female Quixote,* Fanny Burney—another of Johnson's protégées—would still be trying to erect philosophical barriers against the rebellious energy of romance; but though Don Quixote was dead and Arabella married, adventure was not yet at an end.

5

Fanny Burney's Novels
Romance with Regret

The puppy Men said She had such a drooping Air, & such a timid Intelligence; or a timid Air I think it was, and a drooping Intelligence.

—Hester Thrale

FANNY BURNEY's[1] writing career began with the publication of *Evelina* in 1778 and was in a way the opposite of Eliza Haywood's. Haywood courted fame in her youth and published anonymously in her chastened middle age; Burney began in anonymity and struggled all her life with the unexpected attention that came with her success. In a similar way, Burney's heroines instinctively dread adventure; they are "born" with the inhibition their mid-century counterparts painfully acquired. Lennox's Arabella learned that she did not have the power of life and death over her suitors; Burney's Cecilia, in a sense, has it—Belfield almost dies fighting over her, and her money and attention help to cure him—but she fears to exercise it (163). Her power, like her creator's talent, is a sort of black magic dangerous to the possessor; each use of the wand adds a new spot to her reputation.

Other novelists described in this study used the gap between romance and reality to satirize one or the other, or both; to Burney, the deeper satire lay in the frightening similarity between the two—at least with respect to the romance heroine's isolation and undeserved suffering. Yet however realistic the adventure of romance might have seemed to her, she disapproved of its philosophical implications even more seriously than Lennox had. Like Arabella's Johnsonian clergyman, she had a Tory dread of anything that might inflame readers' passions and encourage recklessness and egoism. For she was a Tory—broadly speaking, in that she believed in the importance of society and order, and specifically, in that she supported royalist causes during the tumultuous years of the French Revolution and its aftermath.[2] Not that Burney had no liberal leanings (we know she was miserable as a courtier to Queen Charlotte); she was the sort of conservative Claudia Johnson describes as fairly common in her time, sympathetic with individualism in theory, but increasingly uncomfortable with it as it became associated with "jacobinism" in the 1790s (19). Burney, connecting romance with quixotic individualism, found herself condemning it with increasing vigor as the decades passed. And yet, ironically, in a world going mad with selfishness, she gradually came to feel as alone with her social values as any beleaguered heroine and to speak out against the times as sharply as any jacobin polemicist.[3]

The adventure of romance seemed to Burney realistic but wrong; in contrast, the romantic happy ending seemed implausible—like the "jolly chorus that makes all parties good and all parties happy" in "hack Italian operas"—but right (*Diary* 2:80-81). The closing wedding appealed to her, not because it was about love—on principle, she disapproved of "mere love stories" (*Journals* 3:117)—but because of what it symbolized: the individual's need for restraint, relationship, and structure.[4] This symbolism had enabled Lennox, paradoxically, to use the romance ending to make an anti-romantic point: once Arabella marries Glanville, her adventures are over and her life will be calm and orderly. Burney gave her heroines the same reward, but without Lennox's suggestion that it is common or ordinary. With each of Burney's novels the happy marriage—the long-awaited end of the story and hence of the suffering—becomes harder to arrange without magic; and so, in the growing darkness of Burney's fictional worlds, the denouement takes on more and more of its old romantic splendor.[5]

Burney's situation was thus full of paradox: disliking romance, she nevertheless needed it to explain the reasons for her dislike and to express the traditional opinions that circumstances had made unorthodox. Her novels are therefore difficult to classify by ideology. They are conservative like those of Lennox but unconstrained by the older author's feeling that she had an obligation to assert, despite the evidence, that all was well. They bear some resemblance to Manley's radical Tory satires, as well as to many novels that are classified as "jacobin."[6] The novels are, in other words, as complicated as their author's beliefs, and, as in *The Female Quixote,* those beliefs can be traced in the novels' confusing mixtures of romance and realism. This chapter will present an overview of Burney's "radical conservatism" as it appears in a variety of her writings, and will then consider how that complex ideology generated formal conflicts and problems in her novels.

First, however, since much has been written about Burney, the differences between my own approach to her work and that of other critics of the past and present must be examined. The tendency of

eighteenth-century criticism to create neat, antithetical categories
has persisted, in Burney's case, up to the present moment—and so
have the paradoxes and contradictions usually caused by dialectical
thinking. Two centuries of commentators have accounted for
Burney's complexity by seeing her as two people. Critics had already
begun during her lifetime to distinguish the lively, "artless" voice of
Evelina from the conventionally respectable third-person narrator of
Burney's last three novels. Fame was supposed to have forced the
more interesting, "real" Burney underground, and much critical attention was directed to the discovery of this submerged free spirit; but
each new excavation—the publication of her diaries, Joyce Hemlow's
work with unpublished manuscripts—led to new accusations of pho-
niness and hypocrisy.[7] The search continues in more recent criticism
that treats Burney as a "paradigm" for the crushing effects of public
opinion on the late-eighteenth-century woman novelist (Simons 135,
Straub 19).[8] The contrast between her public and private selves has
indeed provided a critical model for a "double" approach to the study
of other women writers of her period.

It is undisputed that women of Burney's time had to lead double
lives; it is also undeniable that a "woman writer" could sometimes
write what no "proper lady" could say.[9] Pressures on women had been
steadily increasing since Behn's day, and by Burney's time they were
immense; some evidence of covert rebelliousness, of text and subtext,
can be found in Burney's later novels.[10] When the "Queen of the
blues," Mrs. Montagu, objected to the "boisterous" humor of *Evelina,*
for example, Burney managed to include such humor in her second
novel without seeming to sanction it, becoming in her own phrase
more "finical" (*Diary* 1:461, 1:231).

But as Kristina Straub points out, the text-subtext model raises a
number of questions (6, 24). How, exactly, does the subtext relate to
the text? Who are these two Burneys? Did the author "internalize"
some of her age's prejudices about women, or did she conform for
"pragmatic" or "prudential" reasons?[11] Simply bisecting the author
and the text stops short of the ultimate goal of criticism: to put the
parts back together. And it leads to several further distortions.

First, it polarizes the contradictions in Burney's writing without
explaining her obvious attempts to reconcile them.[12] It is not accurate
to say that the diaries and *Evelina* show by their "zest" a real, private
Burney at odds with the conservative voice of her last three novels
(Simons 135). Burney's diary was not so much an outlet for the
publicly inexpressible as it was a forum where her various selves
could come together and argue out workable compromises—where
fears of the egotism of writing could be modulated into written self-

satire: "This year was ushered in by a grand and most important event . . . the first publication of the ingenious, learned, and most profound Fanny Burney!" (*Diary* 1:21). Nor is the narrator's voice in the last three novels—the voice that speaks the surface text—consistently conservative. Like the diaries, the novels show clear attempts at integration. Earlier women novelists such as Manley, Haywood, and Lennox had accepted the submerged self and preached conformity while strongly hinting its unfairness. I see Burney as the first woman novelist to try to create some consistency between her characters' theoretical and practical values—between what they should do and what they can do. Though a satirist, Burney was not essentially an ironist; her satiric characters, with their single vision and simple, truthful expressions, merely expose the doubleness of hypocrisy or self-ignorance in others.[13]

And here one sees a second problem with "doubleness" as an approach to Burney's writings and to those of other women writers of the eighteenth century: it exaggerates their passivity and deference to the opinions of others. Spender's observation about Haywood serves equally well for Burney: "She was part of the society she was writing about and writing for, and she helped to *shape* as well as to reflect the social values of her period. It is absurd to think solely in terms of her reaction to public demand, and to omit any consideration of the role she played in stimulating, extending and developing the tastes of her audience" (90).[14] It is especially easy to oversimplify Burney's domination by patriarchal males—her father, "Daddy" Crisp, and Dr. Johnson—for these men usually intended to encourage her, though in a misguided and authoritarian way.[15] When she rebelled against them it was to avoid writing, because of what today would be called fear of success. So highly did some men regard educated women— assuming that they could read Greek and Latin, for instance—that Burney doubted she could sustain the role (*Diary* 1:207).

As a juvenile writer, Burney was more directly and consistently censored by women than by men: as a diarist she had to defy the scoldings of her stepmother and the warnings of her friend Dolly Young, continuing to write despite her guilt only because, as she wrote at the time, "I cannot help it" (*ED* 1:18). Burney also had a formidable dread of the female critical establishment—the Bluestockings—whom her male mentors also feared to offend when they advised her to suppress her first comedy, *The Witlings,* which seemed to satirize them. Such women, after all, guarded the gates of respectable society—something Burney's ideology would not let her ignore or disparage. The Bluestockings, as we have seen, tended to the conservative view that women in general should not write, at least for publication; they saw themselves as exceptions to the rule. Men (such as Boileau) may have originated the idea that learning in women is connected to lasciviousness; Burney's sister Charlotte wrote of an "insolent wretch" who tried to compliment her by assuring her that she was no "précieuse" (*ED* 2:297).[16] But in practice men were far more tolerant of this imagined looseness than women were.

Johnson laughed at Burney's fears of appearing "studious or affected" and advised her to learn Latin (*Diary* 1:135-36).[17] Only another woman—Burney's sister Susan—could understand what was wrong with this advice; after being asked if she knew Latin, Burney wrote to her, "I wonder, my dear Susy, what next will be said of me!" (*Diary* 1:207). She was right to wonder, since later someone asked her if she had read *Les Liaisons dangereuses,* a question that "hurt" her more substantially than the novel's contents ever could (2:178).[18] Questions like that one, as she knew, could have turned the "world's wife" against her and locked the gates of society in her face. Her awareness of women's social power explains why she sometimes presented matriarchy in her novels as more malevolent and threatening than patriarchy.[19]

Burney's problematic relation to the female writing establishment is a third reason for revising our approach to her novels—for the portrait of her as a repressed radical seems to imply that she identified herself as a lady author and therefore felt a need to sublimate her rebellious self to conform to feminine restrictions. Critics from her own time to ours have seen Burney as "feminine" in contradictory ways. Ignoring the "boisterousness" noted by Mrs. Montagu and so many other commentators, William Hazlitt praised Burney's feminine reverence for manners and conventions, identifying the subject of her humor as "violation of the rules of society, or a deviation from established custom" (336).[20] More "liberated" critics of our own century have censured her for the same reason, Lord David Cecil for instance calling her work "intensely feminine, using the word, it must be owned, not wholly in its best sense" (78). More recently some feminist critics have taken her concern with decorum as a sign of her domination by patriarchal males (Simons 28-30).[21] Paradoxically, when Burney penetrates surface manners to satirize them from a moral perspective, the resulting didacticism is also regarded as stereotypically feminine or subservient—though not long before, in Manley's time, moral seriousness would have been associated with male and not with female novelists, and not long after, in the works of Hannah More, didacticism would be seen as "reformist" rather than conformist (Myers 265, 269).[22]

Burney herself resisted being categorized as a lady author because she wrote novels, and ladies' novels were presumed to be "mere love stories." Though the dedication of *Evelina* to Dr. Burney is "feminine" and deferential—abjectly so, according to Doody (*Frances Burney* 32)—the preface unabashedly places the author in the male counter-tradition of the novel as Fielding had defined it in *Joseph Andrews*. Her first critical statement to the public carefully avoids any hint of femininity, citing "Rousseau, Johnson, Marivaux, Fielding, Richardson, and Smollet [*sic*]" as her literary ancestors, with whom "no man need blush at starting from the same post, though many, nay most men, may sigh at finding themselves distanced (7)." [23] Even after her gender was known, Burney did not introduce her novels with the apologies typical of women writers such as Sarah Fielding, instead using the space for serious critical statements on the status of the novel and on her own artistic goals (Tompkins 117). In *The Wanderer* she celebrated the novel's didactic possibilities, and she used the advertisement to *Camilla* to define it as a "work" rather than a novel.[24] She was as aware as feminist critics are today that women's writing was "marginalized" in a way she did not want hers to be; her desire for a larger reading public suggests more a sense of self-importance than the "diffidence" attributed to her by critical tradition (Spencer 95).

Burney's unwillingness to be regarded as "merely" feminine leads me to a fourth problem with the text-subtext approach: it seems to imply a lack of conscious control. Just as Schofield refers to Haywood as "unconscious," Simons calls Burney "an unsophisticated artist, unaware that she is projecting her own mechanisms for survival through her fictional characters" (Schofield, *Quiet Rebellion*, 10-11; Simons 59). This view is uncomfortably close to the eighteenth century's own conception of the woman writer as "artless," discussed most perceptively by Spencer (79).[25] Yet Spencer herself reasons from Burney's "diffidence" (95) as it appears in her diary that the author "almost denies her artistry" (98), although Burney's public statements in the prefaces to her novels are designed to assert it.

Finally, the text-subtext approach to Burney's novels is usually based on oversimplified assumptions about the ideological meaning attached to fictional patterns. The model usually identifies Burney's surface text as stereotypical romance, corresponding to her conscious, conformist self, and the subtext as realistic, corresponding to her unconscious, rebellious self.[26] But one must take a warning from the number of excellent recent critical analyses that have come to opposite conclusions about the conservatism or progressivism of novelists such as Fielding, Austen, and Burney.[27] As we have seen, the romance plot, ending in marriage for love, gives value to feminine will while also confirming the social order, and therefore it lends itself to both conservative and subversive purposes.[28] Furthermore, although writers in Burney's time often referred to romance, particularly to the happy ending, as conventional and hackneyed, they also associated it with quixotism and hence with radical individualism, as Lennox did when she satirized both associations in *The Female Quixote*. Conversely, realism was not radical without the addition of some critical or satiric apparatus, which romance could supply—though with some difficulty, as Manley's works attest.[29]

My own approach is to treat Burney and her texts as complex unities. I submit that the contradictions in her fiction resulted from her deliberate attempts to reconcile opposing value systems, and to bend the form of the novel, with all its unwieldy and deeply rooted romance archetypes, to her own purpose. The enormous difficulty of this task makes her incomplete success a matter of "tradition and the individual talent" rather than of simple social repression.

According to Burney's own beliefs, nothing could be more absurd and futile than the unceasing attempts of critics to separate her "real" self from her social milieu. In some matters she did "internalize" her age's strictures on female conduct, and in others she did "pragmatically" stifle rebellion. But the imaginary line between self and society that both theories ask us to draw would have been drawn very differently by Burney herself—if she would have drawn it at all. What we call conformity, she would have called self-assertion. For example, her concern for public opinion, such as it was, can be seen as a legitimate artistic choice rather than as a choice of life (or social life) over artistic integrity. She feared publicity, but only an audience could make her achievement meaningful to her. She published *Evelina* willingly, though in disguise, and therefore must have welcomed the enlarged opportunity for self-expression publication offered her.[30] Like her character Belfield in *Cecilia,* she seems to have considered the occupation of publishing satirist, with all its pressures and frustrations, a potential means to freedom (719-21); she listened to her many mentors only when she felt their suggestions had merit—refusing, for example, to change the ending of *Cecilia* to please Mr. Crisp.[31] To Burney, writing for others did not mean surrendering her judgment— for in her judgment, others mattered.

Burney's position on women similarly resists simple classification as "fetter'd" or "free." Critics sometimes see her as "diffident" because whenever she appeared in public she made sure to give that impression.[32] And, as one may judge by Mrs. Thrale's acid comment quoted at the beginning of this chapter, the apparent paradox in this behavior, the Arabella-like studied artlessness, could easily elicit accusations of hypocrisy, which J.W. Croker called "playing off all the little airs and manners of *'Miss in her Teens'"* (255). But it was important to Burney to show that she did not seek the attention she received so that the narcissism that seemed to be destroying society— and feminine manners and character along with it—would not attach itself to her. The key concept in Burney's philosophy of feminine selfhood was "female delicacy," a trait which is itself so ideologically ambiguous that writers as far apart politically as Hannah More and Mary Wollstonecraft preached its importance (More 1:409-411, 418; Wollstonecraft, *Vindication,* 185-86; *Anthology,* 218).[33]

To Burney, delicacy was not merely female; it was related to Scudéry's "tenderness," the sensitivity that makes one sympathetic to others, which is one source of resemblance and attraction between men and women. Hence Lord Orville has *"feminine . . .* delicacy" *(Evelina* 261), as does Edwy in Burney's tragedy *Edwy and Elgiva* (II, ii, ll. 81-90). Delicacy in these works is consistent with masculinity because, unlike male writers such as Steele and Burke, Burney did not connect it with weakness.[34] In fact, she believed it could even stimulate women to quit the private sphere to which they seemed destined "by Nature . . . reason, and . . . custom" and enter the male, public world of politics.

> But in the doctrine of morality . . . their feminine deficiencies are changed into advantages; since the retirement, which divests them of practical skill for public purposes, guards them, at the same time, from the heart-hardening effects of general worldly commerce. It gives them leisure to reflect and to refine, not merely upon the virtues, but the pleasures of benevolence, not only and abstractedly upon that sense of good and evil which is implanted in all, but feelingly, nay awfully, upon the woes they see, yet are spared! It is here, then, in the cause of tenderness and humanity, they may come forth, without charge of presumption, or forfeiture of delicacy. [*Brief Reflections* iv][35]

Burney was acting on her own advice when she wrote this passage, which forms part of a pamphlet on the plight of the emigrant French clergy during the Revolution. Following her example, three of Burney's heroines are led by delicacy to perform rather than shrink from brave deeds. Evelina runs after Mr. Macartney and seizes his gun, preventing his suicide. Cecilia "burst[s] from the shackles of common forms at Vauxhall, to save the life of Harrel," in the phrase of Burney's friend Mrs. Crewe (*Memoirs* 3:186). And Juliet in *The Wan-*

derer ostensibly demonstrates that "where occasion calls for female exertion, mental strength must combat bodily weakness, and intellectual vigour must supply the inherent deficiencies of personal courage; . . . those, only, are fitted for the vicissitudes of human fortune, who whether female or male, learn to suffice to themselves" (204).[36]

Delicacy is composed of the two main ingredients Haywood's and Lennox's lovers found so appealing in each other: intense feeling and self-command. But Burney saw these drives as acting in concert rather than opposition, because she knew that women had other intense feelings besides love, and that suppressing love might lead to greater freedom in the long run. For one thing, it was normally only the man's love that was considered important, and therefore a woman looking for freedom had to get rid of unwanted suitors before she could even think of looking for what Sir Bazil Loveit called the "favourite man."

The right to turn down marriage proposals was important in Burney's life as well as in her novels. As a young girl she dreamed—like any eighteenth-century heroine—of ending her days in pastoral retirement with her favorite sister, Susan—until Susan did what those heroines really do and left her to get married (Doody, *Frances Burney,* 109). Burney herself tended to regard marriage as a trap and mustered all her defiance to avoid it when her family wished her to marry the eminently eligible Mr. Barlow, whose only fault was that she simply wasn't attracted to him.[37] "But, surely," he asked, "is this not *singular?* " "I give you leave, Sir," she replied, " . . . to think me singular—odd—queer—nay, even whimsical, if you please" (*ED* 2:66). Clearly this was one instance in which Burney believed a woman had to ignore convention; women who did not do so failed in a higher duty, as the plot of *Camilla* demonstrates. Because Dr. Marchmont's wife agreed to marry him without loving him, out of a misguided respect for the wishes of others, their marriage was unhappy; the embittered husband then imparts his cynicism to Edgar, who wishes to marry Camilla: "whatever are your pretensions to her hand, do not necessarily connect them with your chances for her heart" (161). Edgar's response to this advice—to suspect and test Camilla—causes her unfortunate adventures. And so an obscure, obedient woman indirectly brings misery on an entire little world.

No one in this novel denies that women have the right to a "negative choice" in love and marriage, but a "positive wish"—though granted as a right "in theory" by Camilla's clergyman father—is not generally "allowed" (359). Therefore, Mr. Tyrold warns, it is likely to lead to frustration and humiliation—and so it does. The greatest danger the heroine faces is her own vulnerability to love (358). Love is not the domain in which Burney's strong heroines exercise their power; in this third novel, which Doody sees as a deliberate "anti-love story" (*Frances Burney* 221), love is an enervating force that prevents useful action and makes Camilla fearful and indecisive, a source of concern to her parents. Mr. Tyrold advises that only "a strict and unremitting control over your passions" can save his sensitive daughter from pain (359). The voluntary sacrifice of "inclination," which Betsy Thoughtless and Harriot Stuart worked so hard to release, may make it difficult today to associate female delicacy with selfhood. But Mr. Tyrold sees this self-renunciation as a kind of self-assertion, a "combat" requiring strength; he advises "constant occupation," as Manley had once recommended cards, to help Camilla overcome the weakness of passion (359).

As long as equality is not "practicable," love for the delicate woman poses a dilemma: if she feels it for a man who has not yet declared himself, she can either say nothing and suffer frustration, or speak out and suffer humiliation. The women deemed inferior in Burney's diary and novels lack either the "good sense" to see, or the sensitivity to feel, that love threatens their delicacy and therefore their selfhood (*Camilla* 359). The complicated nature of female delicacy as Burney understood it helps to explain her ambivalence toward women who did not manage to control their passions. While one ingredient of delicacy—intense emotion—made her sympathetic, the other—self-restraint—pointed out some justice in society's sentence of ostracism for those who gave way.

The diaries show severe inner turmoil in Burney's dealings with fallen women, from her teen years, when she cut "poor Miss L" ("I was afterwards very sorry that I did not speak with more kindness to her"), through her muddled rejections of Madame de Genlis, Madame de Staël, and Mrs. Thrale (*ED* 2:74).[38] The strain of reconciling her opposing feelings is apparent in the style in which the diary disposes of these women, as in this sentence intended to close the file on Madame de Genlis: "How I grieve at the cloud which hovers over so much merit, too bright to be hid, but not to be obscured" (*Diary* 3:17).[39] The self-conscious metaphor helps keep Burney from confronting her responsibility, because her refusal to "countenance" Madame de Genlis helped to darken the obscuring cloud. The tone of sanctified pity shows her recourse to conventional wisdom to convince herself that rejecting such women should satisfy her conscience, though in fact it disturbed it.

Burney's sentence on Madame de Genlis does not reveal a simple, "pragmatic" compliance with an unjust custom, for Burney felt her behavior indicated a lack of something important. Her frank—or, rather, French—manners attracted Burney at first because they seemed to promise warm feelings; but just as Haywood had depicted uninhibited Frenchwomen as essentially heartless, Burney attributed the errors of Madame de Genlis, and of the other fallen women of her acquaintance, to weakness and insensitivity rather than to emotional intensity.[40]

Burney's adolescent descriptions of her stepmother suggest that she was already connecting what she saw as crudity in manners ("laughing so loud, & hooting, & clapping her hands") with lack of sexual control (Hemlow 39). This was, after all, the woman who had seduced Burney's beloved father, and all three of her daughters eloped, one with her own half brother. Perhaps more important, all three in the end were desperately unhappy, more imprisoned than liberated by their surrender to passion. Burney's final letter to Hester Thrale warning her not to elope with Piozzi—a music teacher, an Italian, and a Catholic—should be read in this light. She was not being merely prudish or prejudiced. She feared that the most important part of her friend's character was about to be destroyed by feelings of questionable value, even of questionable reality, and she begged her not to "wilfully deprive yourself of all hopes of happiness but One,—that one so uncertain! so *inadequate* to such a sacrifice" (quoted in Doody, *Frances Burney,* 162).[41]

In *The Wanderer* Burney explored the possibility that free sexual expression was inversely related to selfhood through the character of Elinor Joddrel, a Mary Wollstonecraft figure who attempts to put into practice the theoretical sexual equality mentioned but waived by Mr. Tyrold. Elinor learns that her own innate delicacy is even more her enemy than the double standard she defies. After proudly declaring her love for Harleigh and her plan to pursue him, "She stopt, and the deepest vermillion overspread her face; her effort was made; she had boasted of her new doctrine, lest she should seem impressed with confusion from the old one which she violated; but the struggle being over, the bravado and exultation subsided; female consciousness and native shame took their place; and abashed, and unable to meet the eyes of Ellis [Juliet], she ran out of the room" (141). Because no one in the novel bothers to refute Elinor's assertions, some critics have theorized that by the turn of the century Burney had become something of a feminist; but Elinor's principles have already been refuted, *a priori,* by "nature."[42]

In much the same way, all women in Burney's novels who want to be exceptional and rise above convention—in any fashion—are at war with themselves; they fail to understand that their delicacy is their selfhood and that both depend on social approval. Delicacy requires restraint of the tongue in addition to sexual restraint; the two ideas were often connected in anti-feminist literature.[43] For this reason Burney's novels show a growing disapproval of female wits. Most of her predecessors had had difficulty with these characters, for they knew that they themselves were examples of a type that they could not wholly approve. Manley simply decided that wit was acceptable for herself only; Lennox excused Arabella's unconscious satire but could not thus justify her own. Characteristically, Burney's novels show the author's attempts to determine the right position to take and to hold it consistently. She treats witty women favorably in her earlier novels; but perhaps because of her experiences with Mrs. Thrale and Madame de Staël, neither of whom "could ever withstand the pleasure of uttering a repartee, let it wound whom it might," over time she gradually withdrew her support from the characters who resemble them (*Diary* 6:399-400). Thus the "disowning" of the humor in Burney's later novels was caused not only by the author's surrender to public pressure, but also by her mounting desire to expose the dangerous indelicacy attached to the wit's deceptively attractive talent.

Mrs. Selwyn in *Evelina* already shows the beginning of this theme. Although on the whole she is a virtuous character, voicing the author's own satiric opinions, her sharp tongue makes Mr. Villars and Evelina uncomfortable (275-76, 268-69).[44] In her next novel, Burney began to separate wit from true intelligence. In place of Mrs. Selwyn's "masculine learning," Lady Honoria Pemberton in *Cecilia* has "quick parts and high spirits," but "her mind was uncultivated, and she was totally void of judgment or discretion." The insensitivity latent in Mrs. Selwyn is brought to the surface in Lady Honoria, who has "much levity and . . . little heart," and who can therefore afford to be "careless of giving offense, and indifferent to all that was thought of her" (454).[45]

The connection between individualism, wit, and insensitivity is a central theme in *Camilla*, illuminated by the witty Mrs. Arlbery, an individualist who "had offended or frightened almost all the county around, by a wilful strangeness of behaviour, resulting from an undaunted determination to follow in every thing the bent of her own humour" (194). Mrs. Arlbery believes wits are misunderstood: "Never judge the heart of a wit . . . by the tongue! We have often as good hearts, ay, and as much good nature, too, as the careful prosers who utter nothing but what is right, or the heavy thinkers who have too little fancy to say anything that is wrong. But we have a pleasure in our own rattle that cruelly runs away with our discretion" (780). She turns wit into the venial sin of vanity by connecting it with narcissism; as Betsy and Harriot are in love with their reflections, wits are in love with their "echo." Wits only appear cruel, she says, because they are too honest to create a pleasant facade. But the statement actually betrays that in this instance appearances do not lie: she is, at the moment, apologizing in her way for a crude remark she has just made about Camilla's crippled sister, Eugenia. Wit may be born of a noble independence of mind, but the conceit that makes it grow is a serious moral failing, and so wit gradually hardens into habitual selfishness and coldness.[46]

Mrs. Arlbery is a warning not only of the personal, psychological dangers of wit, but of the widespread damage witty people may cause when they become leaders of society. The paradox of Mrs. Arlbery is that, although she sees herself as exceptional, she is really the epitome of conventionality in the decadent world of Burney's radical/conservative vision.[47] Her willingness to offend everybody has ironically earned her a position as leader of the *"ton,"* a fashionable ingroup that had been described in *Cecilia* as the "insipid, negligent, and selfish" antithesis of real "social felicity" (*Cecilia* 271, 29). By defying fashion Mrs. Arlbery makes defiance fashionable, for everyone wants to be a member of this exclusive club; it is a sort of social cancer, growing from the quirky urban minority it appears to be in Burney's first two novels until, in *Camilla,* it seems to be taking over the world.

Mrs. Arlbery, believing herself unusual, is pitifully common; proclaiming herself a free spirit, she merely perpetuates the worst aspects of the status quo. She is the rule-bound feminine humorist Hazlitt thought he saw in Burney. Mrs. Arlbery is a shrewd observer, and she correctly points out to Camilla that her lover Edgar is "a watcher . . . without trust" who will trifle with her affections (482). But she too is a "watcher" who, like Edgar, thinks that scrutinizing other people's conduct and interpreting it in the most sinister light will put her above the reach of evil, not realizing how much evil this behavior can cause. Edgar, with his mistrust, creates rather than prevents Camilla's worst predicaments. Mrs. Arlbery's cynicism makes the world the ugly place she believes it is by implying that it cannot be otherwise. When she tells Camilla that of course poor, crippled Eugenia will have to buy herself a husband, she may mean to satirize the greed and hard-heartedness of others, but instead she makes it difficult for her charmed listeners to conceive of the possibility that anyone could love Eugenia for herself.[48]

In Burney's last novel, *The Wanderer,* the Mrs. Arlbery type has become both more clearly evil and more eminently respectable. Three such furies torture the heroine in this novel, chief among them Mrs. Ireton, whose name suggests both "ire" and "irony," and whose wit is only "mockery and derision" (37). Mrs. Ireton and her friends comprise a female establishment, a group of non-literary Bluestockings even more formidable than the wives in Manley's novels, the cabal in *Betsy Thoughtless,* and the nuns in *Harriot Stuart,* because they do not need men to give them power. This establishment is a serious obstacle to the comic ending, for it determines who shall and shall not be included in society. "Society," however, in the best sense, no longer exists, for its members are all "egotists, equally wrapt up in themselves, and convinced that self alone is worth living for in this nether world" (518). What calls itself "society" here is merely an unharmonious collection of sneering, self-absorbed individuals.

The vision of harmonious union remains alive in this novel only for the heroine and her hero, who in a better world would be normal and ordinary. In character Juliet is as far as possible from a quixote in the Cervantean sense; she would not dream of introducing chaos into the social order, as Don Quixote does, in the hope of re-establishing God's original meritocracy. But she does innocently bring chaos with her from France into the drawing room of Mrs. Ireton; for the Revolution and the Reign of Terror have destroyed the old signifiers of rank, forcing nature's aristocrats into a new way of showing themselves for what they are: "all that are greatest, most ancient, and most noble, have learnt, that self-exertion can alone mark nobility of soul; and that self-dependence only can sustain honour in adversity" (612). Juliet embodies the paradox of Burney's ideology: she derives her sense of self from her membership in a noble family, but she can demonstrate that she belongs in that family only by surviving on her own. The pillars of English society, rigidly adhering to outmoded forms, are unable or unwilling to adjust to the changes and to read the new signs of aristocracy. Their selfish desire to make "society" an exclusive club makes Juliet guilty until proven innocent—guilty of being an "adventuress," of living a romance.

Juliet's plight is one of the romantic paradoxes generated by Burney's feeling that the world had turned upside down and that society had become individualistic and "normal" social values rare. In this last novel one sees the culmination of the contradictions and problems found throughout her fiction, the complications of her craft at their most extreme. In the paragraphs that follow I will examine these paradoxes as they develop in her novels: first, in her use of romantic adventure, and second, in her use of the romantic denouement.

Romantic adventure creates confusion in the novels' didactic message because it both supports and contradicts Burney's ideology; it is a convenient means of expressing the author's dissatisfaction with reality, but it is unfortunately related to the sources of that dissatisfaction. Juliet epitomizes the Burneyan heroine by showing that romantic adventure could be consistent with realism, for she is both a figure from fairy tales and an inhabitant of eighteenth-century England. All Burney's heroines are Cinderellas; but Juliet is also Sleeping Beauty, literally imprisoned in a "brier thicket of brambles, nettles, and thorns" by Snow White's wicked queen—that is, by Mrs. Ireton, who has been turned into a witch, all too plausibly, by her frustration and anger over the loss of youth, beauty, and male attention (518). Juliet also qualifies as a Burneyan heroine because, ironically, she wants nothing less than to be the center of attention; in contrast, her sometime friend Elinor Joddrel wants nothing more, and therefore her melodramatic bids for heroinehood are doomed to failure. Even her attempted suicide at Juliet's concert is turned by the audience into an episode in Juliet's romance—one more "adventure" or "accident" among many for which the heroine is somehow deemed responsible (407).[49]

Juliet's romantic/realistic situation is fraught with possibilities for the satiric exposition of Burney's opinions about "society," but if her central characters are unwilling to be heroines they are even less comfortable as satirists. In the early novels Evelina and Cecilia do get to expose the follies of fashionable life by describing them with common sense, or by asking reasonable questions, as when Evelina writes to Mr. Villars about the effeminate male milliners of London (27), or when Cecilia tries to pin down the "voluble" Miss Larolles to some definite meaning (40-41). But as wit becomes more dangerous in these novels, satire must be managed more subtly and placed in less vulnerable hands. Increasingly it is assigned to an innocent eccentric, a type of character that abounds in the sentimental fiction of Mackenzie, Sterne, and Goldsmith and that is also plentiful in the pages of Burney's diary (Butler, *Jane Austen,* 17). These characters are romantic in their own way: they are a type of quixote, though not the same type as Mrs. Arlbery, and they convey some of the "wonder" Congreve had attributed to the romance by illustrating the great variety of human personality, the "wilder wonders of the Heart of man" (*Camilla* 7).

Instead of hiding a soft heart with a sharp tongue, the innocent satirist, nearly always a man, speaks satire out of kindness. He makes fun of himself as often as he ridicules others and usually ridicules others only by accident; in this way he manages to voice stringent criticism of powerful people without bringing punishment on himself or on the others for whom he speaks. Burney wrote fondly in her court journal about such a man: Colonel Goldsworthy, equerry to King George, "wag professed of their community, and privileged to say what he pleases" (*Diary* 3:258). He pleased to complain in nearly blasphemous tones about the hardships of royal attendance; and since one could laugh *at* him without revealing how much one was also laughing *with* him, he was an invaluable reducer of stress for his fellow courtiers.[50] Just as Goldsworthy's eccentricity was a shield for himself and his audience, Burney's fictional eccentrics protected their author from blame for "boisterous" humor and what might now be called "strident" satire. As wits declined in value in her later novels, these buffoons rose, and often their unconscious targets are the hard-hearted satirists who mistakenly think they have a monopoly on laughter.

This development begins in *Cecilia,* where Lady Honoria Pemberton first demonstrates the difference between wit and wisdom. She and the members of the *ton* laugh at the "crazy-man" Albany, ludicrously out of place in their fashionable assemblies, but his mad, biblical style of speech enables him to tell them to their faces that they are talking nonsense. He exposes, with his pure, single vision, the doubleness of worldly manners (64).

In *Camilla,* in which the moral danger of wit is a major theme, Burney can arrange to make the victim of a practical joke the innocent agent of the joker's reform. Unlike Captain Mirvan in *Evelina,* Camilla's brother Lionel chooses undeserving targets, and so his pranks are funny only in ways he does not anticipate or understand. He disrupts a family picnic by inventing a mad bull about to attack, only to frighten Miss Margland. Burney uses the incident to aid characterization as the members of the group, including Sir Hugh Tyrold, reveal themselves by their reactions. The elderly Sir Hugh, remembered by Austen's dreadful John Thorpe "playing at see-saw and learning Latin" (*NA* 49), is a ridiculous spectacle. While everyone but Camilla and her uncle runs to safety, nothing can speed up the old man's circumlocutory speech: "There's no need of all of us being tost, my dear girl, because, [sic] of my slowness, which is no fault of mine, but of Robert's not being in the way; which must needs make the poor fellow unhappy enough, when he hears of it" (132-33). But one does not laugh at Sir Hugh as one is meant to laugh at the mud-covered Madame Duval in Burney's first novel; the old man's serene good nature and unselfishness add an element of pathos. As a result, Lionel "felt his heart smite him, . . . and flew to acquaint him that he had made a mistake, for the bull was only angry, not mad" (133).

In *The Wanderer,* the malice of wit reaches its peak, and therefore the eccentric's task is at its most important and most arduous. The "Lionel" of this novel is Ireton, the son of the villainess, and his pranks are as humorless as his mother's sarcasm, consisting mainly of using his superior strength to trap Juliet. Within the space of two chapters, he "wantonly filled up the door-way," "maliciously placed himself against the door," "declared that he should not suffer her to decamp," and "encircled her completely within the broad leaves of the screen" (579, 581, 583, 586). With this family established as the epitome of respectability, the only source of true humor and of the sound moral vision that produces it is the clown, Mr. Giles Arbe. We laugh at Arbe's accounts of his absent-minded *faux pas,* as when, intent on catching a gnat, he slapped the face of a lady on whom it had landed, and then "ran away as fast as I could; for I had not a word to say for myself" (272). Whereas in *Evelina* such gaucherie was something for the heroine to overcome, here it frees Arbe to speak the simple truth, incidentally exposing pretension and hypocrisy. Thus he can say of his cousin, whom he was to chaperon at a ball, that she was "looking better than ever she did before in her life, as she told me herself," without seeming to be aware that he is pointing out the lady's vanity (272). More important, he can tell off an entire roomful of Juliet's unpaying harp students and make them so ashamed that they decide to go home early, though without settling their bills (303).

As the world gets worse with each novel, the heroines show an increasing respect for the opinions of these "crazy" men. Cecilia lets Albany command her purse, but she is not as willing as he is to ignore public opinion and all forms of politeness.[51] Juliet, on the other hand, takes Arbe's advice and agrees to "sing those songs" in public in order to pay her debts (284). Nevertheless, none of these quixotes has the final answer to the heroine's moral problems. Because they are "crazy" in one way or another, they are incomplete. Albany is just one of a large assortment of one-trait characters in *Cecilia*—like the heroine's three guardians, the supercilious aristocrat, the rich miser, and the prodigal urbanite—whose fragmented personalities prevent them from achieving self-fulfillment through meaningful relations with others. Sir Hugh, kindly as he is, cannot be trusted with the upbringing of his nieces and heedlessly causes Eugenia's accident. Arbe similarly wounds the innocent along with the guilty with his habitual absence of mind (332); even more serious, he is unable to balance one clear duty, such as paying one's bills, with others that may conflict with it, such as not accepting money from a rejected suitor. All three men are finally too "shallow in judgement, and knowledge of the world" to be consistently helpful (*Wanderer* 312).

Marilyn Butler describes characters like Arbe in earlier fiction—

Sterne's Uncle Toby, Goldsmith's Vicar—as part of the "radical inheritance" of the jacobin novelists of the Revolutionary period. Though the jacobins deplored these characters' sentimentality, their idiosyncracies implied a respect for human uniqueness that would prove useful to proponents of radical individualism (*Jane Austen* 55). This latent individualism made Burney's eccentrics as inappropriate to her purpose in one way as they were useful in another, for it was impossible to exploit their position as outsiders without seeming to endorse that position. She preferred to deal with the problems of trying to live on the inside, which were problems these characters could know little about.

Life is finally more complicated for the Burney heroine than it is for the Burney buffoon, for the heroine exists in the crux of her author's complicated ideology. As a social being she can neither defy nor accept "society" as it has become without betraying herself and her ideals. In essence, she is faced with an unanswerable question: How far may a conservative go in defying a corrupt world? It is not only permissible but mandatory, from a Christian perspective, to defy the world in the direction of self-denial; as Hannah More quotes scripture, "the friendship of the world is *enmity* with God" (1:449). This is the Christ-like self-sacrifice that, as we have seen, made the lives of actual women so far from comic. But may one defy a corrupt world in the direction of self-gratification? Burney's heroines suffer because the author in good conscience cannot say yes. Like Manley, Haywood, and Lennox, Burney insists that, though it should not be necessary, her heroines must be ready to give up the "positive wish"; she even goes farther than her predecessors in considering rebellion not only impractical but wrong.

And so, in these intentionally didactic novels, the author can offer no practical advice on how her readers might get out of their own predicaments. This problem is first apparent in *Cecilia*—in a sense, it is what that novel is about, thematically and formally. The theme is how to maintain one's integrity in a corrupt world, and the plot consists of the heroine's search for the "golden mean" (127). The form, with its moderate romance ending, is appropriately a compromise: Cecilia defies the terms of her uncle's will, which stipulates that her husband must take her name, and gives up her inheritance in order to marry Delvile, who defies his father in order to marry her.[52] But the ending does not fully resolve the conflicts the author has raised. Allusions to *Romeo and Juliet* are frequent as a subtle acknowledgement that the situation is essentially tragic and cannot be resolved in this life (500, 535-36, 831). At the end of the novel Burney asserts the couple's right to marry. But she questions this right earlier when

Delvile proposes a secret wedding even though the objections of Delvile's parents, and by analogy the conditions of the Beverley will (677), are clearly shown to be unreasonable, the result of "pride and prejudice." Theoretically, Delvile is right, as Cecilia admits: "he had truly said that their union would be no offence to morality" (553). If the world were fair, she would not hesitate; but as it is, clandestine marriage "seemed to imply . . . impropriety" (554); she feels "degraded" that he would even suggest it (543). Cecilia cannot justify herself if others blame her, even wrongly.

The conflict is partly one of theoretical versus practical morality, familiar from Manley's novels on—for, practically speaking, Delvile might abandon Cecilia without proof of their marriage, as Mrs. Dormer's husband abandoned her in *Harriot Stuart,* and as Sir John Belmont abandoned Evelina's mother (*Cecilia* 544-45). But just as prudence had begun to take on absolute value for Haywood, Cecilia regards her reputation as theoretically as well as pragmatically important. She would not blame Delvile if he ceased to respect her after marrying her in secret, for to risk even "seeming" impropriety is to court adventure and romance, and thus to show real indelicacy. Cecilia demands a higher morality of herself than she demands of Delvile; she blames herself severely for temporarily agreeing to the clandestine marriage, but after her first indignant response to his proposal she never blames him for consistently intending to go through with the ceremony (609). All moral responsibility rests with her, and thus she is the ethical center of the novel. Because her standards are so unrealistically high and impossible to emulate, because she judges herself more harshly than the reader is expected to judge her, her nearly tragic restraint is no more helpful to the ordinary woman than Juliet's tragic abandon.[53]

The same moral paradox occurs in *Camilla,* where it is also left unresolved; here it forms the basis of the heroine's character and therefore of the novel as a whole.[54] Camilla is more or less in the Betsy Thoughtless mold, a good-hearted heroine with minor flaws who gradually learns to realize her potential for perfection, but her "flaws" would be marks of perfection in a more perfect world. Her main distinguishing feature, suggested by her name, which is used to illustrate speed and lightness in Pope's *Essay on Criticism,* is her vivacity, referred to variously as "airy thoughtlessness," "gaiety," and a "playful good humour." This trait, "a source of perpetual amusement" to her family, also "raised a fear for her discretion" (51-52).[55] But Camilla would not need discretion if she never came into contact with the world that makes women responsible for the romances people create about them.

In fact, if Camilla were to become "discreet" it would be a sign of that loss of innocence Edgar keeps expecting; with each new experience that gives her further knowledge of the world, he prays that "a short time might restore her mind to its native simplicity and worth" (486). The only development he can imagine for her is backward into childhood, like Lennox's unreflecting Arabella.[56] Unless Camilla can remain sheltered from the world, anything she does will be wrong. The novel does contain a character like Harriot Loveit in *Betsy Thoughtless* and the Countess in *The Female Quixote*, a woman who has grown up discreet without being corrupted by the world that forces her to be that way: "Lady Isabella, addressed only where known, followed only because loved, sees no adulators encircling her, for adulation would alarm her; no admirers paying her homage, for such homage would offend her" (476). But she is as bloodless as the Countess, an embodiment of theory; she is supposed to exert a power over her surroundings that the heroine's experiences show to be impossible. Even if Lady Isabella were believable, she would not be an appealing model for a young reader, for unlike the Countess, whose happiness is not questioned, Lady Isabella's happiness is a facade that may dutifully conceal private misery: "She knows she has not only her own innocence to guard, but the honour of her husband. Whether she is happy with him or not, this deposit is equally sacred" (476).

Arabella's life, we must imagine, eventually resembles that of the Countess; but Camilla does not imitate Lady Isabella. Her novel shows the world to be a moral quagmire in which women can rarely manage to remain good, much less happy. In both novels the heroines' isolation from the world is at the same time the safeguard of their innocence and the source of their errors; but *Camilla* is even less able than *The Female Quixote* to show the reader a safe path out of Eden. The ending does nothing to settle the question of the heroine's moral worth, for Camilla and Edgar are both excessively humble; he apologizes for his suspiciousness, and she for her "false internal reasoning" (896). The author refuses to say which of them has been more at fault. Without ever separating Camilla's virtues from her errors, Burney simply removes the heroine to a country asylum—a pastoral world of perpetual innocence—where she can end her days "smothered," as Spencer says, by patriarchs in the form of father, uncle, and lover, who guard her from reality, and from maturity (Spencer 167).

The pastoral retreat is an evasion because it is more a fictional convention than a realistic alternative; escape is possible for Camilla only because she has people to care for her and plenty of money. Without these resources there is no protection against the world's dangers and injustices; hence the "female difficulties" of Juliet in *The Wanderer.* Juliet is stuck without an identity card in a world that insists on knowing—in the most superficial way—who everybody is. Here the rich can choose how they wish to be known—as art connoisseurs, for example, like Sir Marmaduke Crawley (215) or Miss Arbe (209), even if they have no taste—because no one dares to contradict them. But unable to divulge her name, and lacking the cash to purchase one, Juliet is consistently trusted by no one but the hero, Harleigh, and her half sister, Lady Aurora. The "open, generous, kind-hearted and sincere" Lord Melbury (her half brother, it turns out) makes a pass at her (125-29). The fatherly Admiral, her uncle, pities her, yet says,"But for all that, young woman, I must make free to remark, that the devil himself never yet put it into a man's head, nor the world's neither, to abandon, or leave, as you call it, desolate, a woman who has kept tight to her own duty, and taken a modest care of herself" (28). Correctly identifying Juliet as a heroine, the young people take her for a "princess in disguise" (99), while the old and cautious see her as Moll Flanders. Burney herself refers to her as a "female Robinson Crusoe" (836).[57]

This almost universal suspiciousness is part of a major theme of the novel: how a presumptuous confidence in the "mathematical" self-sufficiency of human wisdom causes the erosion of faith in God and one's fellow man in post-Revolutionary society, causing in turn a loss of all that holds true society together. As Harleigh converts Elinor to a belief in the afterlife, he asks, "has friendship any other tie? has honour any other bond than faith?" (755). Yet Juliet will not permit herself to resent the nearly total lack of faith in her, for she recognizes that the world's blindness is largely caused by her own invisibility: "Appearances have so cruelly misrepresented me, that I have no right to be indignant, nor even surprised that they should give rise to false judgments" (528). The statement shows Burney's unwillingness to undermine the importance of the outward signs that make up one's social identity; Juliet is a romance heroine, an exception, not designed to encourage the reader to take real-life adventuresses on trust.

These novels' unresolved problems indicate that there were limits to the instructive value of "female difficulties," or adventures, realistically described. The dedication to Burney's last novel sounds very much like the conversion chapter of *The Female Quixote* (both echo Johnson's *Rambler 4*) in proposing "to give to juvenile credulity knowledge of the world, without ruin, or repentance; and the lessons of experience, without its tears" (xx). But the goal of didactic fiction was to help readers live happily, not die dramatically, and so the basic structure of an instructive work had to be comic, however severely that structure might strain probability. Furthermore, only the comic plot, with its happy ending, could counteract the potentially dangerous effects of the heroine's unwilling individualism by establishing a new social order; as Frye observes in reference to dramatic comedy: "The movement of comedy is usually a movement from one kind of society to another. . . . At the end of the play the device in the plot that brings hero and heroine together causes a new society to crystallize around the hero, and the moment when this crystallization occurs is the point of resolution in the action, the comic discovery, *anagnorisis* or *cognitio*" (*Anatomy of Criticism* 163). It was crucial to Burney's ideology that her heroines arrive, somehow, at this denouement.

The romantic denouement does not resolve the heroine's moral dilemma, as we have seen; yet it does represent her just reward. The question about the ending is not whether it is right, but how to bring it about; the paradoxes it generates have less to do with morality than with realism. Realism makes Burney's heroines increasingly unfortunate in their adventures and brings them ever closer to tragedy, and so their final happiness becomes more and more improbable and abrupt. Committed to realism, or the "appearance of truth" (*ED* 1:9), Burney tinkered with this problem throughout her career, trying to solve it with minor adjustments. First she moderated the ending of *Cecilia* to fit the dark beginning and middle, then she lightened the suffering in *Camilla* to fit the happy ending.[58] But the more she tinkered the more improbable, or romantic, her endings became.

Juliet would surely have died many times over without the very visible interference of the author; she makes Harriot Stuart with her Indians and sailors look fortunate by comparison. Juliet must rely heavily on magic to supplement her own strength because her novel most dramatically shows Burney's skepticism about the human ability to perceive and interpret character. One sees that skepticism developing gradually in her last three novels. The ending of *Evelina* seems fitting because, although that novel explores the gap between appearance and reality, it is essentially optimistic about the possibility of accurate perception: Sir Clement Willoughby is not really disguised by his sheep's clothing, and Lord Orville can discern Evelina's nobility even when she is walking with prostitutes, or residing in Holborn. But *Cecilia*'s Mr. Monckton does not show his fangs until the end. And in *Camilla*, Edgar not only fails to see the heroine's worth but contributes to the masking of Mrs. Arlbery; his tests confirm Mrs. Arlbery's opinion of him and thus keep Camilla from seeing the danger of trusting her. In such a world, how can the *anagnorisis* of the comic denouement be made believable?[59]

This skepticism about appearances is connected to a growing cynicism about the transcendent power of love, the love that *should* lead Prince Charming to recognize Cinderella despite her rags. Burney's heroes become increasingly ineffectual, even, as in the case of Edgar, unintentionally menacing, while the heroines are ever more in need of male protection.[60] It seems at least slightly possible that Burney's own marriage had something to do with this cynicism, though the evidence from the diary is inconclusive. Since she married in her forties for love, in an obvious assertion of her selfhood at last, most commentators assume the d'Arblays were happy (Straub 65; Doody, *Frances Burney,* 203; Spender 285), and the diary certainly does not contradict that impression. But if, as both Doody and Devlin remark, the novels are sometimes a good source for uncensored auto-biographical information, one may sense some personal disappoint-ment (Doody, *Frances Burney,* 33; Devlin, *Burney,* 64). *The Wanderer,* written mostly during Burney's ten-year exile in France, particularly invites speculation. Having promised at their marriage that he would not separate his wife from her family, d'Arblay later decided they should go to France to recover his estates, and there they were forced to remain during the Napoleonic wars. The diary of that period paints a happy picture, but Burney later admitted that she had been misera-ble.[61] Might her last novel—the story of a woman who flees France and marriage and tries to survive in England, alone—be read as the author's nightmarish fantasy of escaping back to England, perhaps to find her gravely ill father already dead and herself a pauper and an outcast?

Of course this reading is a fantasy of my own that I mention merely to point out how varied are the scenarios that may be built on the available evidence. Both the diary and *The Wanderer* do strongly suggest, however, that if Burney was happily married it was not because she found in d'Arblay a savior knight. Their married life was "romantic" in precisely the way she most disliked: full of exciting incident. In England, she could share with her appreciative family loving mock-heroic portraits of her husband "mowing down our hedge—with his *Sabre!*—& with an air, & attitude so military, that if he had been hewing down other legions than those he encountered— i:e: of spiders—he could hardly have had a mien more tremendous, or have demanded an Arm more mighty" (*Journals* 2:73). The heroics she had to write about in his native country were all too real, as d'Arblay resumed his commission in the army in late middle age. Ironically, the general was like a real-life version of Manley's imaginary lover, sweeping his wife off against her will to the land of Manley's dreams, making Burney, like her characters, a reluctant heroine. It is not surprising, then, that Burney's last novel puts forth the proposition that a woman should depend on herself instead of passively waiting for her prince to come.

Nor is it surprising, given the power of the wicked stepmothers and stepsisters in that novel, that Juliet finally cannot save herself. The heroine proves her nobility by her resourcefulness in trying out all available occupations and by her endurance of poverty, insult, and even physical abuse. But she does not by her own agency get her name, her inheritance, or Harleigh; and she must get all those things in order to demonstrate Burney's belief that happiness is finding one's proper place in the lives of others. And so the happy ending leaves the reader with an uneasy feeling—the same feeling Brecht found in the ending of *The Beggar's Opera*.[62] Juliet in the midst of her sufferings—including the many rapes she only *almost* suffers—is finally a more vivid picture than Juliet happily married to Harleigh. And as the final happiness of Oliver Twist inevitably puts one in mind of all the poor orphans who remained poor orphans, Juliet's miraculous rescue reminds one of all the poor nameless women who did not live in novels. Like the women writers before her, Burney could not make the comic ending believable as long as real good women could not get the reward she felt they deserved: a husband and a home, but more important, a sense of connection.

The nearest Burney comes to a realistic resolution of this problem, ironically, is the pastoral retreat in *Camilla;* this was the sort of resolution Burney habitually sought for herself. The smaller the society she had to deal with, the less she was forced to notice its sad contrast to the Tory ideal, and the less her integrity and comfort were endangered by complying with its ways. "The World" was often troublesome to her; she wished it "would take more care of itself and less of its neighbours" (*Journals* 1:123). In hopes of reducing this interference, she settled in Bath rather than London in her old age, a town that from her description would have welcomed even the Wanderer: "Respect does not hang either upon the lackey or the attire; and admission is as easy without the one, as reception is good or bad without the other. There is something nearer to independence from the shackles of fortuitous circumstances in the society of *Bath* than I have ever witnessed elsewhere" (Hemlow 383).[63] But Bath was no utopia. The only place Burney had ever been really happy was in the circle of her family and a few close friends. Having outlived nearly all of them, including her only son, she was often alone in her last years. She would never have used such an ending in one of her novels.

Burney's heroines are finally luckier than she was, and luckier than the average reader. But they do not make the reader jealous in quite the same way that Betsy Thoughtless and Harriot Stuart did, because unlike their vain predecessors they do not wish to compete, to be set above their peers, to be called goddesses—to be heroines. They wish only to be understood and accepted, a wish that is "romantic" only because the world is so unfeeling and blind. And so, instead of threatening to reject the reader, the heroines seem rather to fear rejection themselves, at least as much as Burney feared her "daddies," the Bluestockings, and the public.

By inviting the reader's friendship, Burney's heroines helped her to serve the young people—particularly the young women—the author envisioned as the primary audience for her novels.[64] In the dedication to *The Wanderer: or Female Difficulties,* Burney announces her intention to show how these readers may grow up happy and uncorrupted. To fulfill that promise, she would have had to create some consistency between what is and what should be—to resolve her novels' formal and philosophical conflicts—and that, as we have seen, was impossible. But her novels do show some signs that women's fiction and women's lives were having an improving effect on each other. In 1751 Betsy Thoughtless had to marry Munden in "Recognizance" for his unwanted attentions; but in 1782, under similar pressure, Cecilia does not even consider rewarding Sir Robert Floyer in this way (226). Her refusal has unpleasant consequences, and for her martyrdom she, like Harriot Stuart, does not receive the "fame and applause" she deserves (151). Nevertheless, because of these novelists' efforts to expose and then to resist the tyranny of courtship, Jane Austen would soon be able to treat the "negative choice" not as a rebellious dream, like Betsy's premarital "splenetic" nightmare, but as the bare minimum to which every woman was entitled. And readers would begin to see how strangely affirmative the word "no" could be.

6

The Italian
A Romance of Manners

I, a poor unprotected being, wander about in darkness and in dread,
and, though I do nothing wrong, undergo the terrors and alarms of
guilt.—But, do I not act wrong? Alas! I am afraid I do—It *must* be
wrong to carry on a clandestine correspondence.

—Charlotte Smith

IF Fanny Burney's novels were as romantic as the previous discussion
suggests, then they had something in common with the Gothic novels
that became popular during the course of her career, novels which
proclaimed their authors' appreciation for the old romance conventions so long discredited by realist criticism. But until quite recently
a powerful tradition, dating from the eighteenth century, has prevented critics from seeing her works in this light. That tradition set
Gothic apart from other contemporary fiction in much the same way
that novels had once been too-neatly distinguished from romances.
The motive for this exclusiveness was much the same as before—to
dissociate serious male literature from women's popular writings.
During this period, the old battle merely changed its ground as men
entered what they had themselves fenced off as feminine territory—
the romance—and built critical fortifications as they went. The
boundaries they put up between Gothic and other types of fiction
(called "novels of manners," or "sentimental novels," or "didactic
novels"), and those between men's fiction and women's, were observed
more in theory than in the practice of either male or female novelists.

Some fine recent criticism restores hidden connections between
Gothic and other fiction contemporary with it by studying together
novelists such as Ann Radcliffe, Jane Austen, and Sir Walter Scott,
who are traditionally treated separately (Cottom 31). But links connecting women writers such as Fanny Burney, Charlotte Smith, and
Ann Radcliffe (Figes 62), who are traditionally placed in different
categories, are clearer and easier to uncover than cross-gender connections, because for women the Gothic phenomenon was an es-

pecially small step away from what they had been doing for over a century: using romance to describe their experience of life.

Radcliffe in particular owed a great debt to Burney—and vice versa, since their writing careers overlapped—particularly in her "radical conservatism," her belief that in the real world people and values that ought to be ordinary, and that once were, had become rare and "romantic." The similarity of their vision and ideology made it possible for Radcliffe to write *The Italian* (1797), a Gothic novel remarkably close to Burney's still-popular *Cecilia* (1782). In fact, it was closer to that didactic, sentimental novel of manners than to the novel more usually identified as its source, Matthew Lewis's *The Monk* (1796). *Cecilia,* with its realistic setting in the London of Burney's time, expresses its romantic themes largely through symbol and metaphor; in the openly romantic setting of *The Italian,* those symbols are realized and given form and substance. The criticism of the state of society implicit in Burney's tortured uses of romance continues relatively unchanged in Radcliffe's Gothic transformation.

This chapter will examine how the similarity between these two novels confounds traditional categories such as "novel of manners," "sentimental novel," "didactic novel," and "Gothic novel," how readily Burney's novel lent itself to Gothic treatment, and how extensively Radcliffe made use of it. First, however, it will be necessary to trace the origin of "Gothic novel" as a distinct category of late eighteenth-century fiction—to restore some sense of women's rightful place in it, and of its connections to the romances and novels that flourished before, during, and after it. (To avoid confusion of terminology, I will use the term "Gothic novel" throughout this chapter, although the same works so named here are sometimes referred to by other writers as "Gothic romances" or "romantic novels." I will also distinguish "romantic," an adjective I use to refer to the romance as a form of fiction, from "Romantic," referring to a movement in the arts at the turn of the nineteenth century.)

When Horace Walpole officially launched Gothic fiction in 1764 by publishing *The Castle of Otranto* (Varma 41), it may seem to a twentieth-century observer that he declared war on neoclassicism.[1] But although he boasted of his freedom from Aristotelian rules (*Otranto* 12), he was actually objecting to their narrow application in criticism such as Voltaire's. At about this time other writers were also at work trying to stretch the boundaries of classicism without attacking its foundation. Edmund Burke's *A Philosophical Enquiry into the Origin of Our Ideas of the Sublime and Beautiful* (1756), a critical text often credited with starting the Gothic revolution in the arts, was based on a work by Longinus that had been translated by the vehemently neoclassical Boileau in 1674 (Murray 51). Richard Hurd's *Letters on Chivalry and Romance* (1762), another text credited with making Gothic fashionable, also had a French neoclassical source; in it Hurd praises the classicist Addison, in contrast to Voltaire, for his willingness to take romance seriously (53-54, 91-92).[2]

The Gothic "movement" was part of a larger romantic revival that was by no means limited to an interest in British feudalism or Germanic folklore. Even Lewis, an avid collector of German tales, names the pastoral romances read by Don Quixote among his sources for *The Monk* (6).[3] This was the literature that inspired Aphra Behn's picturesque lyrics, the poetic equivalent of baroque paintings by such artists as Claude Lorraine and Nicolas Poussin, who were two of Radcliffe's favorites and sources for her own descriptions of landscape. Although the baroque style is now often contrasted with Gothic, particularly in architecture—the one southern European and elaborate, the other Germanic and "rude"—in the late eighteenth century they seemed related.[4] Hurd's notion of "Gothic" design, in gardens as well as in romances, emphasizes elaboration of detail (67).[5] Not surprisingly, he was less interested in medieval romances, which seemed to him barbaric, than in Renaissance narrative poetry— works by Tasso, Ariosto, and Spenser—that took the feudal society of the past as subject matter. Into the nineteenth century, readers continued to associate the British romantic revival with the continental tradition; Maria Edgeworth refers to Scott as the "Ariosto of the North" (*Helen* 117).[6]

Those continental romances had much to do with love. And for women writers, as we have seen, the pastoral love-romance did not have to come back; it had never gone away. Through the medium of the seventeenth-century French romance, particularly *L'Astrée*, its influence was continuously felt in the works of the women novelists discussed in the previous chapters—sometimes directly, sometimes covertly—and it was therefore ready to be of use to women Gothic writers. Thanks to Behn's and Manley's baroque eroticism, Radcliffe could evoke an atmosphere of passion, subtly and chastely, simply by mentioning the scent of orange blossoms (*Italian* 292; see also *Romance of the Forest* 87, 164). And terms such as the "tenderness" and "esteem, friendship, tender affection" that describe Ellena's feelings for Vivaldi remained in use far into the nineteenth century; some are still alive today in popular music (*Italian* 9, 122). This vocabulary retained its resonance as a form of shorthand for the metaphysical concepts that had been painstakingly worked out by d'Urfé and Scudéry.

The new spirit of acceptance of romance gave women writers every reason to hope that at last they might be taken seriously. Now that English men were recognizing that romances were not "proper furniture only for a lady's Library"—something Clara Reeve, in *The Progress of Romance* (1785), says other nations had always recognized (xi)—men and women might have been able to discuss literature as they once had in the salons of the précieuses.[7] Indeed, women might have hoped to receive credit for anticipating this critical development. Reeve points out that women had continued reading Sidney and Spenser long after men had stopped (*Progress* 1:77-78), and before Hurd told them to start again. She even suggests the existence of a female scholarly tradition, including Madame de Genlis and Lady Mary Wortley Montagu, running counter to a largely male anti-romantic tradition (*Progress* 1:24, vii-viii). But the pat on the back Reeve may have expected women to receive for their astuteness never came.

It was not through overconfidence that women lost their bid for inclusion in the new literary mainstream; confrontational statements are rare in *The Progress of Romance* and in women's novels of the period. Reeve claimed insight into the modern-language domain of romance, as Aphra Behn had claimed the theater and Charlotte Lennox had claimed Shakespeare scholarship, but she did not presume to pass judgment on recent fiction (2:5). Women novelists frequently attempted to gain acceptance by pointedly limiting their ambitions, usually replacing the issue of artistic merit, as measured by classical standards, with an aesthetic of sensibility that would make their artistic efforts seem decorous and unpresumptuous.[8] (Jane Austen ridicules this idea nicely by having Lady Catherine de Bourgh brag about how well—that is, with how much feeling—she would have played the piano, if she had ever learned how [*PP* 173].) The female characters' humility extends outward to the author as a sort of apology for having written a novel. Thus, in Radcliffe's *The Romance of the Forest*, the narrator praises the "sensibility" of Clara's singing, despite her ignorance of the "intricacies of execution" (249), in much the same way that T.N. Talfourd recalls in his memoir of Radcliffe that she had a "sweet" voice with a "limited" range (99).[9] In *The Mysteries of Udolpho*, the narrator raises and then dismisses the question of the merit of Emily's little poems, which, of course, were really Radcliffe's, saying only that they were dear to those who loved her (16-17). And Ellena in *The Italian* paints with "genius"—copying the designs of others (24).

If feeling had been enough—if, as Sir Walter Scott believed, the worth of a book had been the "pleasure" it gave readers (*PW* 3:363-

65)—then these humble solicitations for favor would have worked. But in practice other standards operated, with remarkable inconsistency, to suggest that women writers, by virtue of their gender, were unable to see what Gothic was really all about. The word "romance" from a woman's pen still conjured up images of the French romance only, which the increasingly anti-Gallic English—including Reeve—were not prepared to include in the revival (*Progress* 1:16-7, 95-96).[10] But it was not so much as romance writers of any sort that women were now disparaged, but as realistic novelists.

Walpole is usually described as having written *Otranto* as an escapist gesture connected with his giving up a career in Parliament and retiring from the world of serious purpose; his doing so may have been the source of later critics' association of Gothic with anti-realism.[11] But though realism was going out of style, it remained an important concept in criticism during this period; and it remained as tricky and elusive a concept as ever, reliable only in leading to the foregone conclusion that women's work was inferior to men's.

The concept of realism remained important because, no matter how fond of "wonder" English readers became, they had no intention of giving up their commonsense awareness of the difference between life and fiction.[12] Reeve's definitions of romance and novel in *The Progress of Romance* show how much—and how little—the notion of realism had changed between 1692 and 1785.[13] Reeve preserves Congreve's distinction between romance as "an heroic fable, which treats of fabulous persons and things," and novel as "a picture of real life and manners, and of the times in which it is written": "The Romance in lofty and elevated language, describes what never happened nor is likely to happen.—The Novel gives a familiar relation of such things, as pass every day before our eyes, such as may happen to our friend, or to ourselves."

The departure from Congreve lies in the evaluation of the categories: "the perfection of [the Novel], is to represent every scene, in so easy and natural a manner, and to make them appear so probable, as to deceive us into a persuasion (at least while we are reading) that all is real, until we are affected by the joys or distresses of the persons in the story, as if they were our own" (1:111). Congreve noted how foolish the reader felt after being taken in by romances, not novels, as if the "deception" of novels were understandable or desirable. Reeve's comments rather suggest that the smart reader of her time could enjoy fiction without being a dupe and was thus in a better position to accept the fantastic. A key concept for both Reeve and Hurd was "poetic truth," which Aristotle had set above the literal, factual truth of the historian (Hurd 1:92, Reeve 1:17). Renaissance critics had reversed this judgment in order to explain the inferiority of contemporary romances to Greek and Roman epics, which were supposed to be based on historical events. In reviving the romance, Reeve questioned the historicity of epic and denied its importance, thus restoring Aristotle's original judgment in favor of the poet.

But "poetic truth" had a number of meanings to the defenders of romance—many of which had little to do with Aristotle. It could mean observing the laws of probability, or of psychology, or accurately describing the manners of a society; or it could mean something deeper and therefore antithetical to any or all of these. To illustrate, let us examine three "debates" between men and women writers of the romantic revival. "Debate" is perhaps not quite the word for these skirmishes, for although in each case the woman did try to engage in a public dialogue about the nature of Gothic fiction, the man's "response" was usually dismissive.

The first argument about realism began when Reeve, in the introduction to *The Old English Baron,* suggested that instead of making pictures come off the wall and walk away, as Walpole had done, it might be more effective to keep the supernatural within the bounds of probability (4-5). Those bounds are hard to define, since for Reeve they included a groaning corpse under the floorboards that is never explained. But Walpole felt she had observed her own restrictions, all too well, and disdaining to "return that attack" in public, in private letters to friends called her novel "so probable, that any trial for murder at the Old Bailey would make a more interesting story"; "the most insipid dull nothing you ever saw" (Walpole, *Correspondence,* 28:381-2, 2:110).[14] From this point on, men and women writers divided into camps on the question of whether supernatural occurrences should ultimately be explained, either as natural or as psychological phenomena.[15]

Male writers, it seemed, felt they were at war; and for a time, it appeared that women were winning. In the 1790s it was the feminine Gothic, as practiced by Radcliffe, that held sway. And so in the second skirmish I wish to describe, the first shots were fired by a male writer—Matthew Lewis—in an attempt to regain some lost ground. In his private writings, Lewis expressed "an aversion, a pity, a contempt for all female scribblers" (quoted in introduction to Ferrier, xv).[16] *The Monk* may be seen as his public effort to masculinize, or remasculinize, Gothic fiction.[17] *The Monk* assumes a male audience, addressed in jokes against women reminiscent of those told by dense men in Manley's novels: "She was wise enough to hold her tongue. As this is the only instance of a Woman's ever having done so, it was judged worthy to be recorded here" (Lewis 34). And he deliberately follows *Otranto* rather than *Udolpho* in giving his demons a reality of their own, outside the disturbed imaginations of the characters, though Lewis had read the latter with pleasure (Summers 210).

Radcliffe disapproved of what Lewis was doing to the Gothic novel. In an "essay" on the supernatural that she decided not to publish, she borrowed terms from Burke in order to distinguish "horror," an effect produced by shock, from "terror," an effect produced by suspense and suggestion. The strong implication is that Lewis's masculine "horror" makes his novel less "sublime" than her own feminine "terror."[18] Her more direct response to Lewis was to publish *The Italian* the year after *The Monk* and, by preserving enough superficial similarity to his theme, to point up the differences. Where Lewis showed an imprisoned woman clutching the decaying, worm-eaten corpse of her dead child (368-70), Radcliffe showed a bed of straw with an indentation where the previous tortured prisoner had lain (140).[19] This, she implied, was the way true Gothic was done.

It might seem that Radcliffe had the last word in this "debate," for whereas both men and women continued to read Radcliffe throughout the nineteenth century, Lewis was read mostly by men—and men of a certain sort, such as the brutish John Thorpe in *Northanger Abbey* (48) and the Marquis de Sade (quoted in Summers 106); in the 1930s Montague Summers felt he needed to rescue Lewis from almost total neglect. But even after the Gothic craze of the nineties had "gone to seed" (Varma 73), Radcliffe and Reeve found a third authoritative male opponent in Sir Walter Scott.

In his memoir of Reeve, Scott reasons that once ghosts are introduced into a work, probability is out of the question; since Reeve was unable to see this, she wisely "confined her flight within those limits on which her pinions could support her" (*PW* 3:330-31). His memoir of Radcliffe is far more complimentary—on the surface. He praises the strength of her imagination and acknowledges that the supernatural poses almost impossible problems for every novelist. Yet he also finds it necessary to apologize for her rational expliqués, which he likens to being told at the end of *Macbeth* that the witches were "only three of his wife's chamber-maids disguised for the purpose of imposing on the Thane's credulity" (*PW* 3:371n). The implication is that Radcliffe thus sacrifices deep, "poetic" truth to petty realism. In the preface to *Waverley,* Scott further develops this concept in defense of his own practice by distinguishing "men" from "manners," associating the latter metaphorically with clothes. His own subject is to be "those passions common to men in all stages of society, and which alike have agitated the human heart, whether it throbbed under the steel corslet of the fifteenth century, the brocaded coat of the eighteenth, or the blue frock and white dimity waistcoat of the present day" (*Scott on Novelists* 433).

Neither Walpole, Lewis, nor Scott consistently held to this opposition to explaining the supernatural. Radcliffe could have gotten the idea for her explanations just as easily from Walpole's *The Mysterious Mother,* to which she alludes frequently, as from Reeve's novels; and George Haggerty notes that Lewis also psychologized a ghost in *The Monk* ("Fact and Fancy" 386).[20] It was only when women observed this "stupid convention" (Summers 139) that men saw it as a sign of their absorption in petty detail.[21] In any case, Scott's objection is a misrepresentation of Radcliffe's opinion, for she agreed that historical realism could be dull and banal. She also used *Macbeth* to make the point that the viewer with the truest taste would not want the witches to appear as ordinary old Scotswomen, but rather in the poetically true guise of old crones—or, ideally, would prefer to imagine them by reading the play instead of seeing it ("Supernatural" 146-47).

Unfortunately, women writers were criticized just as severely for such attempts to "soar" above manners as they were for pedestrian realism. Although Gothic had come to mean "supernatural," it had started out meaning "medievalist" (Varma 13), and both meanings could be used to women's disadvantage. Though Walpole sneered at Reeve's literal-mindedness, he had undertaken, in *Otranto,* to "be faithful to the *manners* of the times [his emphasis]" (4); he did a good deal of research in preparation, and the castle itself was probably "real" (Strawberry Hill, if not the "real" Castle of Otranto in Italy, or perhaps Trinity College, Cambridge).[22] Furthermore, at least in the first edition, Walpole seems seriously to have wished his readers to believe that the story was transcribed from an ancient manuscript (3-5). Scott praised Walpole for his scrupulousness and criticized Reeve for her comparative carelessness, a difference he attributed to the fact that ladies of her day read French romances, which were notoriously free with the truth (*PW* 3:332).[23] Scott himself was later praised by Charles Eastlake in his *History of the Gothic Revival* (1872) for his accuracy in describing ancient manners (112); Eastlake drew a line directly from Walpole to Scott, keeper of the "Lamp of Memory," from which "Mrs. Ratcliffe" was only a minor deviation (43, 115).

A final twist to the realism problem was that if Scott chose to bend history to his own purposes, he could be forgiven, as Reeve could not, because he was obviously in pursuit of higher truths (Eastlake 113). Ladies, on the other hand, despite their apparent interest in the psychology of the supernatural, were believed to know as little of "men" outside of novels as they knew of history, and therefore one could not expect them to create fictional characters that were anything but derivative, artificial, and identical (Scott, *PW*, 3:334).[24] Though Scott did praise a few of Radcliffe's characters, on the whole it was in this regard that he ultimately judged her novels to be second-rate (Devlin, *The Author of Waverley*, 15-16). In light of this judgment it appears unlikely that the true reason for men's objections to women's explanations of the supernatural had anything to do with theories about probability in narrative; as many critics, including Scott, have pointed out, Radcliffe's ingenious explanations were so contrived that they could actually seem *less* probable than a ghostly visitation.[25] Instead, these objections seem to be based on a mistrust of women's psychological insight. Scott measured this insight, or lack of it, by the author's ability to create three-dimensional or "mixed" characters; his literalism did not permit him to recognize the psychological depth of Radcliffe's romantic symbols.[26] And so we find ourselves back at the beginning of the "Catch-22" that provided that realism, of whatever sort, denoted seriousness and spirituality in men's writing, but only banality in women's.

Critics of our own time have shown some awareness that the lines male writers were attempting to draw in the eighteenth and early nineteenth century were artificial. Robert Kiely is "amused" at the Walpole/Reeve debate (25), in which the question of probability was really one of degree.[27] Nevertheless, some of the old, shifty exclusiveness has found its way into recent studies of the Gothic. Scott had partly excused Reeve's and Radcliffe's rational expliqués by blaming them on the demands of the unimaginative readers of their time (*PW* 3:370); Talfourd added that as a delicate lady Radcliffe could not defy even so "arbitrary" and silly a convention (115-16). Early in our own century, when ladylike compliance was passé, Summers would see Reeve's plea for probability as "prosaic" and "crass," the "finicking cavil" of a "prim and precise lady of fifty-three" (Introduction to *Otranto* and *Mysterious Mother*, xxix-xxxii). Even more recent critics with a stronger feminist consciousness often imply that Reeve and Radcliffe retained conventions that seem to us quaint, absurd, and un-Gothic because as women they could not fight custom and take control of their material (Murray 13, Howells 29).

Some recent criticism has worsened the problem of seeing Gothic in all its connections and discovering where women fit into it, by looking at it backward through the nineteenth century. In the 1960s and 1970s, scholars routinely commented on the newness, even the courageousness, of their own attempts to treat this "pop culture" phenomenon seriously (G.R. Thompson 1-2, Hume 282, Howells 2), particularly since it was outside Leavis's Great Tradition of the novel. And so they reminded readers of what it was all leading up to: the Romantic poets on the one hand, and nineteenth-century realistic novelists on the other (Murray 167, Howells 2).[28] Two main effects have followed from this approach. Instead of the heroine, the male villain was seen as the essential character, as a sort of Byronic Manfred or Heathcliff in embryo. And romance, in all its ancient complexity, became identified with Romanticism, especially in its transcendence of moral and aesthetic rules.

The sublime, as Burke describes it, has a masculine ring, as some modern critics have observed (Kiely 14-15, Howells 52). Since the source of the pleasurable pain that is the sublime in Gothic novels is the villain, he has become the focal point of critical definitions of Gothic as "one kind of treatment of the psychological problem of evil" (Hume 287), or a "literature of nightmare" that explores the "place of evil in the human mind" (MacAndrew 3). Women are crucial to these fictions, James Twitchell notes, only so there will be someone to experience "sexual distress"—that is, to scream (44). It is the monster who is the real "villain/hero" (Varma 110, 117-18) or the "self-divided hero" of the "demonic quest romance" (G.R. Thompson 2). Heroines are largely ignored, even in studies of Radcliffe; but to such critics it is not Radcliffe but Lewis, whose Ambrosio really is the center of his novel, who seems "most Gothic" (Howells 62, 69; Summers 14).[29]

This development would have surprised both men and women in the eighteenth century, and even far into the nineteenth. In masculinizing Gothic, Lewis deliberately made his subject male sexuality and sexual guilt, in the process reviving the old debate of Manley's day regarding men's and women's sexual language by eschewing what seemed to him feminine, sentimental euphemism in favor of a more visceral style.[30] But men and women accustomed to the "novel of sensibility" would not have found "feminine" language evasive. Like many novelists from Haywood on who wrote about women, including Richardson, Radcliffe used language that conveyed how difficult it was for "inclination" to develop under the constant threat of rape or forced marriage; what a woman needed first was not sex but a way to lock her door from the inside. Following this tradition, Radcliffe did not evade sex but treated it holistically as a complex moral problem, thus winning the approval of her own contemporaries and of the Victorians, who found Lewis offensive.[31] To these readers, sentimental and Gothic fiction were not opposites; during the eighteenth century terror as well as pity was believed to have its source in "sensibility" or "delicacy of feeling" (Radcliffe, "Supernatural," 148, 145).[32]

It was not until our own "sexual revolution" that Lewis began to look, to some readers, like the way of the future, whereas "sensibility" was the way of the past (Murray 164). Critics of our time tend to see the Gothic as replacing the sentimental, substituting the "shudder" for the "tear" (Twitchell 39-40).[33] Robert Hume dislikes Summers's creation of separate Gothic categories such as "sentimental-Gothic" and "terror-Gothic" (Summers 28-30), preferring simply to exclude the former (such as Reeve's *The Old English Baron*) (Hume 282-83); for him, Radcliffe only narrowly redeems her too frequent "Mackenziesque" moments with key antisentimental speeches (283). Kiely also insists that the emotion of Gothic fiction—or as he calls it "romantic fiction," a term he applies narrowly to the novels of this period—is darker than sensibility; he believes Radcliffe failed to see the distinction and refers to her typical heroine as "the creature of a second-rate Richardson in fancy, foreign, and vaguely antique dress" (10). And so she is implicitly marginalized, along with many other women writers who combined sentimental and Gothic elements in their novels (Murray 44-50). Also thus relegated to the margins is Fanny Burney, whom many critics have characterized as a "second-rate Richardson" (see James Thompson 69).

In defining Gothic as a study of evil, some twentieth-century critics are led to regard didacticism as an intrusion—like sensibility, a vestige of earlier, inferior fiction. Thus, although Walpole and even Lewis insisted on the importance of the moral of their stories, recent critics consider the moral framework "conventional" and "moribund" (Murray 60, 14, 161).[34] Characters who are "good" according to eighteenth-century standards are present, in Hume's view, only to provide a "moral norm" against which to measure the villain/hero's distance from it (287)—in other words, as moral "screamers." And so women writers, for whom the norms themselves were interesting, seem "prim" (Murray 19-20), "prudish," (Varma 77), "conscientious and humorless ladies" (Kiely 25), whose basic principles are "antiromantic" (Kiely 78). Lewis, on the other hand, can be read as a herald of modernism who treats the moral frame of his novel as a symbolic type of imprisonment (Kiely 102).

The ultimate tendency of this sort of criticism is to define "Gothic" and even "romance" as the force or spirit opposed to classicism, the Dionysian in revolt against the Apollonian (Varma 209), which finds its best, least hampered expression in Romantic poetry. Gothic fiction is made to symbolize the Romantic tragedy: a soul struggling against the limits of mortality, a flame barely contained by the lamp of rationality, or of narrative structure (Kiely 24-25; Haggerty, "Fact and Fancy," 379-80; Tompkins, introduction to Varma, xiv-xv). Closure in particular is this spirit's enemy (Kiely 252), dooming to failure the demonic hero's quest for the "Absolute" (G.R. Thompson 2, 6) or the "numinous" (Varma 211), so that the ending inevitably feels like a "flop" (Twitchell 41). Thus Radcliffe is praised for deferring explanations, but criticized for finally providing them (Chard, introduction to *The Romance of the Forest,* viii).

The Gothic novel is undeniably full of tensions, a "schizoid phenomenon" (Kiely 26) of "pervasive ambivalence" (Kahane 52), in which "fear of anarchy . . . runs side by side with expressions of frustration at conventional restraints" (Howells 6). This line of thinking has enabled feminist and historicist critics to note how ably it both preaches repression and releases frustration (Figes 73) and how it has helped illuminate the moral and ideological confusion of the 1790s (Cottom 27-29, 50, 53-54; Haggerty, "Fact and Fancy," 379). But similar points can be made—have been made in this study, in fact— about novels from periods other than the 1790s, and bearing labels other than "Gothic."

If we remind ourselves of what eighteenth-century writers already knew—that the Gothic craze was part of a revival of many types of romance and that novels themselves are a kind of romance—the tensions so often noted by critics of Gothic begin to look familiar. Happy endings no longer seem like "sentimental commonplaces" or "didactic" impositions on romantic, transcendent subject matter (Howells 56). As Robert L. Platzner notes in his reply to Hume, and as Judith Wilt also asserts, closure is as basic to romance as adventure is, especially as romance was understood in the eighteenth century.[35] We have seen that romance is about both seeking and finding, about individual experience and the need for others, and thus it is well adapted to exploring tensions in complex ideologies such as Fanny Burney's. In other words, romance, whether Gothic or otherwise, is equally about fear—or terror, horror, or "dread"—and love.[36]

By recognizing the importance to Gothic fiction of both adventure and closure, of both fear and love, one begins to get a very different sense of where it came from—and of the role women novelists played in its development. If Burke's sublime is really masculine, then while one experiences it one is inevitably in the feminine or receiving role, frightened, not frightening (which is not to say that Gothic villains like Lewis's Ambrosio can't be both).[37] One might thus be tempted to reverse Twitchell's formulation and assert that it is the "screamer's" position in the story that is most truly Gothic, and that the monster is merely there to give her something to scream at. And women had been screaming, in one way or another, ever since they had first appeared in romances to be carried off by villains.

Heroines had always had an affinity for pain that gave their stories tragic overtones, if not always tragic endings. When the Gothic movement brought with it a renewed interest in tragedy—not the tragedy of a Romantic ego in frustration, but that of an unprotected soul suffering adventitiously in an unjust world—women were ready. As for love, which had been made over to women as their special province during the Restoration, that had been kept alive in the romance endings that had been rescuing heroines from tragedy in women's novels ever since the 1740s. And so, through many decades of critical disdain, the women writers we have already discussed helped to preserve both basic elements of romance—fear and love—for the convenience of Gothic novelists of both sexes at the end of the eighteenth century.

One segment of the unbroken line leading to and through Gothic fiction can be seen in the close relationship between Burney's *Cecilia* and Radcliffe's *The Italian*. For although Radcliffe's novel is "Gothic" and Burney's has been variously called a "novel of manners," a "sentimental novel," and a "didactic novel," to borrow Hume's terms, both works criticize reality from a similar vantage point, dramatizing how women's lives had all the unpleasantness of romantic adventure with none of the rewards of the romantic ending. In some respects, the style Radcliffe chose gave her some advantages over Burney in expounding this world view; but as we shall see, it also had some unavoidable drawbacks.

The simplest possible view of both novels would label Burney's as realistic and Radcliffe's as romantic. But as we have seen, try as she might Burney could not separate her realism—or her moral vision—from romance. This was a continuing problem for anti-romantic women writers such as Mary Wollstonecraft and Mary Hays, whose novels show their inability to deny romance's "poetic truth."[38] In Hays's *Memoirs of Emma Courtney*, for example, the father who forbids Emma to read romances lest they make her mistake "my rational care for your future welfare for barbarous tyranny" is in fact a tyrant and a brute (20); the author fears that reading romances will make young women too sensitive to the pains of a world filled with such men.

Clearly, according to this novel, men and women have different ideas of reality, a theory that helps to explain not only why men once called women's realistic fictions romantic, but also why they later found women's romances too realistic. In Radcliffe's time, the romance or nonrealistic plot was often defined as one in which the heroine is carried off (*Scott on Novelists* 230, *Wollstonecraft An-*

thology 220), although for women then as now the fear of rape in one form or another was an inescapable aspect of life. Women may well have preferred terror (suspense) to horror (shock) because for them, Gothic was not a sensation-seeking response to the dullness of life (Ellis 7), but an aesthetic distancing of "the fears and dangers uppermost in the society of [their] time, especially as that society appeared to women" (Cottom 66)—that is, the fear of violations of the will, of various direct and indirect types of rape.[39]

That men in our own century still have trouble believing in these fears and dangers is apparent in the facetious tone used by Richetti in discussing Manley's heroines and by Kiely in discussing Radcliffe's Emily St. Aubert (73).[40] But perhaps even more appalling from the woman's viewpoint is the occasional recognition by male critics, albeit Victorian ones, that this fear *is* real and therefore not sufficiently interesting for romance. For example, "the whole persecution and death of Madame Montoni," according to Talfourd, is interesting only in the way Radcliffe handles it, "for there is nothing extraordinary in the fate of a despicable woman, worried into the grave by her husband, because she will not give up her settlement" (128). Talfourd was correct that Madame Montoni's persecution was ordinary; Maria Edgeworth based an episode in *Castle Rackrent* on a similar real-life story (29-30n). But to Edgeworth the truth of it made it neither unromantic nor unsuitable for fiction—just as it did not prevent Mary Wollstonecraft from building a realistic-Gothic novel *(Maria, or the Wrongs of Woman)* on a similar theme.[41]

And so it was inevitable that Burney's *Cecilia,* however realistic in intention, would also be romantic. As a "novel of manners," it adheres to the rules of human probability that Samuel Johnson used to distinguish the new fiction from the old. But it also has some of the episodic structure Johnson attributed to the older romances, a structure also common to the "sentimental" novels of Mackenzie and Sterne, which are organized and unified by the emotion of the main character as he moves from one experience to another. Burney was so adept at organization by mood and contrast that her practice more than anticipates Gothic techniques. Harrel's suicide amidst the merry-making at Vauxhall is more dramatic—perhaps more Gothic—than the corresponding scene in *The Italian* in which a miserable Vivaldi attends a carnival (194).

As I remarked at the beginning of this chapter, it is not usual to think of Burney as a Gothic novelist, but Margaret Doody has observed recently that perhaps it should be *(Frances Burney* 251). Doody points out many "Gothic moments" (51) in Burney's novels, some of which predate Radcliffe's by more than a decade, so that Burney as well as Walpole and Reeve may have been sources for Radcliffe's own Gothic techniques. In the 1780s Burney was in an especially Gothic mood; four years after writing *Cecilia,* while immured at court, she wrote in her journal that she felt she was living in a "monastery" (quoted in Doody, *Frances Burney,* 173-74). Her best known tragedy, *Edwy and Elgiva,* written during that time, is about a mad monk whom Doody notes resembles Monckton in the earlier *Cecilia* (180-81) as well as the later monk villains of Radcliffe (182) and Lewis.

It is possible, then, that in choosing the name "Monckton" for her villain Burney intended a subtle evocation of Gothic atmosphere that was not inconsistent with her story's basic realism. Dressed impeccably in contemporary manners, Cecilia "glides" matter-of-factly through a plot full of terrors that ought to happen only to heroines of romance (662, 666). ("Gliding" is a popular Gothic verb; see *The Italian* 1, 76, 105.) Her uncle's will involves her in a conflict about her surname that links her to the most ancient romance archetypes regarding identity. During the course of the novel she visits a "Gothic," "romantic" castle (497, 522), the "antique mansion" of the Delviles (447), which reminds the satirical Lady Honoria of a "gaol" (495). And later in the novel she is literally imprisoned, something Austen's Henry Tilney will later say could never happen in England. Improbable, emotionally charged, even supernatural events abound. The turning point of the plot, the interrupted wedding, leaves Cecilia "aghast and struck with horror," because the woman who calls out her eerie warning "glide[s]" away unseen (611). The "terror" (613) and mystery of this event cast a shadow over the rest of the novel. Yet all this is presented as if it were not only possible but probable.

If this is reality, then the romance enclosed in Burney's realism could be let out without producing the dramatic difference men such as Talfourd might have expected. Radcliffe's story is set even nearer to her own time than the "sixty years hence" of *Waverley,* a distance Scott chose to make his story both real and romantic, familiar and remote (*Scott on Novelists* 432-33). She uses Walpole's device of the found manuscript to preserve the English narrator's credibility and her female modesty, since the author was a student at Padua who was "very young, as to the arts of composition" (4). But the device is more than the obligatory bow to English common sense, for it is nearly an exact reversal of the frame device used by Delarivière Manley. Manley romanticized reality by filtering true stories through the perceptions of a sympathetic foreigner; Radcliffe realizes a foreign romance by passing it through the perception of an Englishman whose reliably level head ironically gives the story its dash.[42] She thus implies that a true appreciation of romance depends on clear vision and common sense. Italians, it appears, are too blasé about crime to enjoy its Gothic possibilities. When the Italian owner of the manuscript points out the confessional where some "very extraordinary circumstances" took place, it is his English, Protestant companion who finds "the view of it . . . enough to strike a criminal with despair!" "We, in Italy," he is told, "are not so apt to despair"(3).[43]

The setting for these "extraordinary" crimes is another kind of rational frame for the story. It is not baroque, having "nothing of the shewy ornament and general splendor, which distinguish the churches of Italy, and particularly those of Naples"; nor is it Gothic in the sense of rude, wild, gloomy, and austere. Rather it is almost classical, with "a simplicity and grandeur of design, considerably more interesting to persons of taste, and a solemnity of light and shade much more suitable to promote the sublime elevation of devotion" (2). As habitual crime jades the moral palate, excessive architectural decoration blunts religious emotion, so that, paradoxically, an English Protestant is better able to experience the drama of Catholicism than an Italian Catholic.[44]

The frame device of *The Italian* provides just enough conscious artifice to enable Radcliffe to uncover the "poetic truth" of *Cecilia*'s plot. For instead of the tale of a horrible crime promised in the opening pages, the story into which the reader is immediately plunged is a love story about an orphaned heroine, the rather spoiled only son who rescues her, his parents' opposition to their marriage, based on "pride and prejudice" (*Cecilia* 908), and the subsequent debates, in words and action, about the propriety of clandestine marriage. The romance setting gives the characters more fairy-tale simplicity than they have in Burney's novel: the Marchesa Vivaldi's objections to Ellena begin as Delvile-like snobbery but are eventually revealed to be plain, unmotivated evil (295-98). The heroine, at times, seems almost to dwindle into the old heroine-as-object left over from male romances. But *The Italian* has a psychological complexity of its own that becomes apparent when one regards all the characters and events of the story as embodiments of the heroine's consciousness. The fears that were inside Cecilia are located outside Ellena, given form, and, in the process, validated, along with those of her fictional foremothers. In Radcliffe's world, anxious dreams really do predict danger; they are one type of supernatural occurrence that is never explained away. The dread of being carried off, represented as paranoid in *The Female Quixote,* is completely appropriate. In *The Italian* a woman "carried from her house," in Arabella's delusional romantic euphemism, is indeed assumed to have been raped (*Italian* 340).

The plot of *The Italian* literalizes Burney's Gothic symbols and

metaphors. Monckton here is really a monk, and the white domino
that figures so prominently in the masquerade scene in *Cecilia* is not
a costume but the real robe of a white friar (*Italian* 81, 352-53). As
Delvile dresses up as a monk to "save" Cecilia from annoyance—by
Monckton, we learn later—so Vivaldi dons a lay-brother's habit to
rescue Ellena from Schedoni (125). And the metaphorical "unmasking" of Monckton at the end of *Cecilia* really happens at the fair
in *The Italian* when a juggler turns a monk into a devil before
Schedoni's eyes (274). In the same way, Schedoni's crimes are merely
more visually dramatic versions of Monckton's, with the crimes of
some of Cecilia's other guardians thrown in for good measure. In one
person he represents the theme of perverted fatherhood that is quad-
rupled in *Cecilia,* maybe even sextupled, as one counts the number of
father figures who let her down. When Schedoni believes Ellena is his
daughter, he tries to "sell" her to the Vivaldis as a bride for their son
in much the same way Harrel tries to sell Cecilia to his friend. Schedoni's attempt to stab Ellena is only a more personalized version of old
Delvile's nearly murdering Cecilia by ignoring her plea for shelter.
But Schedoni most closely resembles Monckton, the "father" Cecilia
chose for herself, and who, she is shocked to find, has all along been
plotting to trick her into what to her would be a spiritually incestuous
marriage to him. The picture Radcliffe offers of Ellena withdrawing
her hand in fright from the "father" who has seated himself on her bed
in the middle of the night, though in its own way decorous, allows the
reader to visualize Burney's delicately hinted fear of paternal rape
(*Italian* 236).[45]

By thus realizing Burney's symbolism, Radcliffe uncovers wom-
en's problematic relation to what men had determined to be reality.
Gothic fiction is often described as containing two "worlds": a "real"
world of comparatively ordinary and probable events, which appears
at the beginning and the end, and a "romance" world, the world of the
villain and the castle, in which anything might happen.[46] But in
women's realistic fictions, which also contain two worlds, the villain's
world is "real," because the villain believes in it, and his word is law;
to him, the perceptions of the heroine are romantic illusions. The
literary fathers of the Montonis and Schedonis of Radcliffe's novels
are thus realistic rather than romantic; they are the fathers and
brothers of Clelia, Betsy Thoughtless, Harriot Stuart, and Arabella,
whose oppression of women was their denial that women were oppressed. When Radcliffe moved these characters from realistic novels
to an avowed romance, she laid bare the falseness of their position.
When Vivaldi's father sneers at his son's quixotism, he is also demon-
strating why the world needs knights-errant (121-22). More impor-

tant, Schedoni constantly stirs up in Ellena and Vivaldi, and in the reader, emotions which he believes are nonexistent:

> The callous Schedoni, by a mistake not uncommon, especially to a mind of his character, substituted words for truths; not only confounding the limits of neighbouring qualities, but mistaking their very principles. Incapable of perceiving their nice distinctions, he called the persons who saw them, merely fanciful; thus making his very incapacity an argument for his superior wisdom. And, while he confounded delicacy of feeling with fatuity of mind, taste with caprice, and imagination with error, he yielded, when he most congratulated himself on his sagacity, to illusions not less egregious, because they were less brilliant, than those which are incident to sentiment and feeling. [289]

To achieve this "callousness" in a world so full of emotion is no mean feat, and so the villain is engaged in a constant struggle against the "weakness of compassion" (223), a struggle that has made him the most interesting figure in the novel to generations of readers (Wilt 37, 41). But Schedoni provides the novel's heart of darkness less because he is its "center of consciousness" (Ellis 125) than because, as vision is defined here, he is totally blind.

Schedoni's energies are so inwardly directed that he often quite literally cannot see what is in front of him. He is indifferent to the lovely scenery that cheers and invigorates the captive Ellena (255), a blindness he shares with the Marchesa, who while looking out a window sees only "the visions that evil passions painted to her imagination" (292). Both villain and villainess are often deaf and mute as well, beyond the reach of conversation. He speaks in an "inward voice" (284) and at times cannot be spoken to because it is clear he would not notice or respond (286). And she has trouble paying attention even when Schedoni is speaking to her (296-97). There may be a sort of telepathy between the two on the subject of their crime, as Murray says (144), but the disjointedness of their conversations suggests that no real communication, or society, exists between them. Not seeing or hearing, they are also determined not to be seen or heard; and so they must go about veiled, because in this world of realized symbols their evil would otherwise be plainly visible in their faces.[47] (The reading of countenances is called a "romantic notion" in *The Romance of the Forest,* but in a romance that phrase does not discredit it [256].[48]) The Marchesa's veils tend to be verbal, as when she "veil[s]" her desire to have Schedoni murder Ellena in "flattery" about how highly she values his friendship (176). Schedoni's veil is literal: his monk's cowl.

Schedoni and the Marchesa in their cowls and veils are right in style in this novel, just as Monckton is only the worst of a majority of blind and selfish people in Burney's. The fashionable world that wrongly calls itself "society" in *Cecilia* is personified in *The Italian,* or rather institutionalized, into the Catholic Church; individual, corrupt convents and monasteries, devoid of love, are connected into a web by the overarching authority of the Inquisition, creating an organization of arbitrary power that destroys all real human connection. Vivaldi is astonished above all at the terrible impersonality of the place; hatred and revenge he can understand, but "that any human being should willingly afflict a fellow being who had never injured, or even offended him; that, unswayed by passion, it should deliberately become the means of torturing him, appeared to Vivaldi nearly incredible!" (311-12). That the Inquisition is ultimately successful in finding the truth about Schedoni and meting out a sort of justice neither excuses its brutal practices nor negates its main purpose in the novel: to provide the climax of terror and suffering.[49]

The villain is the blind center of this false society, first because he uses the Inquisition for his own purposes, and later because he becomes the focus of its investigation. In contrast, the heroine is the seeing center of the true society. Like Cecilia, Ellena is a figure of common sense—which in neither novel is really common—who quietly exposes the doubleness and absurdity in the speech of less self-aware characters. When Schedoni commands his garrulous guide to be silent, the servant answers, "That is what I say, Signor:—silence! for the people make such a noise that I cannot hear a word you speak." And Ellena responds, with a restrained pertness similar to Cecilia's, "Considering that you could not hear, you have answered wonderfully to the purpose" (274).

The heroines see and hear clearly, but because almost no one else does, they spend much of their time alone. Ironically, they are isolated by their uniquely sane awareness that sanity loves company. Their need for society puts them under constant pressure both from without and from within to enter the world of shadows and deceptions that surrounds them. Cecilia goes to London determined to form her "society" on a rational plan and to exclude all meaningless connections, but loneliness eventually drives her to compromise, just as bereavement began her intimacy with the evil Monckton. But her most serious temptation, which is also Ellena's, is to enter into a clandestine marriage with the hero, a temptation that would bring about a tragic fall from innocence.

Clandestine marriage with its attendant miseries is the theme of *Romeo and Juliet,* a play used extensively in both *The Italian* and

Cecilia not only for the atmosphere of its death scene, which made it a favorite with Gothic writers (Howells 73), but for the tragic plot about lovers separated by parental opposition. Eighteenth-century readers were especially attuned to the moral ironies of that play, which can be interpreted in terms of 1790s debates about individualism and society. The love Friar Laurence tries to use to reform Verona has a selfish, "fire and powder" dimension not unrelated to the love mixed with hate that keeps the two houses in a state of feud. The lovers lose their innocence and betray old social bonds in establishing their new one, and yet that new one does contain a seed of *agape* that ultimately does reform their society once the most violent part of its eroticism has spent itself in mutual suicide. The question of whether their marriage is finally "right" has no answer that can be of use to the lovers themselves.

This moral problem is inseparable from the romantic distress of Burney's and Radcliffe's heroines. The didactic framework of *Cecilia* naturally finds its way into *The Italian* along with the plot, not as the "moribund" relic of Augustan rationalism, but as the very source of Gothic terror.[50] Like Lennox or Johnson, who praised fiction that teaches by supplying an "antidote to example" (*FQ* 420), Burney believed that novels are chiefly valuable in supplying "the lessons of experience, without its tears" (*Wanderer* xx)—that is, they acquaint young readers with evil by removing it to a safe distance. Thus the same technique that satisfies this didactic goal also fulfills the demands of the sublime aesthetic.

The frame device of *The Italian,* in fixing the Cecilia story at a middle distance, renders this abstract principle in concrete terms, just as the rest of the novel realizes Burney's more metaphorical vision of women's moral suffering. A woman in the throes of a moral decision is a perfect conductor of suspense, something Radcliffe observed years earlier in *The Romance of the Forest* (1791), where she used Adeline's conflicting modesty and self-preservation to tease readers with the possibility that she will not meet Theodore in the woods, and therefore will not find out what the reader is dying to know (106). The heroine's inner debate about clandestine love affairs was also made to yield up its Gothic energy by Charlotte Smith in *The Old Manor House* (1794), as may be seen by the quotation that introduces this chapter.

Because the Romeo and Juliet problem has no satisfactory solution, it epitomizes the moral situation of eighteenth-century women, who often found that though they were given few choices, their "female delicacy" made all of them wrong in one way or another. Female delicacy was a key concept in Burney's morality, and even to possess it required a dangerous tightrope-walk between emotion and restraint. Radcliffe's novel supports Burney's in pointing out that excessive emotion will inevitably produce a dramatic plunge; the Marchesa and Mrs. Delvile are both unsexed and demoralized by their "passion" (*Italian* 174-75, 291, 292), and Mrs. Delvile's resulting stroke is one of *Cecilia's* most Gothic moments. But the subtler peril that threatens to overset the heroine is "sensibility," for that cannot simply be put aside or repressed. Depending on its intensity, sensibility can be either a means to sanity or a threat to it. It makes one able to empathize and form ties with others; yet it also makes one shrink from pain, so that one may become isolated and withdrawn.[51] The balancing act between these extremes is almost too much for Talfourd in his eulogy of Radcliffe, for he wants to endow her with exquisite sensibility while dispelling rumors that she eventually lost her mind. He finally has recourse to a doctor's testimony that the sort of "sensibility" she possessed "would serve to increase the warmth of the social feelings, and effectually prevent the insulation of the mind, either as regards the temper or the understanding" (104-5).

For Talfourd, this is simply a verbal problem; for Cecilia and Ellena, its perfect resolution is a condition of their existence, visible in the beauty that is supposed to reflect their excellence of character. Cecilia's "countenance announced the intelligence of her mind, her complexion varied with every emotion of her soul, and her eyes, the heralds of her speech, now beamed with understanding and now glistened with sensibility" (2). Where feeling and reason simply mix and alternate in Cecilia's face and voice, in Ellena they are shown in a more complicated relation. Vivaldi observes of Ellena's features that *"though* they expressed the tranquillity of an elegant mind, her dark blue eyes sparkled with intelligence [my emphasis]" (6), and her voice "modulat[ed]" with "sensibility of character" (5). This description suggests that feminine perfection is not simply a matter of using reason to restrain emotion, for both heart and mind are active, "modulating" in the voice, "sparkling" in the eyes; "tranquillity" must then result from mental and emotional forces colliding with each other in just the right way.

Ellena, though in repose, is thus alive with energy—fortunately for her, because like Cecilia she has much to enact as well as to endure. Radcliffe follows Burney in making courageous action consistent with delicacy, so that as Cecilia rushes after Harrel at Vauxhall to try to save him from suicide, Ellena runs after Schedoni when he has disappeared into the darkness at the site of an old, horrible crime (264).[52] Both women need all the active heroism they can muster, because the heroes are only sporadically up to the role of gallant knight. Though Delvile does save Cecilia from an overturned teapot, getting scalded himself in the process (280-81), in serious matters the heroes are more a hindrance than a help. Where Ellena is clear-sighted, Vivaldi has the susceptibility to terror and delusion that are supposed to be the hallmarks of Radcliffe's heroines. This expansion of the hero's role, as Murray sees it (135), is more of a contraction to the traditional feminine role of "screamer."[53] Like Delvile, he regularly loses control over his reason and judgment in the intensity of his love, a tendency that further diminishes him into a male "sex object" whom no one expects to be able to cope with the novel's central moral question.

The men do pause, briefly, over the problem of "selling" the scrupulous heroines on clandestine marriage, as may be seen in Delvile's careful preparation of his case and in Vivaldi's momentary reluctance to ask Ellena to "condescend to enter a family who disdained to receive her" and "his fear of offending her" (13-14). But it is the role of the man here to prove his manliness by pressing the heroine to consent against her better judgment, like a teenager in the back seat of a Chevy. Of course, this "gentle violence" (*Italian* 135) is necessary to break through the heroines' delicacy, part of the love game men and women had been playing long before Behn described it in her pastoral lyrics. But in accepting the role of wanton shepherd in such a complicated moral landscape, the heroes sacrifice their right to be treated as the heroines' spiritual equals. When the women do waver, in the height of their self-blame they never think to be disappointed in the men who brought up the idea of the secret marriage in the first place.

The men's freedom from responsibility in these novels is a far cry from the chivalric code found in some men's romances, even in Lewis's *The Monk,* in which Raymond gallantly bears all the blame for Agnes's lapse from purity, begging her forgiveness for offending her while she denounces him as a "monster of perfidy" (*The Monk* 186-87).[54] Instead, *The Italian* and *Cecilia* operate according to the double standard of real life that gave men the privilege of testing women's virtue and discarding those that were damaged in the process. Both Vivaldi and Delvile complain about their ladies' self-control; Ellena, Clelia-like, will admit to feeling no more than "gratitude" toward Vivaldi (151-52). Yet their admiration for these women is fed by their resistance or "delicacy," just as Trueworth loves Betsy Thoughtless all the more as she struggles from his embrace (571). With no need to be consistent or principled, the heroes can drift along following their inclinations and leave the steerage of their course to the heroines, so that even when the men look most heroic they are really most passive. Delvile fights a duel for Cecilia, but it is for her to decide what they ought to do in the aftermath of that impulsive act. And Vivaldi rescues Ellena from prison but then must rely on her to rescue him from himself, and to make him quit stopping along the road to talk of love when "our situation is yet perilous, we tremble on the very brink of danger" (145).[55]

In the world of these two novels it is the man's role to push, and the woman's role to apply the moral brakes. As a result, the heroine is left alone to agonize over the problem of reconciling selfish desire with social impulse; of enclosing erotic love in a larger love of family, fellow humans, and God. That agonizing takes the form of an endless circle of contradictory moral propositions. When Ellena, like Cecilia, temporarily consents to the secret marriage, with more excuse than Cecilia, perhaps, in that she needs a husband's protection from Schedoni, she feels exactly what Cecilia feels as soon as her lover is out of her sight: "remorse." "[N]ow, that the sound mind of Ellena was left to its own judgment," she decides "I deserve punishment, since I could, even for a moment, submit to the humiliation of desiring an alliance, which I knew would be unwillingly conferred. But it is not yet too late to retrieve my own esteem by asserting my independence, and resigning Vivaldi for ever." Yet, like Cecilia, she realizes that to do so would be to suffer and to make the man she loves suffer for his parents' "pride and prejudice." "O! miserable alternative!—that I can no longer act justly, but at the expence of all my future happiness! Justly! And would it then be just to abandon him who is willing to resign every thing for me,—abandon him to ceaseless sorrow, that the prejudices of his family may be gratified?" (69). As Cecilia fears her morality may be mere "unnecessary punctilio" (553), Ellena begins to wonder about the true labels of her virtues, which, "now that they were carried to excess, seemed to her to border upon vices; her sense of dignity, appeared to be narrow pride; her delicacy weakness; her moderated affection cold ingratitude; and her circumspection, little less than prudence degenerated into meanness" (181).

Both heroines ultimately decide to marry, because that will satisfy themselves, their lovers, and perhaps God, if not the world. Both do so with at least as much foreboding as Friar Laurence felt in joining the hands of Romeo and Juliet; and neither is surprised to find her wedding interrupted by a "ghost" that seems to embody her own troubled conscience. But the attempt is a step toward reforming the world through love. And thus Ellena and Cecilia are agents of their authors' radical yet ideologically complex critique of a world in which love was badly needed. Schedoni and Monckton are typical of this world, and stereotypical of male villains in women's novels, in considering love of any kind a romantic fiction, or "silly rhodomontade," in the phrase of the parody-Schedoni in Barrett's *The Heroine* (263). (This hackneyed allusion to Rodomonte in Ariosto's *Orlando Furioso* points to the irony of one romantic villain's taking an anti-romantic attitude toward another.)

A "society" held together without love is rotten, and thus both Burney and Radcliffe share some ideology with the "progressives" in the "war of ideas" of the 1790s.[56] When one looks from the central characters up the scale of power, one sees nothing but persecution and abuse of authority. Both Radcliffe and Burney, like the "jacobin" Robert Bage, associate the Gothic castle negatively with a debased aristocracy attempting to preserve its outmoded and undeserved privileges (Bage 11, *Cecilia* 447). Most of the convents in *The Italian,* like the one in *Harriot Stuart,* are merely extensions of that power, places where evil lords and ladies, or marcheses and marchesas, can imprison anyone they want to punish for the crime of presuming to have wills of their own (67, 121). In contrast, the rank of the hero and heroine is less important than their personal merit; Vivaldi's desire to marry Ellena despite her lowly condition reminds the hero's father of the romance's subversive tendency, a view also set forth in *The Female Quixote.*[57] *The Italian* even prefigures Burney's last novel, *The Wanderer,* in its praise of the heroine for earning her own living (9, 46).

Yet, paradoxically, this radical critique is also conservative in the broadest sense, in that individualism has produced this chaos, and the love that is meant to cure it is not selfish but social. The heroines do not wish to be individualists. Ellena's job is not an outlet for self-expression but a heroic labor; she would much prefer to be a dependent, or rather an interdependent, member of a family group. Cecilia rejects the advice of her evil and foolish guardians, but she continues to look for a worthy father in Monckton and a mother in Mrs. Delvile and is desolated by her lack of success. As Adeline complains in *The Romance of the Forest,* the overprotective parents most romance heroines are supposed to want to escape would be a comparative blessing to a woman on her own: other, luckier young women "have friends and relations, all . . . watching not only for their present safety, but for their future advantage, and preventing them even from injuring themselves. But during my whole life I have never known a friend" (242).

While sharing Burney's basic philosophy, Radcliffe altered Burney's fictional approach, and thus inevitably altered the way that philosophy would be presented. Though sharing a great deal of both realism and romance, each novel is ultimately governed by different laws, so that even though *Romeo and Juliet* is central to both, the patterns of allusion produce contrasting effects. In Burney's novel, Delvile must "deny his father, and refuse his name" to marry Cecilia, or she must "no longer be a Beverley," or rich; hence the heroine often has occasion to ask, "What's in a name?" (504). Just as Romeo, after marrying, learns that this is not an idle question, Delvile also fights a duel and must go into exile just after Cecilia has promised to "follow thee my lord throughout the world" (831). In his absence, Cecilia nearly dies, and a tragic conclusion seems inevitable. Radcliffe, on the other hand, makes more use of the romantic comedy in Shakespeare's play. There is an early balcony scene in which Vivaldi climbs a garden wall to spy on Ellena and hears her calling his name (10-12). Immediately afterward the mysterious monk appears, whom Vivaldi alternately considers as a friend, like Friar Laurence, and a foe, as he eventually proves (12). Later the servant Beatrice, like Shakespeare's nurse, in her garrulity leads Ellena to believe that Vivaldi may be dead (373), but he is not. And unlike Romeo, he is still alive at the end of the story. For although Ellena descends to veils and secrecy by consenting, on Schedoni's insistence, to hide in a convent under an assumed name and write to him under cover (289-90)—much as Juliet descends to lying to her parents—in the world of her novel this fall is not irredeemable. It is rather the world in which Romeo and Juliet's story would have turned into triumphant New Comedy, in which the stratagems of servants eventually do foil the *senex iratus* and unite the lovers.

At a key moment in each novel, the heroine is brought so low that she begins to question the nature of reality. Under the pressure of acting as Delvile's moral arbitress, Cecilia's head begins to ache and her mind wanders (828). A few pages later, she is raving mad, having been refused shelter by her father-in-law/guardian and left to roam the streets alone. Ellena's affairs come to a similar crisis; having learned, she thinks, that Schedoni is her father, she asks herself whether her life up to now has been merely a "romance," and if real life means having a father with whom there can be no exchange of affection (302). But the "sound mind of Ellena" (69) is spared Cecilia's Gothic disintegration, for in her novel her instincts are correct, Schedoni is not her father, and it is the "romance" that proves real.

Both *Cecilia* and *The Italian* contrast the romance world, the world of love, with the real world, the world of the villain and his persecution, the world of fear. Burney's realism leaves her free to explore the evil world of Monckton, and that is one reason *Cecilia* may seem so Gothic to readers who think of Gothic as villain-centered. But there is little room in her novel for development of the romance world, which exists only in the little corner she manages, with difficulty, to contrive for her lovers at the end. For this reason her realism sometimes strikes readers as defeatist, and critics have differed widely in their sense of her radicalism or feminism. Radcliffe, on the other hand, having labeled her story a romance from the beginning, is free to use whatever magic is necessary to bring about the conclusion Ellena deserves without having to worry about probability or consistency with contemporary manners. The happy ending in *The Italian* is thus more than a tacked on device. It is the culmination of the pastoral romance motifs that have been part of the story all along. The fuller development of the romance world of the lovers gives Radcliffe, as it once gave Behn and Manley, a broad utopian base on which to stand in judgment of reality.

At the end of the eighteenth century, women were once again writing openly of the romance's potential for utopian projections and social reform. Reeve reminded her readers that during the reign of Elizabeth romances had been considered morally inspiring, and so she believed they could be again in her "low" and "mercenary" age (*Progress* 1:97-98, 103). She revived the old charge of "vanity" that was once used to damn medieval romances and later French romances and English novels, but she gave it a positive twist, noting that romance flatters the world by making it appear better than it is and thus gives readers an ideal to strive for (*Old English Baron* 3). The higher morality of this ideal world was as ideologically ambiguous as romance itself, encompassing both liberation of the individual and social harmony. In particular, women's romantic utopias eliminated the gender gap by liberating women and putting more restrictions on men. Manley had presented two ideal worlds in *Atalantis:* one that gave women the same sexual freedom as men, and one that bound men's sexual conduct as tightly as women's.

Because sex was such a heavy moral burden for women in Reeve's time, it is not surprising that it is this second utopia she took up as a corrective of the too-realistic *Tom Jones,* in which "fornication" is given the name "gallantry" (1:67-68, 1:141, 2:95).[58] But the sort of story she felt should replace it might not seem much of an improvement to a male reader. The example she appended to *The Progress of Romance* is about the virgin queen Charoba, who piously kills an entire nation of men, poisoning them an army at a time, to avoid marriage and the surrender of her throne. Apparently, when women of Reeve's time fantasized about solutions to the sexual double standard that oppressed Cecilia and Ellena, they were more likely to think of genocide than of "free love."

The idea of women uniting to protect themselves against lying, lustful men goes back to the shepherdesses of d'Urfé. In *The Italian* they take the form of the nuns of Our Lady of Pity. As Lewis had his Ambrosio talk of the monastery as the last stronghold of real society (54), Radcliffe makes this retreat a female utopia ruled by a "mother" who is as "christian" as a Protestant could allow a Catholic to be: "she conformed to the customs of the Roman church, without supposing a faith in all of them to be necessary to salvation," an "opinion she was obliged to conceal, lest her very virtue should draw upon her the punishment of a crime" (300). Vivaldi finds a serious rival for Ellena in this community, for whereas Ambrosio's religious feelings are really sublimated lust, Ellena's are connected with women's fantasies of escaping the problem of sexuality altogether. Ellena parts from her "sister" Olivia (who is really her mother) more painfully than any heroine we have yet encountered, tearfully proclaiming, "farewel! O farewel, my dear, my tender friend! I must never, never see you more, but I shall always love you," prompting Vivaldi to remark, "Ah Ellena! . . . do I then hold only the second place in your heart? . . . I envy your friend those tears . . . and feel jealous of the tenderness that excites them" (135-36).

Of course, in pastoral romances the shepherdesses only *almost* retire together in single blessedness, and so Ellena does have to leave the sisters for Vivaldi. But her romantic life with him also represents a female utopian vision. For despite Vivaldi's masculine tendency to lose control, he is in many respects Ellena's twin or mirror image, possessing a similar sensibility and a voice of "exquisite delicacy" (17). Polarized, brutal masculinity is the province of the villain, who enforces the artificial opposition of the sexes with a specious moral double standard. In attempting to bring out the Lady Macbeth in the Marchesa, Schedoni makes a distinction between feminine love and pity, which he calls "weakness," and masculine "justice," founded on "clear perception" (168-69); yet as we have seen, his vision is far from clear, and in this instance he is consciously lying. He knows very well that real "virtue" cannot exist without compassion and that therefore morality is both "feminine" and "masculine," the same for women and for men. Ellena and Vivaldi may not be moral equals, but they are sufficiently alike to become one, even if the brains of that one are mostly Ellena's.

Vivaldi is delicate not only in feeling and voice, but in character; to use Scudéry's terminology, he is "tender." In other words, he makes a serious effort not to exploit Ellena's predicament in order to force her inclination, and his conduct wins her "esteem and gratitude" (160). His partial success in this endeavor gives the heroine just enough freedom to permit the growth of her inclination for him, modestly and unobtrusively, within the boundaries of their mutual tenderness, so that in their marriage sex is subsumed and rendered benign by love. This social love is symbolized by the architecture of their final home: its style "was that of England, and of the present day, rather than of Italy" (412); with its classical "marble porticoes and arcades," it is far from Dionysian and by no means unique or impossible to build. But it is, nevertheless, romantic, "in truth, a scene of fairy-land," "a fabric called up by enchantment, rather than a structure of human art" (412, 413), because the Apollonian values it stands for have become so rare.

These values are rare within the novel, and rare, Radcliffe believed, in the society of her time, but Ellena and Vivaldi are not quite as alone as they feel. For Radcliffe asks her readers to join her in appreciating the good taste of their villa. According to *The Italian*, everyone involved in storytelling—like it or not—is a member of a community with shared values. Within the novel, storytelling is represented as a social activity that connects narrators and listeners across several generations. One measure of Schedoni's spiritual autism is his unwillingness, or inability, to form a link in this chain. Like Betsy Thoughtless before her "socialization," he lacks curiosity about others and thus becomes increasingly impatient when the peasant who tells the pivotal tale of murder continually brings into it the other members of the group that produced it: his father, who told it to him, and old Marco, who began it (279). The peasant keeps Schedoni's attention only by hinting, like a father telling a bedtime story, that he is really talking about Schedoni: "He looked as white, Signor, as you do now" (284). The villain's constant demands for assurance that this is more than a "delirious dream" (284) show to what degree his dislike of imagination ironically cuts him off from what the reader and author know to be reality.[59] This lack of interest in stories exists at the heart of what passes for society in this novel, for the Inquisitors are similarly uninquisitive. Instead of encouraging the prisoners to talk, to reveal themselves, the officers are more concerned with silencing them before their words can shake their own preconceptions (314), before any real meeting of minds can take place. But these characters' chosen isolation within the story finally does not matter, because all along they have been participating in the social transaction going on between Radcliffe, the young student at Padua, the Englishman who reads the manuscript, the Italian who gives it to him, and several generations of readers.

This is a community that, in the true spirit of the romantic revival, could embrace and harmonize diverse and even contradictory elements. It could contain and neutralize the danger of women's lives and turn it into sublime art. Within this safe enclosure, even the randomness of adventure could be pleasing, like the ruins and rocky eminences Radcliffe liked to explore in company with her husband and her favorite dog, Chance (Talfourd 41). Because Radcliffe was at peace with her chosen form, the happy ending of *The Italian* is so aesthetically satisfying that one may forget that the central problem of the clandestine marriage, unsolvable as it is, remains unsolved. Like Cecilia, Ellena is never allowed to feel justified in defying the prejudices of the world and does not marry until at least one parent relents, in this case, even "solicit[s], in due form," her mother's consent (410).

Once the book is closed, however, readers do sometimes feel let down. By including something that corresponds to the real world in her novel, Radcliffe seems to promise a sustained treatment of real difficulties. *The Italian* is in some respects like a *bildungsroman,* in which the reader is invited to follow Ellena's growth "from passive submission to active self-command" (Hennelly 3); as a result, some critics comment on its didactic failure in the same way Patricia Spacks comments on that of *Camilla,* an education novel in which the heroine never grows up (*Imagining* 183).[60] Education novels about women inevitably failed in this way, because there was so little useful advice one could give women, and none that did not immediately raise contradictions between worldly and ideal moral codes. Ellena may work for a living, but she is too sensitive to simply brush aside "the sneer of vicious folly, and to glory in the dignity of virtuous independence" (9), because to do so would show a most unheroinelike indifference to the opinions of others. And in the long run it hardly matters what she or even the more "normal" heroine of the education novel does, because the universe of all their novels is too "deterministic and unpleasant" to leave much room for moral action, even if the right action could be ascertained (Durant 521).[61]

One is aware of these difficulties in Burney's novel long before one has closed it. They are especially noticeable in the denouement, which she made as believable as possible by a "realistic" compromise, the sacrifice of Cecilia's inheritance and name. It takes a miracle to bring about even this moderate happiness because of Burney's less than wholehearted embrace of the art of storytelling. In *Cecilia* the "inquisitors" are what the name implies: curious about people, eager not only to hear stories but to tell them. But these stories are not welcoming, as romance was supposed to be, but exclusive, like critical definitions of romance. For the heroine, they mean not benevolent acceptance but scandal and ostracism, just as by writing and reading novels women risked scorn and rejection. Cecilia is understandably reluctant to take part in this process, and Burney seems equally reluctant to compromise her, and herself, by telling her story. She does, however, want to celebrate Cecilia and express her own talent. The problem is how to give the heroine and herself at least some of the reward they deserve when neither believes that problems can be even temporarily erased by being enclosed in romance.

Burney's artistic dilemma at the end of *Cecilia* is very much like her heroine's dilemma within the novel. Each is forced to deal with the conflicting demands of two worlds: the romance world of love, and the real world of double standards and suffering. Cecilia is unable to choose, because even her own desires would not be fulfilled by any course of action that cut her off from family and friends, however misguided their notions are. Dreading above all else to be *thought* wrong, she ultimately decides to accept what so many previous women's novels, sadly, recommend: obedience to whichever code is stricter. At least then she may seem to deserve a heavenly crown, and maybe someone will write her story and contrive to find her a little happiness despite herself. Women following this example in real life, as Talfourd claims Radcliffe did, had to die before they were rewarded in this literal way, and then only if they were among the extremely small group who managed to achieve fame without seeking it.[62] Burney was also unable to choose between bestowing that crown, in true romance fashion, and remaining true to the manners of her time and the rules of the realistic novel. Neither choice satisfied her, and in trying to mediate between the two she provided no effectual ending at all. The reader is left instead with a vague sense that the tragic fate that seemed to hang on Cecilia throughout the novel has not really been averted.

That is not to say, however, that Burney's novel is a failure, either as art or as a gesture toward social reform. It was only by trying to make happy endings believable within the confines of realism that the injustices of life could be exposed. To be truly useful to women, the romance ending had to look like the anomaly it was. This exposure could ultimately help reveal where society was falling short of its own proclaimed ideals—for example, in its perversion of the "holy sacrament" of marriage into the sale of daughters to the highest bidder. One cannot, consistently, proclaim the importance of love from every pulpit and then make true lovers marry in secrecy. As the next chapter will show, the efforts of novelists such as Burney did help to bring about the awareness that was needed for social change, at least enough to create greater harmony between worlds in the fictions of writers such as Jane Austen.

This harmony could also be brought about by working from the other direction—that is, by bringing women's romantic desires closer to what the real world might be willing to offer them (Poovey 179). In this effort women would have to use their reason to guide their emotions, and they were encouraged to do so not only by the realist Burney but by the romantic Radcliffe as well. This type of advice, which at first glance makes its proponents look more "fetter'd" than "free," was to become the foundation of Mary Wollstonecraft's feminism and of Jane Austen's novels, the feminism of which critics are now busy trying to define. To these women it was clear that uncontrolled desire was the surest route to imprisonment as long as women's sexual conduct was judged more strictly than men's.

Austen's awareness that women's lot, though improved, was still full of hazards requiring a cool head permitted her to make light of the distinction between Burney's realistic novels and Radcliffe's Gothic ones. In *Northanger Abbey* she satirized them both with the same stroke—as did Scott, Wollstonecraft, and Barrett, apparently feeling that both had become equally quaint.[63] But Austen also saw that both Burney and Radcliffe, in different ways, revealed a "poetic truth" about women's lives, a truth that to her was not obscured by changes in literary fashion. And so she gave her Catherine Morland a Burneyan social life filled with Gothic terrors—terrors of being misunderstood, of offending people by mistake, of not being permitted to act. Austen did not use Radcliffe's exotic locales because she would not have been satisfied with a merely aesthetic handling of these romantic realities (Gilbert and Gubar 135). To her the job of a novelist was to discover whether a life of such unavoidable intensity could be made not only tolerable but happy.

7

Jane Austen's Novels
The Romantic Denouement

The romance of real life is beyond all other romances; it's [sic] coincidences beyond the combinations of the most inventive fancy.
—Maria Edgeworth

CATHERINE MORLAND, the heroine of Jane Austen's *Northanger Abbey,* is the first heroine in English fiction to carry on a "clandestine correspondence" (250) without suffering agonies of conscience. In fact it hardly counts as "clandestine," because Catherine's parents look the other way when she receives a letter from her unofficial fiancé, Henry Tilney; they forbid only an official engagement, and only until the groom's father can be brought to give "the decent appearance of consent," which they are sure "could not be very long denied" (249). General Tilney's objections must be temporary because they are clearly wrong—so wrong that Henry can spare Catherine "the necessity of a conscientious rejection, by engaging her faith before he mention[s]" that he has come to her proposing in defiance of his father's command. No "punctilio" leads him to doubt for a moment that defying so tyrannical a father is in perfect accord with "honour," "reason," and "conscience" (247). Far from forming the basis of a long and tortured plot, the secret engagement problem arises a mere ten pages before it is happily, inevitably resolved.

This offhand satiric treatment of a difficulty so many other women novelists, including Burney and Radcliffe, had treated seriously suggests that Austen believed far too much had been made of it. Not that she always dismissed it quite so summarily. In *Sense and Sensibility,* Edward Ferrars's disastrous entanglement with Lucy Steele creates a widening circle of misery among those he loves. Yet the secrecy is ultimately good in that it makes him seemingly, and then really, available to Elinor; only Edward's mother sees it as a "crime" (371), and her abuses of parental authority throughout the novel excuse Edward's conduct to the reader. As soon as Edward is free of Lucy he engages himself to Elinor, also without his mother's permission, and can hardly be persuaded even to seem to apologize for doing so: "I know of no submission that *is* proper for me to make" (372). His mother's eventual consent, even in her own mind, is a foregone conclusion. *Emma* presents something more like the moral dilemma of *Cecilia* and *The Italian;* the man's guardians are clearly "proud and prejudiced," yet the woman blames herself for consenting to defy them. But as in *Sense and Sensibility,* the problem is a tangent. Here it belongs not to the heroine but to Jane Fairfax, and is important less in itself than in its effect on Emma, whose moral progress is evident when she decides that Jane deserves extra compassion rather than further punishment for her mistake (419).[1]

In her handling of secret relationships between men and women, Austen implies that, at worst, secrecy is a venial error that should be unnecessary because even the most unreasonable parents know in their hearts, and eventually will be forced to admit, that their children have a right to choose spouses for themselves. This idea is in the spirit of Charlotte Lennox's *The Female Quixote,* one of Austen's favorite novels, which also asserts that love need not conflict with filial obedience.[2] By crowning Arabella's anti-romantic nonadventures with a romance ending, Lennox implies that women's lives have all the advantages of romance and none of the drawbacks. But her novel undermines its own premise in so many ways that romance and realism fail to blend. In this endeavor Austen is far more successful. While describing "female difficulties" in plentiful, believable detail, she nevertheless manages to envelop women's lives in romantic comedy.

This feeling of harmony at last is what prompted me to choose Jane Austen for the "denouement" of my own study—despite the fact that everything and its opposite has been said about her already. To this mountain of scholarship I wish to add merely the sense of an ending to some of the hidden lines of development I have traced in this study. No matter how thorough readers' knowledge of eighteenth-century fiction may be or how deep their commitment to the rescue of neglected texts, they have not been able to avoid feeling that with Austen they are suddenly dealing with "genius" of a higher order than had yet been shown by a woman novelist (Konigsberg 213)— either the beginning of Leavis's "Great Tradition" or the point to which, according to Ian Watt, the eighteenth-century novel "rose."[3] The purpose of this chapter is to suggest that the way had been cleared for the expression of Austen's talent by the struggles of her female predecessors to develop a fictional form that would contain women's lives, lives that themselves had been changed in the process of being described in more than a century of novels.

"How eloquent could Anne Elliot have been," we are told in

Persuasion, ". . . against that over-anxious caution which seems to insult exertion and distrust Providence!" (30). Exertion on the one hand and a trust in Providence on the other work together to bring Austen's suffering heroines, along with their sailor brothers and lovers, to their safe harbor—that is, to the traditional happy marriage of the romantic and comic denouement.[4] Both forces were available to her heroines as they had not been available to their fictional foremothers.

Many social historians have pointed out that in the eighteenth century domestic industry was vanishing, and a family's gentility was increasingly measured by the leisure of its females; in *Pride and Prejudice,* Mrs. Bennet brags that "her daughters had nothing to do in the kitchen" (65).[5] "Exertion" could thus seem déclassé, especially if it connoted "business," a word that for Aphra Behn was negatively associated with a male world of violence and greed. Yet as Behn well knew, the "iron age," commercial world had forced an unwanted leisure on women by reducing them to mere counters in financial transactions. This economic fact precludes "exertion" for the heroines of Haywood, Lennox, and Burney; they can only wait to be bought. Yet these novelists insisted that the heroines' growth depended on their ability to feel desire or, to use Scudéry's term, "inclination"—a term that can also stand for will in a broader sense. It is not until Austen's novels that "business," though not in the mercantile sense, is both positively associated with "exertion" and recommended for women as well as for men.[6] Her predecessors' halting and reluctant assertions that women do have wills enabled Austen to take that fact for granted. Thus, despite the reactionary times in which she lived, she could give her heroines permission to act in small ways—and often only "a word, a look" is needed (*P* 238)—to bring about their happiness. Though that happiness is the traditional one of marriage, it rewards the heroine for having a will and therefore suggests possibilities beyond those of husband and home.

Of course, like their predecessors, Austen's heroines are often forced to suppress their desires; but often, paradoxically, in doing so they move toward rather than away from the happy ending. The little wheels in which their exertions take place are connected to the larger wheels of Providence, represented within the novel by the author. Austen's providential interference in the lives of her characters is not like the miracles that save earlier heroines from their impossible dilemmas, because her conception of God is more hopeful than that of her predecessors. Earlier women novelists, unlike the male authors of typical "providential novels" (Duckworth 10-12) could not easily imagine their own acts of narration as imitations of the Creator. His power permeates novels such as *Betsy Thoughtless* and *Harriot Stuart,* "authorizing" patriarchs to accept women's sacrifices as their due, but the role of the authoress is to correct this bias by handing out the rewards of love and fame. And her power to do so is severely limited, working only for the heroine, and only, it is clear, in the realm of fiction. Austen, on the other hand, believed God demanded more of women than self-sacrifice and gave more in return; therefore as author she could stand in for him, working with the heroine to bring about a happiness that is nearly probable, and directing the "chance" that supplements her efforts.

Austen's endings are only nearly probable; if they strain belief, the reader is to accept them as the author's means of showing how the story, and life, are informed by religious symbolism, just as Austen's characters must know that "chance" is really Providence.[7] No doubt there were still plenty of undesirable readers who lacked the imagination to read this way; Austen called them "dull elves," a name for them she borrowed from Sir Walter Scott (*L* 298). But those readers who, like the Austens, had been reading current and older novels all their lives, and reading them intelligently, were well prepared to find in fiction "poetic" rather than "historical" truth. Marriage in Austen's novels is not only the "career" most real women of the time had to look forward to. Rather, it is a way of grounding in familiar reality a powerful old romantic and religious symbol. In romance it is not only the heroine and hero who marry, but, as we have seen, self and society. In Austen's novels many other seemingly opposed principles are wed as well, including humanity and God.[8]

By asking her readers to bring old novels with them as they entered hers, Austen invited them to explore with her the boundaries between fiction and life. All her heroines learn how their reading does and does not apply to their experience and thus show the reader how and how not to apply the novel in hand. Some characters come almost to understand that they *are* characters in a novel and try to comprehend their relationship with the author in the same way the reader must come to terms with God. All Austen's oddly assorted and often disputatious predecessors and contemporaries are thus gathered up into a tradition, partners in a spiritual quest. "Let us not desert one another," she wrote to her fellow novelists in *Northanger Abbey;* "we are an injured body" (37). Austen wanted to form an alliance to achieve a common goal: a comedy wide enough to embrace tragic suffering, a romance flexible enough to contain the unpredictable adventure of real life.

Before examining the ways that exertion and trust in Providence contribute to Austen's happy endings, we will need, first, to take one last look at the terms "romance" and "realism," the meaning of which continued to change during Austen's writing life, and, second, to discuss Austen's own critical attitude toward romance.

Jane Austen is often written about as a "Romantic," concerned with questions of epistemology and sympathetic to rebellion against authority, but she is not often seen as a "romantic," someone who used the conventions of older fiction.[9] In her own time she was thought of as a realist, and that label has stuck. Not that the concept of realism was any better defined then than it had ever been; the word itself was not yet in use, and the terminology of fiction was in one of its loosest phases. Every work of fiction was called a "novel," and there was some understanding that romance and novel were related, if not identical. Austen herself used "novel" to describe Scott's and Radcliffe's works as well as her own, unless there was a particular reason to make a distinction. Satires such as *The Heroine* and *Northanger Abbey* ridiculed as a single category sentimental novels, novels of manners, Gothic novels, and historical romances.[10] (I will continue to use "romance" to refer to the old type of fiction of which the novel was a modern and "realistic displacement" [Frye, *Secular Scripture,* 38].) One reason Barrett and Austen could lump so many types of "novels" together in their satires was that as works aged they came to seem more "romantic," that is, less realistic. By comparison, to her contemporaries, Austen was a realist, but the label hardly seems adequate to describe her practice of the novel, for two main reasons: because the concept of realism during her life was undergoing yet another shift in meaning, especially as it related to probability, and because Austen was not consistently a realist by any definition.

In eighteenth-century terms, Austen's novels are the antithesis of romantic; but during the nineteenth century they gradually came to seem romantic in a new way. In the eighteenth century novels were considered more realistic than romances because of their concern with everyday, commonplace affairs. Their plots were "natural," as Johnson said in *Rambler 4,* because they were explainable in terms of the laws of probability rather than amazing coincidence or divine intervention. When later in the century writers such as Richard Hurd and Clara Reeve praised the romance, they had to justify its improbable plots, and so they invoked a rather free interpretation of the Aristotelian term "poetic truth." Aristotle had distinguished "poetic truth" from "historical truth," or factual accuracy, to give the poet freedom to observe the laws of probability that often fail to operate in life (*Poetics,* chapter IX).[11] But Hurd argued that because a poet has liberty to create "a world of his own," he is also free to determine the laws that govern it (92-93).

In the early nineteenth century one begins to see a separation between the concepts of probability and realism that nearly becomes an alliance between probability and romance. In 1821 Richard Whately, reviewing Austen's novels, reminded readers of Aristotle's original words, emphasizing how unlike life is a novel with a probable plot.[12] Whately seems to be looking back nostalgically at the neoclassicism against which Hurd had reacted in 1762, at the days of Pope's *Essay on Man,* a time when probability, or the rules of "nature," could be considered more "real" than mere specific facts. Throughout the nineteenth century, as reality came to seem more violent and random, eighteenth-century England became a sort of historical idyll where life was calm and simple and understandable. (Of course, the Augustans were similarly nostalgic for the original Roman Augustans, who also did their share of bemoaning the decadence of their own present.) Gradually the idyll came to include the turn of the century as it appears in Austen's novels. In 1871 Paul Elmer More saw in *Emma* "an ideal centre of calm which was conceived, and for a time and in certain places actually realised, by the eighteenth century" (quoted in Southam, *Critical Heritage,* 2:86), and during World War I Austen's novels were used as therapy for victims of shell shock (Kent 59).[13]

We have already seen how an early phase of this romanticization of history complicated the realism of Burney's novels. Just as the Victorians could imagine Austen's world as an idyll compared with their own, Burney could look back wistfully at the way Richardson had been able to reward his heroines with both personal happiness and far-reaching public influence. She believed that in her own time, self and society could not be reconciled; in the years of the American and French Revolutions and then of their reactionary aftermath, so-called society was really selfish individualism, and true society had become merely an ideal in the mind of a besieged minority. With every man and woman in a Hobbesian state of war against all others, real life did not lend itself to orderly exposition. The laws of probability, if they operated at all, did so without reference to any moral order; greed was winning, unselfishness was losing, and life seemed to be without moral or mechanical design. From the point of view of the Burneyan central character, whose actions produce little result, events seem to be caused by neither probability nor Providence but chance, the mainspring of the supposedly unrealistic romance plot.

Austen's allusions to Burney, though often satiric, do not contradict this view of society or of romance. In the reactionary England in which she grew up the privacy of women's lives was assumed, so she naturally smiled at the grand, public sufferings of Burney's heroines and, perhaps, failed to see why her "sister author" (*NA* 111) made domestic life in a small country village look like a compromise. For all Austen's heroines except Elizabeth Bennet, this was plenty of happiness, almost more than can be believed.[14] But she was also conscious that "society" was becoming more and more of a paradox, existing on a smaller and smaller scale, and therefore she also regarded the Richardsonian wedding of the public and the private as an idyllic dream.[15] As Tony Tanner notes, Austen crossed out the phrase "social order" in the manuscript of *Sanditon,* which she was writing at the time of her death, as if she no longer believed it existed (12).

Thus by the end of the eighteenth century orderliness and realism were at odds; only in the past did reality seem to operate by logical and moral rules. In 1821 Whately believed that to describe such a world was to be "poetic." Yet the converse, that "improbable" romances were thus more like life than novels, did not follow. Whately continued the traditional association of "chance" or improbability with romance, and of probability with realism, the novel, and Austen.[16] Even more than Whately, Sir Walter Scott, known for his poetry and historical romances, helped establish Austen's reputation as a realist. Most readers are familiar with the comment from Scott's journal, recorded in James Edward Austen-Leigh's *Memoir* of his aunt (1869), praising her for leaving the "big Bow-Wow strain" of historical romance to others and claiming to envy her the "exquisite touch which renders ordinary common-place things and characters interesting from the truth of the description and the sentiment" (370). Even during her life, Scott had publicly admired her originality in writing about ordinary social life.[17]

Yet Scott, unlike Whately, did not believe Austen found "poetic truth" in the commonplace. Though his review seems at first to be favorable, and on the whole Austen was pleased with it (*L* 453), the distinction it draws between romance on the one hand and Austen on the other is not to her advantage, for her "realism" to him was superficial. As we saw in the previous chapter, he considered "manners" to be no more meaningful than clothes.[18] Comparing Austen's novels to Flemish paintings, which Joshua Reynolds had found wanting in the "great style,"[19] Scott finds not much "deep interest" in them: "Upon the whole, the turn of this author's novels bears the same relation to that of the sentimental and romantic cast, that cornfields and cottages and meadows bear to the highly adorned grounds of a show mansion, or the rugged sublimities of a mountain landscape. It is neither so captivating as the one, nor so grand as the other, but it affords to those who frequent it a pleasure nearly allied with the experience of their own social habits" (*Scott on Novelists* 235). The judgment finds its way into Austen-Leigh's monument to his aunt, in which the biographer praises her as a "photographer" of her time while assuming her gift was "humbler" than Scott's (373, 305). The sentiment is later echoed by Coventry Patmore (1886), who sees Austen's "photographic" limitation as feminine (quoted in Southam, *Critical Heritage,* 2:39). Scott's imagery also anticipates a similar metaphor in Charlotte Brontë's 1848 letter to G.H. Lewes criticizing Austen's "carefully fenced, highly cultivated garden, with neat borders." Both correspondents agreed that whatever Austen was, she was no poet (Southam, *Critical Heritage,* 1:126-28).[20]

The issue of whether or not the deep truth lies in the commonplace is moot, however, when one considers how fitfully Austen observed the realism for which she was alternately praised and blamed. Her novels are full of amazing and convenient coincidences only partially explained as "contingencies" (Duckworth 10).[21] Captain Wentworth comes back to Anne Elliot's neighborhood after eight years to visit his sister, but why of all people has *she* become the tenant of Kellynch? Such examples have prompted Darrel Mansell to consider Austen less a realist than an allegorist. But the terms are not necessarily opposed. The author's manipulation of events to make a point may be a mimetic rendering of what she believed God does in actual life.[22]

Austen describes a world organized in such a way that events only appear improbable because of our limited vision. Believing ourselves the center of the universe, we discern no orbital pattern in the events of our lives and thus conclude not that there must be a God, but that life is random. That is why Johnson and Lennox feared that reading improbable romances would erode faith in God and leave only faith in chance. But if one can locate the real center, a new pattern emerges. Austen's vantage point is earth, where robbers often prosper; her novels provide only a glimpse of the pattern. But she can show just enough of it to encourage faith in the rest. She depicts God's hand turning partial evil—Crawford's elopement with Maria Rushworth, Lady Catherine de Bourgh's snobbery—to universal good, symbolized by the heroine's happy marriage.

The allegory that informs Austen's realism is both Christian and romantic. When Cherry Wilkinson in *The Heroine* opens her story with the announcement that she intends to suffer in the present in order to live happily ever after later on, Barrett may mean to ridicule her quixotic application of the romance plot. But what Cherry describes is both real life as a Christian must see it, and romance as practiced by poets such as Spenser.[23] In Austen's novels, to trust that all will be well in the end, if not necessarily on earth—though it is only on earth that she can describe it—is to be neither reckless nor passive, for trust cannot come until the heroine rightly understands her place in the scheme of things and recognizes the work she must do.

By stating that Austen used romance as religious allegory I do not deny that she made fun of romance conventions, old and, especially, new. When asked to write a "historical romance," she refused: "I could not sit seriously down to write a serious romance under any other motive than to save my life; and if it were indispensable for me to keep it up and never relax into laughing at myself or other people, I am sure I should be hung before I had finished the first chapter" (*L* 452-53). There was much to laugh at in the popular romantic fiction of her time, which included abysmal imitations of Radcliffe and Scott such as the novels of Sir Egerton Brydges, a family friend.[24]

Gothic fiction, even at its best, was a particularly easy target, as may be seen in *Northanger Abbey*. Characters take time out from their tragedies to discuss the weather (*NA* 83), they occupy huge mouldering castles in which two women do all the work (184), and daughters look exactly like their mothers (191).[25] Characters are "un-mixed" representatives of good or evil, and villains commit crimes, such as wife-murder, which would be unthinkable in a civilized country where they are only permitted to bully their wives into an early grave. We have seen that Radcliffe's novels are like big-screen projections of the intense problems Burney saw in ordinary life; in *Northanger Abbey* Austen is able to use each of these writers to satirize the other through contrasts in scale. Incidents turned down toward the trivial are narrated in language turned up toward the heroic, as when Catherine, without a partner at a Bath assembly, learns what it means "[t]o be disgraced in the eye of the world, to wear the appearance of infamy while her heart is all purity, her actions all innocence, and the misconduct of another the true source of her debasement" (53).

Nevertheless, it is rarely argued now, as it was once by Q.D. Leavis, that Austen waged "conscious war" on Burney and Radcliffe, or on older romantic fiction.[26] A more relevant "war" may be the old one between male critics and women novelists, which helps explain Austen's refusal to imitate Scott. Although the "Great Tradition" may have passed Scott by, in his time he was to Austen as Dryden had been to Behn, as Pope had been to Manley, as Fielding had been to Haywood, and as Johnson had been to Lennox and Burney.[27] It was J.D. Clarke, the king's librarian, who asked Austen to write a historical romance about the royal house of Saxe Coburg; he also asked her to write a novel about a model clergyman, to be based, it appears, on his own experiences. She refused both requests with humorous humility, calling herself "the most unlearned and uninformed female who ever dared to be an authoress" (*L* 443). The response recalls similar mixtures of modesty and pertness in statements of purpose by Aphra Behn and Clara Reeve; she implies both that she is too flighty and ignorant to follow his suggestions, and too intelligently alive to their potential silliness to want to. For her family's enjoyment she did create a satirical "plan of a Novel" about Clarke's clergyman, in which all the characters are perfect and their sufferings highly improbable (Southam, *Manuscripts,* ch. 5).

Whatever her real reasons for not sitting "seriously down to write a serious romance," Austen certainly did sit humorously down to write comic ones, using romance conventions, both old and new, as Cervantes had done, to point satire in various directions. If Catherine lacks the articulateness of an Evelina to write down everything that happens to her in her "entrée into life" (19, 20, 26-27), if Mrs. Thorpe is incapable of a lengthy digression about her "past adventures and sufferings" (34), if Isabella is not the "tender friend" she pretends to be, the fault is not in romance but in reality. And of course romance does turn out to be like life in a number of ways,[28] some fortunate (marriage for love), some unfortunate (cruelty of husbands and fathers), some amusingly transformed (the hero, not the heroine, won by "Recognizance" or gratitude).[29] In the end, the clear delineation of good and evil found in the Gothic novels that Catherine learns to distrust still provides a useful framework for placing General Tilney, or at least her feelings about him: "in suspecting General Tilney of either murdering or shutting up his wife, she had scarcely sinned against his character, or magnified his cruelty" (247).

Austen's respectful borrowings from Burney and Radcliffe in particular have been demonstrated in recent research. Marilyn Butler, for example, suggests that if Austen's intended volume divisions for *Northanger Abbey* had been observed, the first volume would look more like an homage to Burney than a burlesque ("Sense of the Volume" 56). Several critics have pointed out that Radcliffe's sense of place, of the psychological importance of atmosphere, and even the veils and suggestiveness so basic to her style have analogues in Austen's techniques.[30] And of course Burney and Radcliffe themselves used romance conventions critically, to warn readers against excessive sensibility and imagination. And so in satirizing romance, *Northanger Abbey,* unlike *The Female Quixote* and *The Heroine,* does not take a stand against it. It acknowledges freely, as those anti-romances do not, that the realistic narrative surrounding the heroine's quixotic delusions is itself a fiction, or, in the author's mock-humble phrase, "only a novel" (38).

Austen did share some of Lennox's moral concern about the effects of romances on those who read them badly, but her quixote, unlike Lennox's and Cervantes's, errs from having too little imagination rather than too much (Susan Morgan 62). Catherine has not been trusted to tell her own story, as Barrett's Cherry Wilkinson does, because she would never be able to speak like a heroine; like the Female Quixote's maid Lucy, she fails even as a romantic confidante to the would-be heroine Isabella Thorpe.[31] The novel suggests that moral education comes not from burning romances, but from learning how to read both romances and reality accurately. A "wedding" of fiction and life takes place when the main character has learned the right relation of head and heart, or sense and sensibility.[32] Austen treats emotion rationally in her novels, but not necessarily as a reactionary Augustan,[33] for her analysis of love into the components "esteem," "gratitude," and "passion" owes much to Scudéry and her English followers (*PP* 265, 279; *SS* 378).

The title and basic conception of *Sense and Sensibility* make it an excellent paradigm for the marriage of life and fiction, reality and imagination, head and heart. Austen's juvenile burlesques confidently treated romance as absurdly unreal, but this complex novel acknowledges that even intelligent readers can be led astray by romance and that romance, when read properly, can be a guide to life. Two romance conventions in particular, both of which appear in the juvenilia, are closely examined in *Sense and Sensibility:* the symbolic meaning of physical beauty, and the quest for a twin or mirror-image lover.

In the juvenilia, Austen had great fun playing with the impassable boundaries between romance and reality, particularly in the absurdity that occurs when symbols are taken too literally. Physical beauty, for example, in romance symbolizes goodness, but in life it is more apt to indicate conceit, as when Charles Adams of "Jack and Alice" says, "I look upon myself to be Sir a perfect Beauty—where would you see a finer figure or a more charming face" (*MW* 25). The difference creates a paradox in novels such as *The Female Quixote,* in which the ideal heroine is also supposed to be realistic and is thus alternately, or even at the same time, both vain and artless; hence the lines from "Lesley Castle" that I used to introduce chapter 4: "We are handsome my dear Charlotte, very handsome and the greatest of our Perfections is, that we are entirely insensible of them ourselves" (*MW* 111).

Austen's juvenilia also satirize the twin lover idea, which was familiar from recent sentimental novels such as *Paul and Virginia* (1787), but which also reached back to Behn's pastorals and, of course, to the story of Adam and Eve. In "Frederic and Elfrida," the hero and heroine, "being both born in one day & both brought up at one school," are "so much alike, that it was not every one who knew them apart. Nay even their most intimate freinds [*sic*] had nothing to distinguish them by, but the shape of the face, the colour of the Eye, the length of the Nose & the difference of the complexion" (4).

Sense and Sensibility connects the romance conventions of symbolic beauty and the twin lover, for Willoughby's dashing appearance convinces Marianne that he is her destined mate, the one man whose "taste . . . in every point coincide[s] with" her own (17). One of the clever ironies of this novel is that by being Marianne's false twin Willoughby is in one way a true one, like the male coquets in *Betsy Thoughtless* and *Harriot Stuart*.[34] Willoughby is not a calculating seducer; he is merely led on by "the brightness of her eyes" (47), as she is by his charm, to ignore the questions his "sense," if he had any, would urge regarding the consequences of this flirtation. To grow up Marianne must, like Betsy Thoughtless, find the Trueworth who can be the "mirror of her heart" instead of her folly. The novel finally confirms the existence of such a hero by finding for her the superficially unlikely, and unlike, Colonel Brandon.

To many readers Brandon looks more like a punishment for Marianne than a reward.[35] But he may be regarded as a true hero—and without reading the novel as a rejection of Romantic individualism—if one reads it in the context of the Scudéry tradition. It is important that Elinor is the first to see that Brandon is right for Marianne, though like Nina Auerbach she finds him "depressing" at the beginning ("Jane Austen" 19), and that Elinor's perceptions are established early as both more reliable and more romantic than her sister's. Elinor sees her own love, Edward Ferrars, not with her eyes but with her heart. "At first sight," she admits to Marianne, "his address is certainly not striking: and his person can hardly be called handsome, till the expression of his eyes, which are uncommonly good, and the general sweetness of his countenance, is perceived. At present, I know him so well, that I think him really handsome; or, at least, almost so" (20). That last qualifier shows Elinor's good sense in her reluctance, under the circumstances, to allow herself to be thoroughly in love; but the passage as a whole, which closely resembles Darcy's comments on Elizabeth's "pair of fine eyes" (*PP* 27), shows how, to a trained observer, appearances do reveal inner qualities. Elinor knows how to interpret Brandon's quiet manner as a sign of something far different from the insensibility Marianne and Willoughby choose to see in it.

Elinor sees that beneath the odious flannel waistcoat beats a heart much like Marianne's; Brandon is reserved for the same reason Marianne is at times unable to see anyone: "oppression of spirits" due to mysterious "past injuries and disappointments" (50), specifically the "misery of disappointed love" (55). Marianne looks familiar to Brandon not only because she resembles the two Elizas of his past, as he says, but because she is like a younger version of himself. And she grows more like him, even down to his seemingly unheroic rheumatism, when her own love for Willoughby festers into a "putrid" fever (307). But Elinor roots for Brandon not only because he is Marianne's twin in tragic suffering, but because he is a projection of what she might become if she, like him, can resist the urge to withdraw and learns instead to use her pain to become more compassionate, or "mindful of the feelings of others" (62).

Of course a trained eye like Elinor's is not an easy thing to develop, and the narrator's assurance that in the end Marianne has acquired it may justly be called facile. We have seen Marianne loving Willoughby, but we do not see the process of her coming to love Brandon, the sort of development that in *David Copperfield* takes the whole novel, and that is still the subject of many a self-help bestseller. Yet though it may take time for a sad girl being paid constant, kind attention by a worthy man whom her whole family likes to find that life with him makes her both happy and good, it need not take much space in the narrative—particularly when one has the benefit of Scudérian shorthand. Readers today are bothered by the easy dismissal, or sacrifice, of Marianne's "irresistible passion" for Willoughby (378), but one of the main reasons women writers retained romantic language was to save love from being reduced to mere sex, as it was apt to be in men's "dirty jokes" and satires. For Marianne, *"falling a sacrifice* to an irresistible passion [my emphasis]," riding down the dangerous River of Inclination to the Unknown Lands, would mean a loss of self, for marriage for life to the man one finds sexy at seventeen is not Romantic freedom.

Nor is "passion" necessarily left out of Marianne's life with Brandon, for Clelia's Map of Tender quietly includes it in several places. Post-Freudians have trouble with this map, as we have seen, because it resists any attempt to separate sex from other emotions. One cannot simply equate sex with inclination, because as women writers often pointed out, it is possible to lust against one's will (Manley, *NA*, 2:102). Sex is clearly a part of Clelia's idea of love—the part that seems to frighten her. It is also, in a passive, yielding way, an aspect of tenderness, which is the downfall of many a young woman in Haywood-style novels. When Austen says that "Marianne could never love by halves; and her whole heart became, in time, as much devoted to her husband, as it had once been to Willoughby," her language tells her well-schooled readers that a mild and safe form of sexual passion is part of their union. It may be a gift Marianne bestows on her husband, but in Scudérian terms giving and receiving are indistinguishable in marriages of true lovers, and "Marianne found her own happiness in forming his" (379). Though Marianne is Brandon's "reward" (378), he is also hers, for he has won her by his respect, or as any number of women authors called it, "tender friendship."

The best way to arrive at this happiness, according to Scudéry and Austen, is through "gratitude" ("Recognizance") and "esteem." "Esteem" is an especially important word in *Sense and Sensibility,* particularly in its relation to love and tenderness. At first, Marianne hates the word and threatens to "leave the room this moment" if Elinor persists in using it to describe her own feelings for Edward (21). Marianne, planning only to be Edward's sister-in-law and uncertain whether he is good enough for Elinor, nevertheless claims to "love him tenderly" (17)—as does Mrs. Dashwood, who has "never yet known what it was to separate esteem and love" (16). The problem with this assertion is that in not separating the terms she makes no distinction about which should come first, so that when her romantic daughter falls in love with Willoughby at first sight, esteem naturally—and erroneously—follows. At the end, Marianne is forced to admit that she would not long have been able to "esteem" Willoughby—and that, therefore, her love would eventually have died (350). But for Brandon she feels "strong esteem and lively friendship" (378), which, according to Marianne's own code, must eventually lead to lasting love. By making so much of "esteem" Austen makes the Scudérian metaphysics of love support the moral view that the head should lead the heart: not that it should squash and suppress the heart, but that it should guide it in distinguishing between the false hero and the true.

Heart and head come together in a similar way in *Pride and Prejudice,* in which getting one's heart's desire is not only the "happiest" but also the "wisest, most reasonable end" (347). This "marriage" also creates harmony between self and society; in pleasing herself Elizabeth is confident, as she tells Lady Catherine, that she is offending nobody who really matters. Though not all Austen's endings are so Richardsonian, they are all distinguished by harmony, by "marrying" more than the heroine and hero (Poovey 202). They are even more "romantic" than French romance in extending the marital bond to include the heroine's tender "shepherdess" friend, who traditionally gets left behind at the altar.

In Austen's novels, only false friendships conflict with true love, and only mercenary marriages threaten friendship.[36] In fact, false friends are usually mercenary in these novels, and so their competitiveness with other women makes them untrustworthy. Isabella Thorpe uses Catherine to get at her brother, Lucy Steele lashes out at Elinor Dashwood to keep her from Edward, and Miss Bingley is too jealous of Elizabeth Bennet and too eager to marry Darcy to be a friend to Jane.[37] *Pride and Prejudice* further shows, sadly, that even a good woman who stoops to be mercenary, however understandable her temptation, sacrifices true female friendship. Once Charlotte Lucas has married Mr. Collins, "no real confidence could ever subsist between" her and Elizabeth again, and Elizabeth draws closer to Jane, whose "rectitude and delicacy" she can trust (128). The woman who marries for love keeps her natural sister, as Jane keeps Elizabeth, Marianne keeps Elinor, and Fanny Price keeps, or rather rediscovers, Susan; and she may gain a good sister-in-law, as Catherine gains Eleanor Tilney, and Anne Elliot gains Mrs. Croft.

There is plenty of room in Austen's vision for both a rational assessment of life's limitations and a romantic expression of the desires that transcend them. The romance ending establishes a possible perfection, and the realistic plot explores how, or if, such justice and happiness can be brought about—through "exertion" and "trust in Providence."[38]

What did "exertion" mean for Austen, and how sufficient was it for bringing about the happy ending? To answer these questions, I would like to discuss first how much Austen's heroines are able to do for themselves, and second how much still remains to be done for them. For Austen's comedy, more markedly in the later than in the earlier novels, embraces a harshly realistic account of the constraints on women's lives during her time, and on human life at any time. The later novels are constructed in such a way that humor almost seems to have fled, and only Providence can bring it back.

"Exertion" implies, first and foremost, inclination—wanting something enough to work for it. English women writers after Scudéry struggled long, within the confines of old romance archetypes and real-life double standards, to produce a heroine who loves a particular man and knows it; but their understanding of women's psychology did eventually make this possible. Fanny Burney in particular helped establish that women are just as much inclined to love as men, though for them safety usually dictates strict self-control.

With Burney's novels behind them, Austen's heroines need waste no energy denying or justifying their feelings, though they do often work to suppress them: the question of whether Catherine Morland ought to dream of Henry Tilney before he has dreamed of her is a burlesque of a Richardsonian issue that by Austen's time seemed absurdly out of date (*NA* 30), though Catherine does try to keep her love within bounds until Henry has shown marked interest in her (41).[39]

The new wrinkle in Austen's novels is that not all the heroines' exertion is spent on suppression: inclination can lead to choice. Just as Austen herself, without asking anyone's leave, turned down a proposal from a man she did not love (William Austen-Leigh, 92-93), her heroines are apt to consider accepting or rejecting a husband as their own personal prerogative. To the extent that real women had that right, there is some evidence that, like Lydia Languish in Sheridan's *The Rivals* (1775), they gained it by reading novels.[40] This play, while satirizing Lydia's unnecessary rebelliousness—everyone, it turns out, wants her to marry the man she loves—also ridicules Sir Anthony Absolute's old-fashioned notions of filial "duty" (I, ii), and in doing so it resembles the majority of novels of the 1790s. During this decade Radcliffe was still suggesting that a young woman required the "heroism of romance" to resist coercion (*Romance of the Forest* 136), while Jane West warned that doing so might endanger national security (Claudia Johnson 3-4). Austen ridicules this notion in "Catharine, or the Bower," in which the heroine is told that if she continues flirting with young men "all order will soon be at an end throughout the Kingdom" (*MW* 232).[41] But many other novels, differing widely from each other in ideology, share a view of the matter that makes Radcliffe look outdated and West a little hysterical.

It is not surprising that the "jacobin" Bage's *Hermsprong* treats marrying or not marrying on the command of a parent as masochistic and wrong, but even the more conservative Susan Ferrier in *Marriage* permits her gentle Mary to listen to her mother storming and raging, "determined to judge for herself in a matter in which her happiness was so deeply involved" (367). And Barrett, whose *The Heroine* is built on the conservative, anti-romantic premise that all a girl needs for perfect happiness is to "consult her parents, and make a prudent match" (88), makes Cherry the tyrant who can do what she will with her fond father, including having him imprisoned in a madhouse. Apparently this trend in fiction had some correspondence with life; in 1824, when Sir Walter Scott wanted to praise Richardson's verisimilitude, he had to explain to his readers that "forced marriages in *those* days did sometimes take place [my emphasis]" (*PW* 3:47).

Austen was thus very much in the current mode when she treated parental interference as either a thing of the past (mostly in her early novels) or as at least clearly unjustified (usually in her late ones). In *Pride and Prejudice,* Mr. Bennet would not think of "making" Elizabeth marry Collins (111), and Mrs. Bennet's ranting is pathetically ineffectual. In *Sense and Sensibility,* the trend has almost gone too far: Mrs. Dashwood is "romantic," not as a parental blocking character, but as a vicarious heroine who lets Marianne's love take its course and thus fails in her maternal duty to protect her daughter (85). Even Sir Thomas Bertram in *Mansfield Park* is not quite the tyrannical father we have seen so often in women's fiction, for having always considered himself above making matches for his children he is clearly embarrassed to be forced into this role by Fanny's disobedience (238).[42] In *Persuasion,* a mother figure does prevent the heroine's marriage for love, but Lady Russell's opinion of Wentworth is less ambiguously wrong than any other "persuasion" in the novel. Nor is it the real obstacle between Anne and Wentworth, for if he had proposed again two years after she had refused him she would certainly have accepted (247). Once Anne has made Wentworth understand her, their marriage is said to be inevitable: "Who can be in doubt of what followed? When any two young people take it into their heads to marry, they are pretty sure by perseverance to carry their point, be they ever so poor, or ever so imprudent, or ever so little likely to be necessary to each other's ultimate comfort" (248). The triumph of young love is presented as the least romantic of realities.

All irony aside, Austen's heroines are not merely headstrong in exerting their rights: they are carrying out a sacred duty. Charlotte Lucas in *Pride and Prejudice* may call marrying for love a "romantic" notion (125), but to Elizabeth it is the minimum requirement of decency. Charlotte's decision to marry Collins for a settlement was clearly not unusual, and it may really have been the "pleasantest preservative from want" for many real young or not-so-young women of the time (122-23). But the novel does show that it is both possible and advisable to resist this temptation. Charlotte sacrifices her better self as well as her confidante, and with what we know of the Bennet daughters' situation we cannot help but worry about what will become of the children of such a mismatch.[43] Charlotte has "exerted" herself, but in a way that leaves no scope for the exertion of others in her behalf, for "chance" to bring her something better. She has not trusted in Providence.

The Austen heroine, in contrast, exerts herself properly. By remaining true to her own inclination she preserves "rectitude and delicacy," "principle and integrity," and thus she both deserves help from above and remains available to receive it (128, 136). In *Persua-*

sion, Anne explains to Wentworth that if defying Lady Russell in order to marry him would have been a breach of duty, marrying Musgrove—or, later, Elliot—in order to please Lady Russell would have been a worse one (244). Anne has to be ready for the amazing contingency, or coincidence, of Wentworth's reappearance. And then she must be willing to use every opportunity, once his love seems to be returning, to make her feelings known to him, just as Jane Bennet in *Pride and Prejudice* must "happen to look round, and happen to smile" as Bingley enters the dining room in order to guide him into the vacant seat next to her (340).

Austen's heroines have none of the misplaced patience of Fanny Burney's, whose scruples about using their chances win them hundreds of pages of misunderstandings. When Henry Tilney seems angry with Catherine, "instead of considering her own dignity injured by this ready condemnation—instead of proudly resolving, in conscious innocence, to show her resentment towards him who could harbour a doubt of it, to leave to him all the trouble of seeking an explanation, and to enlighten him on the past only by avoiding his sight, or flirting with somebody else [all of which Camilla does]—she . . . was only eager for an opportunity of explaining" her seemingly rude behavior (*NA* 93). And so when Anne maneuvers herself onto the outside of the bench at a concert so that Wentworth will be able to speak to her as he passes, she thinks of a forward young lady in Burney's *Cecilia,* the "inimitable Miss Larolles,—but still she did it" (*P* 189).

Anne's exertions, however proper, do not guarantee her success; clearly in these novels there *can* be a doubt of what follows no matter how stubborn the lovers. Parental and economic pressures may prove impossible to overcome, as they often were in life, according to feminist critics, who generally feel Lawrence Stone's belief in the growth of marriage for love during this time requires qualification.[44] Austen's novels do convey her respect for the obstacles to romantic love: even in the lightest and brightest of them, Elizabeth's refusal to marry for convenience requires, if not the heroism of romance, at least unusual strength of mind. Therefore, like their predecessors, Austen's heroines spend a considerable amount of exertion resigning themselves to the strong possibility of failure—of never finding love, like Miss Bates, or of learning to love men who are far from ideal.[45] In this way her comedies include the facts of life that made near-tragedies of earlier women's novels.

Jane Bennet's "rectitude and delicacy" are reflected in her comment that a woman should not marry without "something like regard and esteem" for her husband (135). It is hard to imagine a less exacting criterion, or a less romantic one: the man need not be a hero as long as he is not a fool. Part of learning how to see the romance in real life is learning to recognize it in its less dazzling form, which means, inevitably, settling for less than one's dreams. Austen's heroines as well as her secondary characters are willing, to paraphrase Manley, to "compound for some serious defects" in their lovers—more willing than some readers of today, who are led by disappointment to mistrust the endings as a form of bourgeois propaganda (Manley, *R*, 9).[46] Austen's willingness to compromise seems less an attempt to indoctrinate readers than an encouragement to accept life's perennial imperfection. Nevertheless, the strict limitations of happiness in her novels do imply some criticism of a society that blunts personal inclination and thus causes slippage between the little wheels of individual exertion and the larger wheels of the family, the neighborhood, the kindgom, and the world.

The smallness of the "societies" created at the end of Austen's novels suggests the strong Burneyan possibility that soon everyone will be running futilely around her own tiny circle.[47] Some critics argue that the scale of her worlds in itself is a political statement (Monaghan 2). In making the "perfect happiness" of so many of her heroines a moderate income in a modest parsonage somewhere near a "great house," she expresses both a sympathy with Burke's reverence for the family and a skepticism about how far the warmth of the hearth could really be felt.[48] This "political" statement thus contains its own warning against looking for systems-level statements on the home front, beyond the obvious general implication that life outside one's own little corner was apt to be chaos. This is not to deny Austen her place in the "war of ideas," but it does add to the difficulties of placing her in it. Terms such as "conservative," "liberal," and "radical," as we have seen, have general meanings that sometimes conflict with specific applications to historical events and issues. One of the more interesting lines of approach to emerge recently describes how Austen's abstractly liberal or "democratic," yet still Tory, ideas were affected by the polarizing debates of the 1790s.[49]

The critics of the various camps do sometimes come together in granting on the one hand that Austen was highly critical of "society" as it had become and was in that broad sense "radical," or "liberal," and on the other that the ideal of which reality fell so miserably short stressed "communal values" rather than individualism and was in that sense "conservative" or even "reactionary."[50] Romance, as we have seen, is well suited to express this apparent paradox, as the hero's adventures subvert an existing social order and replace it with an ideal one. Austen often criticized the present through references to romance rather than to either the historical past or an existing, dying aristocratic order, as when Fanny Price explains to Mary Crawford why she does not agree that the name "Mr. Edmund Bertram" is "pitiful" or "younger-brother-like": "It is a name of heroism and renown—of kings, princes, and knights; and seems to breathe the spirit of chivalry and warm affections" (211).[51] Similarly, the name "Knightley" in *Emma* alludes primarily to romance and only indirectly reflects on the real landed gentry of Austen's day.[52]

The idea that images of real society could be found only in romance darkens all Austen's novels; but it does not darken them all equally. It is not strictly possible to call the early novels light and the later novels dark, as recent discussions of *Sense and Sensibility* have shown (Susan Morgan 111-12).[53] But on the whole, Austen's later heroines laugh less and suffer more than their earlier counterparts. To explain this change, one need not immediately conclude that her opinions changed or that she became depressed.[54] The difference can be seen in terms of her career-long exploration of the relation between romance and life, which made each of her novels a different kind of technical experiment. Her later novels take as their structural base some of the sad truths that appeared as themes and motifs in her earlier works.

Burney's notion of what was happening to society had a dimension that would prove most useful to the evolution of Austen's art. For if the Apollonian virtues of moderation and order were becoming rare and romantic, it was conversely true that romantic hyperbole was becoming commonplace. Austen's novels suggest that everyone was now speaking in Miss Larolles' superlatives, as when the narrator of *Sense and Sensibility* remarks that "the sweetest girls in the world were to be met with in every part of England, under every possible variation of form, face, temper and understanding" (119). This universal willingness to see heroines everywhere enabled the satirist to ask, what sort of person *is* the heroine next door? The artlessly simple heroine thus becomes Catherine Morland, who is "really" ignorant; and the beautiful and socially important heroine becomes Emma, who tends "to think a little too well of herself" (5).[55] These experiments in combining romance and reality expose not only the limited applicability of fictional archetypes to life, but also the errors of those who believe the archetypes are real—for example, men who are attracted to "imbeciles" (*NA* 111).[56] The later novels—including *Emma,* though at first it does not seem to fit the pattern—have a somber quality because the archetype exposed there is the selfless angel—a fictional ideal that, when mistaken for real, puts happiness beyond the reach of women's exertions.

This ideal was not new. When romances had been written only by men, heroines had been symbols of unearthly perfection, particularly of chastity, and any desire or action would have tarnished and disqualified them. When women writers gave these characters consciousness and will, they automatically challenged the negative definition of feminine virtue and risked censure for their heroines and scandal for themselves. In Austen's time, reactionary views about women made many men, including Scott, sentimentally fond of the old symbolic heroine, who could be molded into a domestic angel more readily than the more recent creations of women novelists; Dickens' Esther Summerson was not far away.[57] But though this archetype was a sign of a polarization of the sexes, a vision of woman as Other, it also began to have some relevance for men as sermons recommending Christian humility for both sexes became more common. And so the selfless heroine was both a traditional and a timely subject for Austen's romantic-realistic exposition.

The study of the selfless woman is not exclusive to Austen's late fiction. *Sense and Sensibility* has a version of her as heroine, whereas in *Emma* she is only a shadowy second female lead, the weak, pale, humble Jane Fairfax, who, of course, turns out to be a little selfish after all.[58] (The well-worn dilemma of the clandestine engagement belongs to Jane because she is partly designed to satirize the sentimental heroine who struggles with a will she is not supposed to have.) Austen's satiric exposition of this type, unlike Mary Wollstonecraft's, is not an all-out attack. The outward sign of selflessness is "sweetness," an appearance of pliancy and powerlessness that puts others off guard and encourages them to reveal themselves. Thus she who seems least capable of positive exertion may be the most knowledgeable. This inverse relationship between knowing and doing is sometimes present in the early novels: Elizabeth Bennet comments that information comes to her only when she cannot possibly use it (227). In *Mansfield Park* and *Persuasion,* the appearance of powerlessness is actually a prerequisite for knowledge. Fanny becomes the confidante of everyone involved in the play only because she has no part (164-65), and she is permitted to see and hear the real Crawfords because at first they carry on in front of her almost as if she were not there. Conversely, one must almost forgive Sir Thomas for being so wrong about everyone, since his almost supreme power puts him out of the way of the evidence. Like Fanny, the heroine of *Persuasion* would not be "too much in the secret of the complaints" of the various Musgroves if she were not "only Anne" (44, 5).

This one advantage of humility and sweetness, however, does not prevent Austen from carefully examining and criticizing these qualities before ranking them on the scale of Christian virtues. These are problem virtues, for by definition they cannot make themselves seen. Where they are involved, appearances not only *may* be deceiving, as they are in Austen's earlier novels; they *must* be. Sweetness may be a sign of a humble character, but it is a negative sign, one that makes its possessor disappear. When Captain Wentworth in *Persuasion* asks for a wife who has "a strong mind, with sweetness of manner" (62), he does not yet know that the "sweetness" he speaks of will hide the strength.[59] Nor does he understand the extent to which sweetness frustrates the strong mind by presenting obstacles to action.

The impossibility of seeing negative virtues is a central theme of Burney's last novel, *The Wanderer,* published the same year as Austen's first "late" novel, *Mansfield Park* (1814).[60] In Burney's novel modesty that can be seen must be false: "nothing is less delicate than professions of delicacy; which degrade a just perception, and strict practice of propriety, into a display of conscious caution, or a suspicion of evil interpretation" (394). In *Mansfield Park,* the Misses Bertram's vanity makes the same point, for it "was in such good order, that they seemed to be quite free from it, and gave themselves no airs" (35). Austen provides an added twist by noting that their success in pulling off this deception gives them more vanity to hide: "the praises attending such behaviour . . . served to strengthen them in believing they had no faults" (35).

The heroines of both novels are overlooked and mistreated because their excellence is such that it cannot be acted out, and so for both the stage is an important symbol. Juliet must decide whether to sing in public to earn money to pay her debts, and Fanny must decide whether to please her cousins by taking a part in *Lovers' Vows.* For each woman acting would mean a sacrifice of virtue. Edmund Bertram explains his own initial refusal to join in the play by saying that "the man who chooses the profession [of clergyman] itself is, perhaps, one of the last who would wish to represent it on the stage" (145), thus implying that virtue by definition is natural and cannot be dramatized. But the issue is complicated, because for Juliet and Fanny modesty conflicts with a higher duty and thus, paradoxically, threatens to become vain and selfish. If Juliet refuses to sing, tradesmen may starve, and if Fanny refuses to act, she will be overwhelmed by her sense of the "debt" she owes the Bertrams (153). Unlike Juliet, who agrees to perform and then is miraculously saved from having to do so, Fanny persists in her refusal.[61] She thus remains virtuous according to the highest ideas of her novel. She refuses to contribute to the damage to her uncle's estate, which, as Alistair Duckworth has shown, has tremendous symbolic importance (55), and she avoids the risk the amateur actor runs of either losing her identity in her role, or exposing her personality improperly.[62] (For Fanny, both risks are the same, because exposure would mean a loss of modesty and hence of personality.) But whatever her decision, she is bound to give up some of her "sweetness."

Both Anne and Fanny do exert themselves in ways that bring them to the hero, with a little help. Both to some degree must exert themselves *against* their own selflessness. If humility makes knowledge possible, knowledge, in the end, makes humility somewhat obsolete. Yet in the case of Fanny, humility is a stubborn opponent that all her exertion is insufficient to conquer, for she is hampered not only by female modesty but by the added disadvantages of youth, poverty, physical weakness, and debilitating shyness. Instead of clouding the moral picture, these seemingly incidental problems help point the satire by partially explaining, or exposing, Fanny's selflessness as not only a moral stance but a disease. They function much like the conceit that goes with Emma's queenliness and the ignorance that goes with Catherine Morland's innocence.[63]

Fanny is like Catherine in many ways. As Catherine expects to find a Gothic castle in the heart of modern England, Fanny is disappointed that the Rushworths' family chapel is not something out of a Scott romance (85-86).[64] The childhood of both heroines is presented in some detail, and both in their young and unformed state are deliberately made unpromising material for heroinehood. Catherine helps Austen burlesque the ideal of innocence, and Fanny's humility is a variation on the same theme. The men in *Mansfield Park* worship her "sweetness" because they do not recognize its connection with knowledge; instead, they read it as a sign not only of pliancy but of lack of consciousness, or ignorance. They believe this much valued quality is "natural" to women: as Crawford says, "though [a man] sometimes loves where it is not, he can never believe it absent" (294). But sweetness, as they understand it, is never present; Fanny as well as the more obviously assertive Mary Crawford demonstrates the falseness of the principle that "general nature" makes every woman "adopt the opinions of the man she loved and respected, as her own" (367). This misapprehension forces Fanny to overcome her humility, to admit that she has knowledge and opinions, and consequently a will of her own—that is, in Scudérian terms, inclination.

The men in this novel range from the idealistic Edmund to the deeply cynical Henry Crawford, with Sir Thomas somewhere in between. But Henry shares some illusions about women, and about Fanny, with the Bertram father and son because, as we saw with Lord

Rochester, libertines are often disappointed romantics. Though Fanny first attracts Henry as a novelty for his jaded palate, he eventually comes to see her as the woman he has unconsciously been looking for all his life, the woman his ultra-cynical uncle, the Admiral, wisely believes does not exist.[65] To him, Fanny's purity resides in what she does not know and hence does not want. When Fanny rejects his proposal, he "considered her rather as one who had never thought on the subject enough to be in danger; who had been guarded by youth, a youth of mind as lovely as of person; whose modesty had prevented her from understanding his attentions, and who was still overpowered by the suddenness of addresses so wholly unexpected, and the novelty of a situation which her fancy had never taken into account" (326). In short, he considers her "ignorant" of inclination, though her "genuine feeling" for her brother, a kind of tenderness, tells him she is teachable (235). Under the delusions of this sentimental theory—"He knew not that he had a pre-engaged heart to attack" (326)—he commits the biggest sin of which man is capable in women's fiction: he has recourse to parental pressure, thus choosing the path of the Scudérian villain who thinks to prove his love by "laying a force upon the inclinations" of his beloved.

Though neither Edmund nor Sir Thomas fancies the role of despot, their belief that Fanny can or should have no inclinations to be forced leads both to decide to exercise a little authority to persuade her to accept Henry. Edmund does momentarily entertain the possibility that Fanny may be in love with someone else when she rejects Henry's proposal, but his personal modesty proves as blinding in its way as is Henry's libido. Because she has seen no men but Edmund and Tom and shows no sign of special feeling for Tom, he assumes he has eliminated all the contenders. He thus urges Fanny to let Henry make his way to Tender on the River of Recognizance: "let him succeed at last, Fanny, let him succeed at last. You have proved yourself upright and disinterested, prove yourself grateful and tender-hearted; and then you will be the perfect model of a woman, which I have always believed you born for" (347). But Edmund's view of the situation is not really Scudérian, for the romance in his mind is not about Fanny but about Henry. Fanny is merely the "reward." And since Henry does not win her in the proper way, by leaving her free, the "reward" herself may be prompted to ask, "What's in it for me?" Fanny does ask this, though Edmund's fundamental error about her humility makes him unable to understand her:

> "He will make you happy, Fanny, I know he will make you happy; but you will make him every thing."

"I would not engage in such a charge," cried Fanny in a shrinking accent—"in such an office of high responsibility!"
"As usual, believing yourself unequal to anything!" [351]

Ironically, it is Sir Thomas, so grumpy at being cast in the role of *senex iratus,* who comes closest to understanding that Fanny has inclination, though that recognition arrives late and leads him to the mistaken, cynical conclusion that she must therefore be corrupt. Without seeing the error of defining female virtue as selflessness, he does see, as Henry and Edmund do not, that Fanny has a self: "I had thought you peculiarly free from wilfulness of temper, self-conceit, and every tendency to that independence of spirit, which prevails so much in modern days, even in young women, and which in young women is offensive and disgusting beyond all common offence. . . . You have shewn yourself very, very different from any thing that I had imagined" (318). Her humble demeanor led him to expect her to be at least as pliant as his own daughter, Maria, whose eagerness to marry just the man he might have chosen for her left him free to worry about whether she liked him enough. Instead, Fanny forces him to confront his "disgust" with female sexuality: "because you do not feel for Mr. Crawford exactly what a young, heated fancy imagines to be necessary for happiness, you resolve to refuse him at once, without wishing even for a little time to consider of it—a little more time for cool consideration, and for really examining your own inclinations" (318-19). Nor does he ever have to forgive Fanny her inclination for Edmund, for when Henry shows his true colors Sir Thomas need look no farther for her motives for refusing him.

The truth about Fanny is that she does "know" love, and that knowledge, rather than corrupting her, forms the basis of her moral vision. Her inclination for Edmund is bound up with her knowledge of his goodness, just as her hatred of Henry stems from her knowledge of his lack of character. Her moral judgments are inseparable from her emotions, her condemnation of Henry from her sexual revulsion or "shrinking," and her distrust of Mary from her jealousy. These feelings, and the knowledge that goes with them, conflict with her humility. The more clearly Fanny sees, the less she displays the "sweetness" these men value so highly, the more unaccountably stubborn—to Sir Thomas and Edmund—she becomes; and as long as humility remains, it threatens her insight. Just as Anne must throw herself in Wentworth's way, Fanny must "come out," both socially, as in Mary Crawford's use of the phrase, and psychologically. Edmund has said that girls whose manners change drastically once they are "out" were never sincerely modest, as Fanny is (50); therefore, when

Fanny is forced to learn to enjoy being the "Queen of the evening" at her very own ball (267), she must not merely feign confidence but must really be able to speak up for herself. She must constantly struggle against her desire to please others and to suppress her own wishes in order to avoid real wrong, such as acting in the play or marrying Henry. But in the end her efforts must be supplemented by the providential elopement of Henry and Maria, because without this contingency, the narrator speculates, in time Henry's persistence and her sweetness would have gotten the better of her inclination (467).

Mansfield Park stretches the boundaries of comedy because Fanny's position is not at all funny. In fact, through the Crawfords the novel seems to take a stand against humor that confirms many readers' sense that the author had become more religious between *Pride and Prejudice* and *Mansfield Park*—or, as it would have to have been, during the process of revising the earlier novel.[66] But the difference may result from the later novel's focus on powerlessness, as one may see by recalling a similar development in Burney's fiction. Burney was always interested in the relationship between wit and power: the way laughing at others is unkind in those with power and foolish in those without it. Evelina, who tells her own story, has great difficulty conveying the ridiculousness of her grandmother, Madame Duval, because the old woman is in serious distress when she is down and a serious nuisance when triumphant (65, 148). Burney may have switched to third-person narrator in part to free her heroines from the awkward responsibility of delivering punch lines, though that could be a heavy burden for a polite lady author/narrator as well.[67] In Burney's novels ridicule is increasingly used as a weapon employed by the privileged to keep the lowly in their place, just as the Bertram sisters as children make fun of Fanny for her ignorance of history and geography. In Burney's last novel the sarcastic jokes of Mrs. Ireton resemble the plain, ill-natured scoldings of Austen's Mrs. Norris.

In treating humor as a problem connected to problems of power and responsibility, *Mansfield Park* is not the opposite of *Pride and Prejudice* but a more focused development of one of the earlier novel's themes. Elizabeth Bennet "dearly love[s] a laugh," and her targets are never "what is wise and good," but only "follies and nonsense, whims and inconsistencies" (57). But Darcy, no doubt suspicious of female ridicule from his too-close observation of Bingley's catty sisters, points out that it may be difficult to be certain one has found an appropriate target. The novel as a whole shows that laughing is a detached response that can be both irresponsible and unrealistic, resting on a misapprehension about the power dynamics of one's social group.[68] Mr. Bennet in his library thinks he is the king of his little world, and so he laughs at his daughters instead of bringing them up. But he learns that they have the power to hurt him, and he is not laughing when Lydia forces him out of his library and up to London. "Thoughtless," "fearless" Lydia not only abuses her power by ignoring the pain she causes but is in turn unaware of her own vulnerability (292, 315). When Mrs. Gardiner wonders that she can be so "lost to every thing" as to elope with Wickham without marrying him, she means "lost" not only to virtue but to any conception of the kind of life she could be letting herself in for as the cast-off mistress of a penniless, reprobate soldier (283). With these bad examples always before her, Elizabeth comes to recognize the limits and proper uses of her own power. To a woman with no library to hide in, a woman who, seemingly, must marry somebody, even the foolish Mr. Collins has power to annoy. When he pauses in his proposal Elizabeth is too busy stifling a laugh to stop him, and thus she gives her absurd mother weapons against her as well (105). More important, as Elizabeth comes to love Darcy she finds that she has been irresponsibly ridiculing "what is wise and good," and has therefore herself been guilty of "folly," or worse.

Elizabeth's errors have been so serious that it is long before she can laugh at herself about them. But the fact that she eventually does so indicates this novel's acceptance of Shaftesbury's belief that ridicule, though dangerous, sheds light and is therefore morally useful (Duckworth 133, 135). As I intend to show, even Austen's darker novels, like Burney's, retain this principle and find new ways to fit humor into the narrative. But Austen continued exploring the way humor can be inappropriate by making this possibility central in her next novel. *Pride and Prejudice* is not "for" wit and *Mansfield Park* "against" it, for neither Elizabeth nor Fanny is Everywoman but a particular kind of woman in a particular situation. Fanny's is a "worst case scenario," a situation in which many things we know Austen liked—amateur theatricals, "liveliness," and humor—are neither right nor possible.

Since Austen wrote later that *Pride and Prejudice* was popular for its "wit" and *Mansfield Park* for its "good sense," it seems likely that to her both terms were valuable but that she was interested in the ways they might be antithetical (*L* 443). Late in 1814, Austen's niece Fanny Knight asked her advice about whether she should marry Mr. Plumtre, a man whose principles she admired but whose evangelical tendencies made him unattractively grave. Earlier, in 1809, Austen had written to her sister, in reference to Hannah More, "I do not like the Evangelicals" (*L* 256); but now, arguing each side of Fanny's dilemma by turns, she commented, "I am by no means convinced that we ought not all to be Evangelicals," for "Wisdom is better than Wit, & in the long run will certainly have the laugh on her side" (*L* 410).[69] Perhaps she was imagining Hannah More and Mr. Plumtre looking down from the great beyond and finally cracking a smile. On earth it was all too arguable that those who could see clearly were in no position to laugh, and conversely, that those who laughed were false wits who misunderstood their responsibility to those beneath them on the power scale and their vulnerability to those above them. That is the possibility that *Mansfield Park* seems designed to examine.

Wit, to fulfill its Shaftesburian function, must be centered in clear moral vision. But as long as clear vision is incompatible with power, amusement must be fleeting. In *Sense and Sensibility,* Elinor Dashwood, watching Mrs. Ferrars try to cut her by exaggerated kindness to Lucy Steele, "smiled at a graciousness so misapplied." But because the crafty Lucy very nearly succeeds in taking Edward away from her, "she could not reflect on the mean-spirited folly from which it sprung, nor observe the studied attentions with which the Miss Steeles courted its continuance, without thoroughly despising them all four" (233). Similarly Fanny has the vision, but not the disposition, for sustained amusement. She is only "not unamused to observe the selfishness which, more or less disguised, seemed to govern" the amateur actors of Mansfield (131), because at any moment they can cause her pain by insisting that she join them, or by making her observe the progress of Edmund and Mary's flirtation.

Fanny might laugh if she could, for wit is attractive. One hardly blames the "matter of fact, plain spoken" Edmund for liking the clever Mary, even if he himself "may blunder on the borders of a repartee for half an hour together without striking it out" (94). But Edmund, as usual, has everything backwards. He is amusing, even while claiming not to be so, because his wit hurts no one, but Mary's wit is false because she is unconscious of the pain she gives and receives when she thoughtlessly ridicules "what is wise and good." When asked whether she may have met William Price's captain at the home of her admiral uncle, she replies, with Miss Bingley-like snobbery, "Post captains may be very good sort of men, but they do not belong to *us*" (60), thus cutting off Edmund's kind attempt to bring Fanny into the conversation. There is a self-satiric grandeur in the remark, hinting Mary's dislike of her uncle, but the snobbery, she shows repeatedly, is her own. Mary is not unlike Mrs. Arlbery in *Camilla,* also a dangerously attractive, snobbish wit who sacrifices the feelings of the present company to the opportunity for self-expression. In this instance Fanny is sacrificed to Mary's greater interest in saying something risqué: "Of *Rears* and *Vices,* I saw enough. Now, do not be suspecting me of a pun, I entreat" (60). The line is funny, yet it would strike oddly on one's ears if one were actually present with the clergyman Dr. Grant, the soon-to-be clergyman Edmund, who "felt grave" when she said it, and three young virgins besides Mary herself. For all her cleverness and social grace, Mary has little awareness of her audience.

Mary's risqué humor is not a sign of her sexual "liberation," as it may seem in our own time, but rather, as such remarks usually were in Burney's writings, a symptom of coarseness and coldness, the female version of the libertine's cynical disbelief in love.[70] Mary's observation of her uncle's and her brother's carryings on has taught her that love is merely sex, and therefore that both love and sex are a joke. The "priggish" Fanny and Edmund, in their disgust and shock over light sexual conduct, regard sex as powerful and serious, acceptable only as an unmentioned ingredient of conjugal love. But in planning a pragmatic match for herself Mary is clearly reconciled to a life in which her own desires, if she has any, will never be fulfilled, because she regards extramarital affairs as "folly" (455). Just as Fanny's principles are bound up with her ability to love, Mary's lack of them is the result of stunted emotional development; "perhaps" she "might be equal to feel" Edmund's worth, but not steadily enough to "discuss [it] with herself," to come to know herself and to grow (65). Edmund understandably sees the waste of such a mind as tragic and feels that losing her is nothing to the disappointment of discovering what she really is. "I would infinitely prefer any increase of the pain of parting, for the sake of carrying with me the right of tenderness and esteem," he tells Fanny (458), though lacking those two Scudérian necessities we know his love for her, like Marianne's for Willoughby, will soon die out. Mary's final saucy smile, contrasted with his own stunned misery as he describes it, has a sepulchral quality. It is a failed attempt to assert an invulnerability she does not possess, to cover the sense of her defeat and loss, which Edmund believes he could see in her face nevertheless.

In the end—and every once in a while, before the end—Fanny has the advantage of Mary, but Fanny is not the girl to press that advantage with ridicule. After making fun of the clergy, when Mary discovers that Edmund is to be ordained, her "countenance . . . might have amused a disinterested observer," but the all too interested Fanny, despite her jealousy, "pitied her. 'How distressed she will be at what she said just now,' passed across her mind" (89). That Mary is distressed mostly at the possible consequences of this *faux pas* rather than at the pain she may have caused makes Fanny's sympathy that much more generous. Fanny illustrates the proper attitude of engagement instead of the detachment that would make laughter possible, and that does make it possible for the reader, and for the author. Elizabeth Bennet's spirit is still present in this dark novel, as it is in *Emma* and *Persuasion,* but not in the heroine. Nor is laughter the only privilege Fanny loses through her involvement in her own story.

If humor is connected to power, the only being in the novel powerful enough to create comedy is the author. *Mansfield Park, Emma,* and *Persuasion* all explore the basic difference between being a heroine and being an author, and thus they help to illuminate man's relationship with God, the Author who, in Austen's view, alone could turn the potential tragedies of individual lives into divine comedy.

All Austen's novels abound with characters who act as "amateur artists," as A. Walton Litz comments, imitating Austen (69-70) and, especially in the later novels, doing it badly.[71] They may be consciously writing their lives as fiction by imitating heroines, like Isabella Thorpe, or even villains, like Sir Edward Denham in the fragmentary *Sanditon,* who sees himself as Richardson's Lovelace (*MW* 404). Or they may be nonreaders who go about creating romances in an unromantic, businesslike way, like the matchmaking Mrs. Bennet in *Pride and Prejudice* and Mrs. Jennings in *Sense and Sensibility.* But however they do it, they represent a danger to those whose lives they are clumsily attempting to shape. Like Burney, Austen was aware that storytelling is potentially sado-masochistic; Catherine Morland creates dramas for herself because the "human mind can never do comfortably without" a certain amount of "solicitude," some "sportive irritations" (*NA* 221), and for the same reason the author has created Catherine's little tortures for the reader's entertainment. But these are nothing to the mischief that can be caused when private persons play author toward their real-life acquaintances. In Austen's time no one was more apt to play this game than the "world's wife," the respectable woman who, in compensation for her lack of basic rights, had been granted the power to write other women's characters. By calling Jane Bennet a "sweet girl" (*PP* 17) Miss Bingley and Mrs. Hurst "authorise" their brother to fall in love with her, and then must spend the rest of *Pride and Prejudice* trying to undo the damage. In a different way Mrs. Jennings has a dangerous power to define Marianne in *Sense and Sensibility,* for while seeing life exclusively in the terms of crude romantic comedy (any husband will do), she helps make Marianne a tragic heroine by publishing Willoughby's defection and then insisting to anyone who will listen that Marianne will "never get over it" (309).

In both these novels the heroines are allowed to thwart these ill-conceived designs by getting the pen in their own hands and writing their sisters' characters themselves. They accomplish this task in opposite ways. In *Pride and Prejudice,* Elizabeth frankly expresses her resentment at Darcy's officiously separating Jane and Bingley, and in doing so she corrects his false impression of Jane. In *Sense and Sensibility,* Elinor's silence and secrecy keep the gossips off her trail and eventually show Marianne a path to greater dignity.[72] In both novels the heroine is virtually the author of her sister's happy ending. In contrast, the later novels are set up to illustrate the difference between living one's story, which means exerting oneself within one's own sphere, and writing it, which cannot be done without controlling the lives of others. The arrangement of events on this higher plane— the harmonizing of each individual's exertions—must be trusted to another author.

The attempt of an ill-assorted group of amateur ladies and gentlemen to stage a play in *Mansfield Park* provides the perfect opportunity to explore this boundary between life and art. With no one to organize their efforts and orchestrate their egos, these characters in search of a director are fortunate that Sir Thomas comes back when he does; he saves them from spoiling their individual, conflicting fantasies of "stardom" with the inevitably messy reality of a performance.[73] The only character with a directorial vision of the whole—not only of the play, but of the various other "plots" afoot—has that vision only by virtue of her lack of authority. Characters are "connected" by Fanny's "consciousness" (163); she knows how Julia Bertram feels when Henry begins to ignore her. But this is not a real connection because Julia does not recognize it. Only the author's consciousness can fit characters together into the same world.

I have said that *Emma* at first may not seem to fit the pattern of the later novels, since it is not built around a selfless heroine. But by making Emma the exact inverse of Fanny (and thus, incidentally, linking Fanny with Emma's foil, Jane Fairfax), Austen leads this novel to the central truth of *Mansfield Park* from the opposite direction. Whereas Fanny is constantly aware of a greater, shaping force in her life—so aware that she is often helpless to act—Emma must learn to notice and appreciate this force and to work within its scheme. Humor is an issue in this novel as it was in *Mansfield Park,* and the climax of the novel occurs when Emma ridicules and humiliates Miss Bates. For the reader, and of course for the author, Miss Bates is ridiculous, just as Mary Crawford is amusing. But for Emma in her position to laugh at Miss Bates in hers is "brutal" and "cruel" (376), an abuse of her power that, as Mr. Knightley observes, sets an example of contempt for others to follow (375).

Emma is usually read as a novel of humiliation or "mortification" (Tave 146), though the exact nature of the heroine's delusions of grandeur is often debated.[74] Some see her as a female quixote who must learn that she is not a heroine, while others note that as an "imaginist" Emma is more of a would-be author. I argue that her humbling consists of discovering that she *is* a heroine, and *merely* a heroine.[75] Jane Spencer compares *Emma* to *Betsy Thoughtless* (141), and the parallel is worth examining. In one important way Emma is the opposite of the mirror-addicted Betsy, for Mr. Knightley admits she is almost unaware of her physical charms (39). Rather than seeing herself wholly as an object, Emma imagines herself as invisible, like God, and is therefore shocked that Mr. Elton should think of possessing her.[76] She does assume she is Frank Churchill's object, but only because she has determined to make herself manifest to him. She is the first Austen heroine whose subjectivity, the result of being the novel's central consciousness, is treated as a technical problem.[77] She reminds the reader that no human being is a disembodied brain, and that therefore no one is above being made a character in someone else's story. But this difference between Emma and Betsy is an effect of a deeper similarity, for each in her way is "vain," unaware of how she appears to others and of how much these others matter. Both are gradually brought to be worthy of "Trueworth" by learning that they are not immune to love. Betsy must give up her cold coquetry, and Emma her matchmaking, and both must allow themselves to be swept up in romances of their own.[78]

From the beginning of the novel, Emma's moments of clearest insight are also her moments of least power, though she mistakenly believes otherwise; she thinks that her "lucky guess" that Miss Taylor would marry Mr. Weston "made the match" between them (13, 11). When she does act to bring about matches, on the other hand, she reveals seriously clouded perceptions, confirming Mr. Knightley's opinion that this is not a "worthy employment for a young lady's mind!" (12). Emma has gotten the idea, probably from novels, that Harriet Smith has the makings of a heroine: the blonde, bovine look, the vacant blue eyes of polarized, ultra-femininity, and a character both "simple" and "modest" (141), or rather "simple-minded and ignorant" (142).[79] Harriet looks like the perfect heroine-as-object, the opposite of Emma as Emma sees herself, until it appears that Harriet is competing with her for Mr. Knightley and likely, Emma believes, to win. When the shocking revelation comes to her, or "dart[s] through her, with the speed of an arrow, that Mr. Knightley must marry no one but herself!" (408), it comes in a Petrarchan metaphor charged with eroticism that succinctly tells us that Emma has found her inclination at last (Steiner 95-96). Without knowing it she has not been the author of *Harriet* but the central character of *Emma,* subject to all the dangerous adventures and eventual happiness of a heroine of romance.

Not that Emma learns to be merely passive; rather she learns that it is her job to mind the turning of her own little wheel. When she stops matchmaking, apologizes to Miss Bates, and then looks for the first chance to let Mr. Knightley know she has done so, she makes herself both morally ready and available for him. She cannot make the Bridegroom appear, but she can and must trim her lamp and go out to meet him. Even in resigning herself to losing Knightley, Emma conducts herself in a way that paradoxically but plausibly helps lead her to him. She controls her distress in order to hear him speak, she thinks, of Harriet, and finds herself listening to his declaration of love for herself. Here one sees a striking difference between the resignation of the Austen heroine and that of the earlier, Betsy Thoughtless type, for while both need a miracle, Austen shows how Providence can make miracles out of the correct actions of humans. And thus the heroine moves closer to her goal even when she has stopped trying to get there.

Resignation depends on self-denial, or according to the titles of Mary Brunton's novels, "Discipline" and "Self-Control."[80] Women novelists ever since Burney, both radical and conservative, often pointed out that emotions conflict with each other, and that therefore expressing one may mean suppressing another.[81] Passion in particular was seen as potentially self-destructive and thus obstructive of real love. When Marianne Dashwood stops short of dying for love and "exerts" herself to recover (*SS* 342), she suppresses her passion and grief for Willoughby in order to preserve her greater and more important love for her mother and sister, and for God (346). And she finally appreciates that Elinor's politeness is not conduct-book correctness but an expression of this love, which holds "society" together, and that, once again, the sister with "sense" has been the romantic one all along. Similarly, in *Persuasion* Wentworth almost comes to see in Anne's rejection the strength of her love for Lady Russell, to whom she owed the "duty" of a child to a parent, rather than the weakness of her love for him (246). A woman who can command her feelings loves more deeply than one who, like Julia Musgrove, simply must have her way; once Wentworth is to be Anne's husband, duty and desire are united into the strongest bond of all.[82]

Self-denial not only makes these heroines deserving of love, it actually lights the Bridegroom's way to their door. Betsy Thoughtless and Harriot Stuart chiefly learn not to flirt, not to chatter, not to stay out all night at balls and masquerades and playhouses, essentially not to be seen by either the wrong men or the right ones. But Austen's heroines perform positive acts of service that, eventually, make their strength and worth shine through the veil of their "sweetness." When Julia Musgrove falls off the Cobb at Lyme, she makes several other members of her party ill, but Anne, though often suffering herself, is a general healer. She shows that quality well before the Cobb incident, when she plays the piano for others to dance, walks herself tired to keep peace among the Musgroves, humors her sister Mary, and nurses her injured nephew, and Wentworth sees it all. Julia's fall merely shows him in a sudden flash that Anne's is the foot that fits his glass slipper. Even in the tiny circle in which she is permitted to move and act, she demonstrates—and Wentworth takes the lesson—that choosing the right husband is not the only meaningful choice a woman can make, and that heroism is as possible for her as it is for the men who protect England from Napoleon.[83]

The happy ending shows that the heroine's world turns not only on its own axis but in a complicated yet definite orbit around some other body that we cannot quite see. This larger pattern provides the comic enclosure for the story and shows how even the darkest life can be lightened with humor.[84] Although humor presents a moral problem, it remains important to the novels' ultimate moral vision in two main ways: as part of the characters' engaged response to their troubles, and as the force behind the narrator's detached satiric judgments.

Humor can make people in Austen's novels cruel, as we have seen, yet a type of humor far removed from wit and repartee is essential to the good characters' humanity. This type of humor is part of a deliberate determination to be happy, for although Austen's heroines spend a significant amount of exertion in resignation, theirs is not the pessimistic stoicism of Samuel Johnson.[85] Stuart Tave notes that in the *OED*'s definition of "exertion," a citation from Austen is preceded by one from a sermon by Secker recommending "a proper Exertion of that Chearfulness, which God hath plainly designed us to shew" (Tave 113). Self-control, which we have seen can lead to love, also helps produce this cheerfulness. The power of the selfish to satisfy their own wants is not absolute; the Christian believes that in time—and within a novel that time can be made conveniently short—greed will overreach itself. The vice brings its own punishment because the greedy by their very nature are unable to bear disappointment. Thus in *Mansfield Park* Julia Bertram, lacking "that higher species of self-command, that just consideration of others, that knowledge of her own heart, that principle of right" that would help her cheer up after

Henry stops flirting with her, can only fume and pout and run off with Yates (91). Her sister's fate is even worse, if possible: unable to do without any of the various conflicting things she wants, she elopes with Crawford soon after marrying Rushworth, and ends up living with her Aunt Norris without the consolation of a humble spirit to make this penance tolerable.

The Christian cultivates cheerfulness as a means of adjustment to the certain yet unexpected pains of life, but that cultivation is a complicated and easily misunderstood process. On this subject Austen's letters provide a useful gloss on the novels. Austen began writing novels in much the same spirit that she wrote her letters, with her family in mind. One reason the later novels may have become darker is that she gradually became aware that her rapidly expanding, heterogeneous audience was missing the dark undertones her family would have recognized in her humor, in much the same way that her Christian cheerfulness could be mistaken for insensitivity or simple good nature. Reading the letters helps restore the sense of the novels' original audience; it also brings out some of the emotional depth of the early novels and shows their consistency in tone and theme with those of her later phase.

First, the letters show that cheerfulness did not mean, in Burney's phrase, "insipid placidity" of character (*Wanderer* 661). Austen believed that good people are highly susceptible to grief; several of her nieces and nephews lost their parents, and she was always relieved to see them affected: "One must hope the impression *will* be strong" (*L* 221); "Edward and George . . . *behave extremely* well in every respect, showing quite as much feeling as one wishes to see" (225). But when that interval of grief was over she was the first to help them bounce back with water parties and games of spillikins and bilbocatch. Second, Austen, like Burney, distinguished between true cheerfulness and mere "buoyant spirits" (*Wanderer* 661). Hence, Mrs. Smith in *Persuasion,* for all her natural "disposition to be comforted," is not a perfect role model (154). In fact, her flexibility in switching quickly from congratulating Anne on her coming marriage to Elliot to revealing his "black" villainy when she learns they are not engaged casts some doubt on the stability of her judgment (195-99).[86] But Mrs. Smith does help Anne acquire true cheerfulness, because as the heroine contemplates the goodness of God in bestowing this "gift" of buoyancy on Mrs. Smith in compensation for her hard life, she reasons herself into optimism and strengthens her faith. This is the adult version of bilbocatch.

True cheerfulness, Burney wrote, is "a disposition of thankful

enjoyment for all that can be attained of good, blended with resignation upon principle to all that must be endured of evil" (*Wanderer*
661); it is a way of coping with the unpredictable winds—or, in the
symbolism of *Persuasion,* the waves—of Providence (Nina Auerbach,
Imprisonment, 46-48). Nor is it only the sailor who is engaged in this
risky enterprise. To ride out Providence successfully one needs, not
the firmness of a nut, as Wentworth believes, but the "elasticity" of a
sail. This too is demonstrated, most poetically, in Austen's letters, in a
passage describing a storm that blew down some of her favorite elm
trees:

> I was sitting alone in the dining-room when an odd kind of
> crash startled me—in a moment afterwards it was repeated; I
> then went to the window, which I reached just in time to see
> the last of our two highly valued Elms descend into the
> Sweep!!!!! The other, which had fallen, I suppose, in the first
> crash & which was the nearest to the pond, taking a more
> easterly direction, sunk among our screen of chestnuts and
> firs, knocking down one spruce-fir, beating off the head of
> another & stripping the two corner chestnuts of several
> branches in its fall.—This is not all.—One large Elm out of
> two on the left-hand side as you enter what I call the Elm
> walk, was likewise blown down, the Maypole bearing the
> weathercock was broke in two, and what I regret more than
> all the rest is, that all the three Elms which grew in Hall's
> meadow & gave such ornament to it, are gone.—Two were
> blown down & the other so much injured that it cannot
> stand.—I am happy to add however that no greater Evil than
> the loss of trees has been the consequence of the Storm in this
> place, or in our immediate neighbourhood.—We greive there-
> fore in some comfort. [86]

Through all the violence of the verbs and excess of exclamation points,
it is clear that Austen's unhappiness about the trees is real; the tone
does not quite rise to mock-epic because the content will not fall to
the trivial.[87] Nevertheless, the next-to-last sentence shows her struggling with duty, and the last shows some self-mockery in the recognition that the attempt is not quite successful and even a little absurd.

Clearly for Austen one route to cheerfulness was the amusement
to be found in such "whims and inconsistencies" as grieving in comfort. But this sort of humor is not cold or detached; it rather assumes
that grief is too common and too deeply felt to need expression, and
that lightness is an attempt at healing.[88] In this spirit Fanny Knight

wrote "kind, amusing letters" to her Aunt Jane on her deathbed when, as Cassandra later wrote, "I know your feelings would have dictated so different a style" (*L* 513). In Jane's own amusing letters to Cassandra she could be sure that the awareness of pain would not be missed. For example, when she was visiting her brother Edward and found herself, Catherine-like, without an escort home, she wrote: "My Father will be so good as to fetch home his prodigal Daughter from Town, I hope, unless he wishes me to walk the Hospitals, enter at the Temple, or mount Guard at St. James. . . . I had once determined to go with Frank to-morrow and take my chance &c.; but they dissuaded me from so rash a step—as I really think on consideration it would have been; for if the Pearsons were not at home, I should inevitably fall a Sacrifice to the arts of some fat Woman who would make me drunk with Small Beer" (*L* 17-18). Cassandra no doubt knew without being told that always being left at the mercy of everyone else's convenience was really annoying (Sulloway 100-101).[89] Finding humor in what could not be helped was her sister's way of cultivating a cheerful spirit.

The satire found in this letter, with its burlesque allusions to sensational fiction, is very much like that of Austen's early novels. And in a similar way the novels' first readers would have needed only slight hints to see that Catherine Morland's experiences are truly Gothic in their way, and to understand, as William and Richard Austen-Leigh did not (264-5), that Elizabeth's determination to be happy without Darcy does not mean she has a cold heart. Austen knew that the feeling behind humor is only properly understood between close friends. While Cassandra was off attending the deathbed of Mrs. Lloyd, Jane wrote to her, "The Nonsense I have been writing in this and in my last letter, seems out of place at such a time, but I will not mind it; it will do you no harm, & nobody else will be attacked by it" (*L* 149-50). And when she tried to refuse Mrs. Knight's gift of a spinning wheel, she wrote, "I had a great mind to add that if she persisted in giving it, I would spin nothing with it but a rope to hang myself—but I was afraid of making it appear a less serious matter of feeling than it really is" (285). Thus, when she wrote that *Pride and Prejudice* "wants shade" (299), she may have been thinking of the need to spell out for the general reader the awareness of pain that her closest readers already knew was there.

In Austen's novels as in her letters, this awareness of pain produces a kind of humor that is perfectly consistent with manners and morality: engaged, sympathetic, human, and in the deepest sense cheerful. This is the sort of humor that can be safely indulged by people, or characters, in the conduct of their social lives. Yet the more incisive humor that comes from a detached perspective has its proper times—when one is reading or writing novels, for example—and its moral uses in honing the judgment. As the reader shares the narrator's broader perspective, she finds that many of the lessons in humor seen from the characters' point of view are reinforced. Clear vision, of course, is supremely important at either level. One sees even more clearly from the narrator's eminence that it is the Christian's duty to cultivate cheerfulness, though from there one sees it chiefly in the stern condemnation of those who fail even to try to do so.

Again, the letters provide a useful gloss. In life the people who annoyed Austen most as she struggled to be cheerful were those who magnified their own sufferings, "look[ing] about with great diligence & success for Inconvenience & Evil" (L 232). Despite Cassandra's excisions, one still sees that in writing letters to her sister Jane gave vent to critical judgments against members of her family that she could not express in her direct dealings with them. During a crisis in her mother's financial affairs, for example, her aunt Mrs. Leigh Perrot, who was directly involved in the difficulties, wrote Mrs. Austen a letter all about her own petty concerns, "among which she ingeniously places the danger of her new Housemaids catching cold on the outside of the Coach, when she goes down to Bath—for a carriage makes her sick." "[T]he discontentedness" of this letter "shocked & surprised" Mrs. Austen, "but I see nothing in it out of Nature—tho' a sad nature" (L 232). In much the same way Jane complained of her brother James: "I am sorry & angry that his Visits should not give one more pleasure; . . . his time here is spent I think in walking about the House & banging the doors, or ringing the bell for a glass of water" (181). Unlike Edward, who made the most of cold weather and became "all alive & chearful," "[p]oor James, on the contrary, must be running his Toes into the fire" (354-55).

Where her own family was concerned, Austen could not be completely detached, even when writing to Cassandra, and hence their doings made her more "sorry & angry" than amused. But when writing stories she could allow indignation to rise into satiric scorn. Seen in this way the narrator's apparent cruelty toward Mrs. Musgrove in *Persuasion,* which many readers like to think would have been softened in a further revision, is perfectly consistent with Austen's ideas and with her later uses of humor.[90] She asks the reader to sneer at Mrs. Musgrove's "large, fat sighings" over the death of her son because we know what no one actually in the room with her can know for certain: that "nobody had cared for" Dick Musgrove when he was alive, and that his mother is doing the opposite of her duty in manufacturing unnecessary grief while the truly suffering but determinedly cheerful Anne sits by, unheeded as usual (68). Our privileged position not only permits but enjoins us to register the "contempt" that Wentworth himself hides from everyone but Anne, who can read even the briefest of his facial expressions, so that we may learn in principle what kind of conduct does and does not deserve pity.

Yet we applaud Wentworth's restraint, his respect for tears that for all he knows may be genuine. The fundamental statement about life in Austen's late fiction is that the engaged and the detached perspectives work properly together only when each is understood to have its own proper occasions. As an author who believed in the supreme importance of social ties, Austen was naturally interested in the way her profession fit into her life, and by extension the way living an examined life affected personal relationships. Her last works, particularly *Emma, Persuasion,* and the unfinished *Sanditon,* show her conviction that the most serious wrong one human being can commit in dealing with another is to assume an authorial power and vision she does not possess. The later novels, as we have seen, are concerned with the problem of using what one knows. They are equally concerned with the problem of using one's awareness of what one does not know. In Burney's *The Wanderer* this awareness is supposed to increase the reader's faith in God and in other people. Similarly, in *Pride and Prejudice,* Elizabeth learns among other things that her moral judgments have been too rigid; Jane's "candour," though it is often naive, makes her admit "one does not know what to think" (86) and thus leaves more room for adjustment to new information (Susan Morgan 101). In that early novel, one does eventually learn what to think; the last works, in contrast, are constructed around the possibility that one may never find out.[91]

Uncertainty belongs more to the Fairfax-Churchill subplot of *Emma* than to the main design. Like Burney and Radcliffe before her, Austen there leaves unresolved the question of what Jane Fairfax ought to have done. She proves her excellence, like Cecilia and Ellena, by being very severe with herself about her secret engagement, but in doing so she ensures the leniency of Mrs. Weston, Emma, and the reader (400), so that the whole affair becomes, to paraphrase Anne Elliot, "one of those cases in which [a decision] is good or bad only as the event decides" (*P* 246). Even more doubtful is Jane's chance for happiness. Frank's willingness to involve her in a painful situation suggests some selfishness and carelessness, which, like Cecilia's Delvile and Ellena's Vivaldi, he puts down to his excess of passion (437). His levity when all has been revealed (480), far more than his tendency to frighten Mr. Woodhouse by leaving doors open, shows him to be "not quite the thing" (249). But though Frank is no

Mr. Knightley, his character is not finally determined, for it is not finally known; his willingness to "look forward . . . to any thing, every thing—to time, chance, circumstance," an inherited "disposition to hope for good" (437), is proved right by the event—and supported by the heroine of Austen's next novel, in which this kind of flexibility is crucial to the main plot. Anne is not perfect, but in rejecting Wentworth she manages to be wrong without being wrong; that is, she comes to see the decision as a mistake and yet, under the same circumstances, she would make the same mistake again. If mistakes are thus inevitable, then human beings must be not only ready to take second chances but generous enough to give them, as Wentworth owes it to Anne to propose to her again. Human judgment should never be considered final.

If B.C. Southam's projections are correct, *Sanditon* would have taken this idea a technical step further by making the characters mysterious not only to each other but to the reader (*Manuscripts* 121-2). Our only way of understanding them would have been the way of the heroine, Charlotte Heywood, "a very sober-minded young Lady, sufficiently well-read in Novels to supply her Imagination with amusement, but not at all unreasonably influenced by them" (*MW* 391-92). That is not to say that she knows the difference between novels and life, but that she is adept at looking for connections and constantly seeks to correct her impressions. She first enjoys imagining Clara Brereton as "the most perfect representation of whatever Heroine might be most beautiful & bewitching, in all the numerous vol:ˢ they had left behind them" at the Circulating Library (391); then she admits that Clara's promisingly dependent "situation with Lady Denham" is unromantically "comfortable" (391, 392); and, finally, she makes a third adjustment back toward romance when she sees Clara privately conversing with Sir Edward Denham (426). But Clara is not the only candidate for heroinehood, for just before Charlotte sees her outside the library she has been considering her own similarity to and determined difference from Burney's Camilla (390). Twenty-one years after the publication of that novel, without furnishing a single detail, Austen still expected her readers to pick up an allusion to an episode in which Camilla overspends. In her last work as well as her first, Austen was relying on other authors' novels to help her heroines and her readers develop the mental and emotional agility to encounter the unknown.[92]

If novels affected people's attitudes and behavior, as Sir Anthony Absolute assumed they affected those of Lydia Languish, they altered the reality they described. Therefore, Austen's contention that it was "reasonable" rather than "romantic" for young women to marry for love was as polemical in its way as Delarivière Manley's fictional autobiography a century earlier: both described people believing something in order to make people believe it. And so fiction and life were not only alike, or related, but intertwined, or "married."

Authors and readers were likewise joined as partners in the very best sort of exertion. Writing and reading novels helped Austen cultivate a cheerful spirit while cementing familial bonds. Just as Elinor Dashwood paints instead of pining over Edward (*SS* 104), Austen discovered a means of creative self-expression that helped her to manage very well in the absence of a hero. But her efforts, like Elinor's, began in much the same spirit of family "usefulness" as Catherine Morland's sewing of her brother's cravats, or Emma's careful superintendence of Mr. Woodhouse's gruel. Mary Lascelles has referred to Austen's writing as "an act of hospitality" (146); in the pages of her novels readers and novelists seem to come together in a family drawing room to converse about what they have all been reading.[93]

In this way Austen made friends with her predecessors and began her own exertions where theirs had left off. If she was able to wed realism to romance in her novels, it was largely because the obstacles to the match had already been exposed and, through exposure, partially removed. If women had not persisted in bringing romance conventions into realistic and didactic fictions, against the better judgment of critical authority, neither life nor the novel would have been in a position for a mutual embrace. If, for example, women novelists had accepted the notion that "real life" is free from "adventures," they would not have been able to construct plots that demonstrated the unfairness of blaming women for their own literal and figurative rape. Nor would a narrative have evolved that was capable of accommodating a vision of life as only partly within human control. And if women novelists had let "realism" suffocate their dreams of a happy marriage to a man of their choice, it would never have become evident that women have a will not unlike that of men. Nor would a fictional form have developed capable of measuring what *is* against what *should be*.

In building her own successes on the achievements of others, Austen helped ensure that the work of eighteenth-century women novelists would affect the direction of the novel in the nineteenth century. This influence is most obvious in the persistence of Scudéry's language of tenderness in Victorian fiction—in Trollope and George Eliot, to name only two—and more broadly in the pastoral and Gothic motifs that continued to appear in the "great" novels, by men and by women, in Europe, Russia, and America (Kiely 255). But perhaps their most important contribution came, ironically, from the disadvantages under which they labored. When critics of the Johnson school recommended that novels provide models of virtue, rendered as believable as possible, they assumed a reader who would go forth into the world and make a life following these examples.[94] But when women writers created female models, the prescribed realistic treatment revealed that morality often had less to do with shaping worlds than with enduring and adjusting to what could not be changed. One result of this discovery was the development of an attitude of critical accommodation, a recognition that one could follow rules, whether of ballroom etiquette or of obedience to fathers and husbands, without necessarily becoming either happy or, in the highest sense, good. The awareness of moral ambiguity, along with female delicacy, produced narrators reluctant to make pronouncements from on high, as Fielding had done, and eventually gave the Austen narrator her unobtrusive, multidirectional irony. In these ways women novelists were of central importance in moving the novel beyond narrow, conduct-book didacticism toward a more subtle and searching, and thus more deeply moral, criticism of life.

Women arrived at this profound, flexible view of fiction and of life not by transcending gender but through the experience of being female. Readers of both sexes may respond to Austen's novels more readily than to those of her predecessors, but her heroines are their heroines' daughters. Austen was able to show that the female condition they all shared was representatively human because to her all human power was limited. Therefore, just as Austen encouraged her readers to take old novels with them in reading hers, one can also profitably take hers along on a backward journey into eighteenth-century fiction. If, as Austen suggested, those with the least power of action can see most clearly, then early women novelists have a good claim to special vision. And if the "universal truth" they could glimpse from their window on the world was how little any mortal can do, they made it possible for others to continue the endless quest to determine what that little should be.

Notes

Note: Unless otherwise indicated, all translations from French to English are mine.

Introduction: A Secret History of the English Novel

Epigraph: Lennox, *The Female Quixote*, 418.

1. There were ancient Greek and Latin stories that are now called romances, but the word in English originally denoted a modern language phenomenon.

2. See D. Kelly 78; E. Auerbach 141.

3. See Frye, *Secular Scripture*, 26.

4. Nelson is quoting the title of a book by F.S. Fussner (41). See also Adams 12.

5. See also Nelson 53.

6. Adams notes that all artists were considered liars in the late seventeenth century (82). He discusses several of the fiction writer's defenses against charges of falsehood (88-93).

7. Hunter, "Novels," 480; Davis 45ff. Both McKeon and Hunter place the taste for "news" in the early eighteenth century, though McKeon sees something like it in the previous century; see, for example, McKeon 47-48, 54-55; Hunter, "Young," 261. This shift in taste has been compared to the change in sixteenth-century Spain that produced *Don Quixote;* see Harry Sieber, "The Romance of Chivalry in Spain from Rodriguez de Montalvo to Cervantes," in Brownlee, 214-17; see also McKeon 292-94.

8. As the encyclopedist Bayle phrased it, "The new Romances keep as far off as possible from the Romantick Way" (Nelson 109; and Davis 38).

9. Not all Scudéry's characters are beautiful; the ugly, satirical Aricidia in *Clelia* is an example of the psychological realism often overlooked in Scudéry's work. See Schofield, *Masking*, 21.

10. Hurd shows that even Boileau's own words found their way into the writings of English critics—including Shaftesbury and Addison—who were sympathetic to the romance (79-86).

11. See Nelson (76-77) on ambivalence in Shakespeare; in Spenser's *The Faerie Queene* (77ff.). In England romance sometimes migrated to the stage; Scudéry's romances were sources for Dryden's heroic dramas. By the 1690s that genre was also largely taken over by women such as Delarivière Manley (Hook, intro. to *The Female Wits*, ii).

12. See Trowbridge, intro. to Hurd, vi.

13. See D. Kelly 77, 87; Nelson 93; Uitti 137, 141. These early claims of truth, which resemble the "naive empiricism" McKeon attributes to readers in the early eighteenth century, show that one cannot simply distinguish "romance" from

"novel" along the lines of Bakhtin's distinction between "truth of idea" and "experiential actual." See Zimbardo 48.

14. The first listing for "realism" in the *OED* is from Ruskin, 1856; Davis suggests that the concept as well as the term did not quite exist before then either (177-78).

15. See Nelson on Scudéry, 100; Adams notes her accuracy in details about foreign countries, drawn from travel literature (113).

16. On theorists' attempts to simplify the novel, see Davis 113; McKeon 88; and Hunter, "Novels," 498. Beasley counts the persistence of romance elements as one of the defining characteristics of the novel ("Life's Episodes" 21).

17. Hunter notes that the "larger cultural embracing of the present moment as a legitimate subject . . . for serious discourse" opened the way for women writers such as Fanny Burney ("News" 495, 504); but a personal diary is hardly "news" in the same way that politics is. See Gardiner 205.

18. If one accepts McKeon's theory that the novel appeared only after a painstaking process whereby readers became able to understand a work of fiction as "realistic" rather than true or false, then women's position may have given them a shortcut to this understanding.

19. See Horowitz 257. This "unisex" romance convention runs counter to that noted by Boone (32-33, 40-42), who also refers to texts that show resemblance between the sexes as anti-romantic (12).

20. See Jane Spencer xi.

21. See Kirkham 37, 165.

22. See Warren's argument that men considered romance reading and writing a desirable hobby for women (368).

23. See Frye on the "revolutionary" potential of romance (*Secular Scripture* 178). Brownstein notes how easily the heroine of male romances could become conscious, since she had nothing to do and therefore had plenty of time to think (35-37).

24. See Spencer 28.

25. Passages from *Clelia* have been taken from the translation by John Davies, the version known to most seventeenth- and eighteenth-century English readers. I suspect that this translation was responsible for Scudéry's bad reputation among some English readers. The original French appears in notes, with only minor changes to conform to modern printing; accents remain unchanged. "Tenderness" and "Inclination" are "Tendre" and "Inclination" in *Clélie*. For a discussion of the Map of Tender, see Brownstein 38; Aronson 93-95; and Doody, *A Natural Passion*, 294-97; the map is reprinted in Doody's book.

"Mais pour ceux que je mets au rang de mes tendres Amis, ils sont en fort petit nombre; & ils sont si avant dans mon coeur, qu'on n'y peut jamais faire plus de progrés" (1:391).

26. "vous verrez qu'elle a imaginé qu'on peut avoir de la tendresse par trois causes differentes; ou par une grande estime, ou par reconnoissance, ou par inclination; & c'est ce qui l'a obligée d'establir ces trois Villes de Tendre, sur trois Rivieres qui portent ces trois noms, & de faire aussi trois routes differents pour y aller. Si bien que comme on dit Cumes sur la Mer d'Ionie, & Cumes sur la Mer Thyrrene, elle fait qu'on dit Tendre sur Inclination, Tendre sur Estime, & Tendre sur Reconnoissance" (1:399-400).

27. "de jolis Vers, de Billet galant, & de Billet doux, . . . Sincerité, Grand Coeur, Probité, Generosité, Respect, Exactitude, & Bonté"; "Complaisance," "Soumission," "Petits Soins," "Assiduité," "Empressement," "Grands Services," "Sensibilité," "Obeïssance," "Constante Amitié" (1:400-403).

28. "Lac d'Indifference . . . qui par ses eaux tranquiles, represente sans doute fort juste, la chose dont il porte le nom en cét endroit"; "mer d'Inimitié, . . . qui par l'agitation de ses Vagues, convient sans doute fort juste, avec cette impetueuse passion, que Clelie veut representer" (1:404).

29. "qui va si viste, qu'on n'a que faire de logement le long de ses Rives, pour aller de Nouvelle Amitié à Tendre" (1:400).

30. "faire connoistre sur cette Carte, qu'elle n'avoit jamais eu d'amour, & qu'elle n'auroit jamais dans le coeur que de la tendresse, fait que la Riviere d'Inclination se jette dans une Mer qu'on apelle la Mer dangereuse; parce qu'il est assez dangereux à une Femme, d'aller un peu au delà des dernieres Bornes de l'amitié; & elle fait en suitte qu'au delà de cette Mer, c'est ce que nous apellons Terres inconnuës, parce qu'en effet nous ne scavons point ce qu'il y a . . . de faire entendre d'une maniere particuliere, qu'elle n'a point eu d'amour, & qu'elle n'en peut avoir" (1:405). Note the mistranslation of the last clause above.

31. Sex can even be against inclination, for one can lust against one's will. See Manley, *NAt*, 2:102; qtd. in Richetti 151.

32. See Newton 8-9, 11, 21; Poovey 241; Schofield, *Masking*, 27; Boone 2, 7-10. Boone does note that the marriage for *love* (37), especially between equal partners, as in Spenser and Shakespeare (56-57), could be subversive.

33. "D'abord tu la verras, ainsi que dans Clélie / Recevant ses Amans sous le doux nom d'Amis, / S'en tenir avec eux aux petits soins permis: / Puis, bien-tost en grande eau sur le fleuve de Tendre, / Naviguer à souhait, tout dire, et tout entendre. / Et ne présume pas que Venus, ou Satan / Souffre qu'elle en demeure aux Termes du Roman" (67).

34. Boileau claimed to have abstained from publishing or even writing down the *Dialogue des Héros de Roman* while Scudéry was alive out of respect (445); but the dates do not bear out this explanation. See notes to the *Dialogue* in the *Oeuvres Complètes* and White, *Nicolas de Boileau* (NY: Twayne, 1969), 19, 77-78. Boileau made other satiric references to Scudéry during her lifetime: in *Satire X*, as we have seen, and in Canto V, the Battle of the Books, in *Le Lutrin* (White 76).

35. "Rit des vains amateurs du Grec et du Latin; / Dans la balance met Aristote et Cotin; / Puis, d'une main encor plus fine et plus habile / Peze sans passion Chappelain et Virgile; / Remarque en ce dernier beaucoup de pauvretez; / Mais pourtant confessant qu'il a quelques beautez" (74).

36. Davis (27) emphasizes that the word "romance" suggests its Roman ancestry; see M.S. Brownlee 220. There is a class issue here: the "moderns" were associated with the middle class, and Boileau's criticism of the précieuses and of romances had something to do with their vulgarity. This may surprise readers of our own time, accustomed to regarding Scudéry and her circle as aristocratic, but it is an important reminder that class is no more reliable as a means of distinguishing romance from novel than any of the other criteria of criticism; see McKeon 268. Frye sees romance as a periodically recurring "proletarian" reaction against elitist literature (*Secular Scripture* 23).

37. Attacks on Scudéry herself in England were not always anti-feminist because not everyone knew how many of the works published under her brother's name were really hers.

38. See El Saffar's comments on Cervantes (249-50).

39. See Poovey xv.

40. On the issue of who was "first," see Gardiner. Although Davis questions the "firstness" of Defoe in the light of Behn's contribution, he misses the fact that she, not Fielding, was the first English novelist to include an account of a contem-

porary historical event, in *Love Letters from a Nobleman to his Sister*—which, though in many respects close to French romance, thus also fits his definition of the novel (see 201).

41. For example: Davis distinguishes novels from romances by noting that novels claim to be true (36) and distinguishes romantic from novelistic verisimilitude (30-33), yet writes later about novels that are avowed fictions (Henry Fielding's, 200) and about something like romantic "bienséance" in the novel (111). He admits that the roman à clef has characteristics he attributes to the novel, but does not include Scudéry in this category although she wrote them (36). McKeon writes about the gradual evolution of realism, the ability to read something that is neither strictly true nor false, through dialectical struggles with the nature of truth; yet Nelson shows that there was a way of doing this earlier, with the Apocrypha (21-22, 35). Hunter writes that male and female young people needed realistic novels to help them understand their daily lives in the early eighteenth century ("Young" 271-72), but I do not see why Scudéry's romances could not have been read for similar reasons, though by a different group of readers. Adams' premise is that from an international point of view romance and novel are impossible to distinguish; yet even he makes the curious distinguishing statement that "no important dramatist in the seventeenth century wrote fiction of any significance" (31), momentarily and uncharacteristically forgetting Behn. His emphasis on travel in both romance and novel also presents a problem for women, who traveled less as the eighteenth century progressed, and whose travel in earlier fiction is more part of the ravishers' quests than their own. Even Clelia's map (which he discusses, 271) mostly points out routes to male travelers; Clelia is the destination.

42. See *The Subjection of Women* [1869]: *Essays on Sex Equality,* ed. Alice Rossi (Cambridge, MA: MIT Press, 1970), 69.

43. Todd criticizes the separate *Norton Anthology* for women writers because of this nineteenth-century bias (*Feminist Literary History* 48). Schofield applies the Gilbert and Gubar type of reading to eighteenth-century novels (*Masking* 9). Other examples of "double" studies: Goreau (5) writes of two Aphra Behns; Schofield refers to Haywood's "double writing" (*Eliza Haywood* 5-6); Straub has entitled her study of Burney *Divided Fictions;* the introduction to *Fetter'd or Free?* calls eighteenth-century women novelists "Janus-like" (1).

44. Conversely, realism is seen as a sign of originality and rebellion. See Simons 24, 32; Spender 21; Figes 16. See also Hunter on the present narrowness of the canon ("Contexts" 128-29, 133-34).

45. "Gynocritics" is a term coined by Elaine Showalter; see "Toward a Femininst Poetics" in *The New Feminist Criticism,* ed. Showalter (NY: Pantheon, 1985), 128-29.

46. Cf. Schofield, *Masking,* 10. In this study I hope to show some of the positive effects of feminism on historicism which Hunter writes about ("Contexts" 133) and also to work within Todd's projections for the future of feminist criticism (*Feminist Literary History* 98-9, 136).

47. See McKeon 14; Hunter, "Novels," 480. Defoe and Fielding are especially praised for their open-endedness by Davis, McKeon and Hunter. Recent criticism on Burney by Straub and Doody has made significant progress toward the reevaluation of her work; see Straub 2-3, and Margaret Drabble's introduction to *The Wanderer,* xii.

48. See Todd, *Feminist Literary History,* 30-33; for French and Anglo-American theories of sexual difference, see 18-19.

1. *Oroonoko:* A Pastoral History

Epigraph: "A Celebration of Charis: Her Man Described by Her Own Dictamen," *Poems of Ben Jonson,* ed. Ian Donaldson (NY: Oxford Univ. Press, 1975), 138-39.

1. Goreau notes that Behn would be the first English novelist if one properly applied Ian Watt's definition (283). Konigsberg considers Behn's fictions too unrealistic to engage the reader as novels do (4).

2. Prior characterizes women in traditional clerical writing as "seething cauldrons of lust" (123); Woodcock notes that Behn's serious treatment of love was rare in the dramas of her day (121).

3. *The Faerie Queene* (New Haven, Conn.: Yale University Press, 1981), Book V; *Metamorphoses,* trans. Arthur Golding (NY: Macmillan, 1965), 8 (Book I, ll. 169-70).

4. See Robert Adams Day, "Aphra Behn and the Works of the Intellect," in Schofield, *Fetter'd or Free?* 375-76, 377-79; he agrees with Behn that lack of education, in her case, was an artistic advantage.

5. See Duffy, 191; cf. midwife Jane Sharp: "It is not hard words that perform the work, as if none understood the Art that cannot understand Greek" (qtd. in Crawford, 227); and religious reformer Mary Cary: "not onely men but women shall prophesie . . . not onely those that have university-learning but those who have it not; even servants and handmaids" (qtd. in Crawford, 215).

6. See MacCarthy 1:226; McKeon 62-63; and Adams 7.

7. The story probably was largely true, though critics have been arguing about this for decades. For a review of the arguments, see Adelaide Amore's introduction to *Oroonoko* (Univ. Press of America ed.), xii-xix. See also Spender 50; Guffey 6-8; and Adams 116-17. Davis points out that if Behn did not really go to Surinam then she was one of the European liars she was writing about (109).

8. McKeon has called Behn a "naive empiricist" (112), but I think this categorization fails to take into account both women's problematic relation to the intellectual currents of the time and the "experiential" detail of earlier romances such as *The Faerie Queene*—in which, as Nelson notes, Spenser strongly hints that Amoret urinates (86-87).

9. See McKeon 240-41.

10. The idea that truth is often more marvelous than fiction is essential to travel literature as well as to the novel (Adams ch. 4). Davis notes that "novels" in the seventeenth century meant both "news ballads" (45-46), which were supposed to be at least partly true, and "tales and jests" (51), which were understood to be fictional.

11. See *The Oxford Companion to English Literature,* 5th ed., ed. Margaret Drabble (NY: Oxford Univ. Press, 1985), 69.

12. See Jean Hagstrum, *The Sister Arts* (Chicago: Univ. of Chicago Press, 1958), 31-33, on the pictorial aspects of Greek romance.

13. Cf. the "man's man" Ben Jonson's rebellion against effeminacy in his "Celebration of Charis," part 9, quoted at the beginning of this chapter. Wiesenfarth contrasts the "affined," twin lovers in romances with the complementary lovers in novels (13-14).

14. Cf. Parker: "Narcissus is the patron saint of courtly love" (90).

15. The abundance of homosexual humor in Behn's comic writings (see Woodcock 63, 114) suggests that homosexuality between men was not uncommon, but a possibly authentic letter from Behn to Hoyle warning him against endanger-

ing his reputation (116) suggests that what passed as sophisticated on stage was less acceptable in life. As for homosexual attachments between women, both Faderman (throughout) and Vicinus (180) comment on the impossibility of determining how much sexual activity may have been included in some of the period's famous sentimental friendships.

16. These seemingly authentic letters may be fictional; for a review of the evidence, see Woodcock 106-7.

17. This dialogue nicely illustrates the romance's traditional inclusion of realism well before the age of the novel, for here the ideal lover addresses the real. See Horowitz (255) on *L'Astrée*.

18. See Goreau 5; Spender 54. Todd credits Kate Millett with first pointing out "the old-fashioned libertine aspects of the libertarian 1960s" (*Feminist Literary History* 22).

19. See Adams, 16.

20. Cf. Poovey on Mary Wollstonecraft's relationship with Gilbert Imlay (93).

21. I don't think Behn really believed poetry must be masculine, and I am less disturbed by her jocular references to her "masculine part" than by Woodcock's praise of the "virile brilliance of her character" (136).

22. See Walker, introduction to *Poems,* xix.

23. It is not certain that she had syphilis. Public attacks at the time are hardly sufficient evidence, and Woodcock seems, chivalrously, to doubt it (193-94). But her description of her symptoms and her slow deterioration make it a likely diagnosis. As Goreau says, considering its prevalence and the company she kept, it would have been amazing if she had escaped it (215-16).

24. See Zimbardo 63. McKeon discusses *Oroonoko* in the context of the French imaginary voyage to a utopian locale, a common feature of which was sexual equality (249).

25. John Milton, *Complete Poetical Works,* ed. Douglas Bush (Boston: Houghton Mifflin, 1965), 278-81 (Book IV, ll. 142-159, 205-87).

26. Davis gives examples of similarly gruesome executions from news ballads, noting that the shocking detail was supposed to attest to their truth (58). And they might have been true; Guffey compares Oroonoko's death to others described in the diaries of Pepys and Evelyn (20).

27. On *Oroonoko* as allegory, see Duffy 267; Guffey iv; Brown 58; and Beasley, "Politics," 221 and "Life's Episodes," 24.

28. See Brownley 174 on *Oroonoko;* and Davis 23-24 on Defoe and the novel in general. For a review of several current theories on the blend of real and imaginary worlds in fiction, see the introductory chapter of Fleishman.

29. Cf. Burney's last novel, *The Wanderer* (1814), in which Juliet considers whether her honor is safe with Sir Jaspar Herrington because he is old and probably impotent (732).

30. See also Woodcock 232-35; Goreau 57; Lore Metzger's introduction to *Oroonoko* (NY: Norton, 1973), xii; Brownley 177; and Guffey 20-23.

31. McKeon fails to see any "tension . . . in [Behn's] dual role as narrator and character" (112).

32. See Spencer 50-51; Goreau 48-49; and Brownley 178-79.

33. Duffy attributes the anonymous "Satyr on the Modern Translators" to Prior (214); Goreau calls the attribution "tentative" (315,n.19)

34. See Brown 43-46, 61. For a twentieth-century appreciation of Behn's achievement, see Virginia Woolf, *A Room of One's Own* (NY: Harcourt Brace Jovanovich, 1957), 66-67.

2. Delia and Rivella: Romantic Autobiography

Epigraph: Burney here translates a line from Madame de Genlis's *Les Mères Rivales* (*Journals* 4:483). See Spacks, *Imagining a Self*, 191, 331 n. 37. E.S. Barrett uses the original French quotation, satirically, as epigraph to *The Heroine*.

1. There no longer seems any justification for considering "Mary" the author's first name; F. Morgan further argues that Manley's first name should be spelled "Delarivier" (14-15), though I follow Patricia Köster's more traditional spelling.

2. Needham calls Manley the "first gentlewoman to gain a living by her pen" ("WB" 259). If birth is the criterion, I think Behn would have claimed this distinction; both authors' fathers were probably lieutenant governors (see F. Morgan 37).

3. The changing times can be measured by the changing fortunes of Barbara Castlemaine, the "royal Whore." See Allen Andrews, *The Royal Whore* (Philadelphia: Chilton Book Company, 1970); F. Morgan 55-56.

4. An episode in Behn's *Love Letters* shows that odor was indeed a concern (226).

5. Romance, which had been used for political satire as far back as Jehan de Saintré (Uitti 139), sometimes used utopias to advocate sexual equality and universal language; see McKeon 249; and Adams 261-62.

6. This use of the moon also recalls Ariosto and Dante, as well as a popular play by Behn, *The Emperor of the Moon,* which has some similarly satirical passages (see Woodcock 188-9). Apparently, Manley's contemporaries recognized that Astrea's judgments are based on a romantic code. In Haywood's imitation of *The New Atalantis, Memoirs of a Certain Island,* Cupid is the divine critic of human affairs.

7. Ironically, as Davis notes, Manley later claimed (falsely, as everyone knew) that *The New Atalantis* was pure invention in order to avoid prosecution for libel (Davis 115, 121).

8. For praise of Manley's realism, see Needham, "WB," 259; Köster xxii. See the introduction to this study and Aronson 10 for discussion of Scudéry's realistic secondary characters.

9. For example, see *NAt* 1:148ff.

10. See Needham, "WB," 264-65.

11. See Spencer 54.

12. See London 103-4.

13. Throughout Richetti's discussion of Manley he treats her rendering of the gender war as "ludicrously unreal" (167)—yet also comments sporadically on its accuracy to female experience (124, 142). See also Paul Bunyan Anderson, "Delarivière Manley's Prose Fiction," *Philological Quarterly* 13 (2 Apr. 1934): 182.

14. Addison quotes Dryden to this effect in *Spectator 62; see Selections from the Tatler and the Spectator,* 2nd ed. (NY: Holt, Rinehart and Winston, 1970), 193-94.

15. Her critique of the cabal has interesting implications for modern feminist celebrations of communities of women, such as Boone's (ch. 6).

16. Todd emphasizes the political implications of Manley's cabal (*Women's Friendship* 340-42). In *The Way of the World* (1700) Congreve had Mirabell use the word "cabal" to refer to a "subversive" gathering of women. Fear of female friendships is also shown in the proviso scene, in which Mirabell demands first and foremost that Millamant "admit no sworn confidante or intimate of your own

sex" (IV, i, p. 79). F. Morgan says the cabal was based on a group of real-life "society lesbians," and gives their real names (104n).

17. Behn had been attacked by Shadwell for her political writing in much the same way; see Goreau 250.

18. Behn had also ridiculed male impotence in a poem called "The Disappointment"; see Gardiner 212, Duffy 184.

19. Cards, like all forms of gambling, offended Manley's Tory reverence for the social hierarchy, for gambling made rich those God had intended to be poor, and vice versa. See *NAt* 2:112-13.

20. See Spencer 53ff.

21. See Richetti 148-49.

22. Boileau personally attacked Mme. de Maintenon and Mme. de Monchevreuil (75), as well as Scudéry.

23. A main idea of Spacks's *Gossip* is that gossip, usually associated with women, is anything the speaker considers trivial. Thus Addison treats what we would call international news as gossip in *Spectator 10*. Steiner has an essay on the *Divine Comedy* entitled "Dante Now: The Gossip of Eternity" (164-85).

24. See Richetti 133; and Beasley, "Politics," 223.

25. Cf. the experiences of Barbara Castlemaine (F. Morgan 59).

26. For a fuller account of this contretemps, see Needham, "TD," 260-61; E.A. and L.D. Bloom, "Steele and His Answerers," in *The Dress of Words* (Lawrence: Univ. of Kansas Libraries, 1978), 167-69; F. Morgan 115-17.

27. Cf. Davis's comment on objectivity in Defoe (173).

28. Cf. Todd, *Women's Friendship,* 340.

29. The Duchess is Hilaria in *Rivella* and the Duchess l'Inconstant in *The New Atalantis*. Interestingly, she is also Clelia in *Zarah*—apparently with irony, since Scudéry's Clelia is spotlessly chaste.

30. London attributes the martyrdom of these heroines to guilt, a desire to be punished for being sex objects (113).

31. Another version of this story suggests that this "sacrifice" may have kept Manley as well as Cleander (John Tilly) out of debtors' prison (F. Morgan 121).

3. Betsy Thoughtless and Harriot Stuart: Unacknowledged Sisters

Epigraph: Boileau, *Satire X,* 67: "Au fond peu vicieuse elle aime à coqueter."

1. There is some disagreement about the date of *Harriot Stuart*. Spender (200) and Margaret Dalziel list it as 1750, though Dalziel gives it as December of that year in her introduction to the Oxford Univ. Press, 1970 ed. (xxi). The title page of the copy micropublished in the History of Women series at Yale reads 1751. See Small 10 n.18.

2. So far was Haywood from influencing Lennox that the younger author would later have one of her heroines refuse Haywood's novels in disgust and pick up *Joseph Andrews* instead (*Henrietta* 1:36); see Whicher 175.

3. The year 1751 belonged to fictional Harriots. Besides Lennox's heroine, there was Harriot Loveit, near-heroine of *Betsy Thoughtless,* and Richardson's Harriet Byron, heroine of *Sir Charles Grandison,* then in progress. The name suggested realism—even ugly, anti-romantic reality in Manley's story of Urania and Polydore. Eventually, in Bage's *Hermsprong* and Austen's *Emma,* it would suggest dull conventionality.

4. Or they end with no resolution at all. See Schofield, *Quiet Rebellion,* 3; and *Eliza Haywood,* 8.

5. See Richetti 154, 168-69; and Hunter, "Novels," 486-87.

6. Nelson notes further that comedy was traditionally the only type of writing which was allowed to be set in the present (48-49). Hunter comments on the falseness of Fielding's literary history here ("Novels" 480; "News" 514) and sees a similar defensiveness in recent "canonical" criticism ("Contexts" 126); but see Adams 25-27 on the influence of epic on the novel. See also Beasley on the male *counter*-tradition of the novel ("Politics" 221-23).

7. Book IX, Chapter XI, from which I have taken the title of this book: "The only excellence of falsehood is its resemblance to truth." It is not certain that Johnson wrote the chapter; see Weinsheimer 7; Small 13; Staves 197; vs. Duncan Isles, "Johnson and Charlotte Lennox," *New Rambler* Serial C, no. 3 (June 1967): 43; and John Fyvie, *Some Famous Women of Wit and Beauty* (London: Constable, 1905), 186. Langbauer notes that the most material point is that the chapter is Johnsonian in both theme and style (42-43).

8. I think this passage shows clearly that there was more to Haywood's literary theory than the "market analysis" Richetti sees in it (126).

9. This is the way saints' lives were typically written; see McKeon 95.

10. The poem is reprinted in Small 233-36.

11. See Schofield, *Eliza Haywood*, 2. By this time "Sappho" was almost a term of abuse. See *Sir Charles Grandison* 1:431.

12. Séjourné confirms that, as far as can be known, *Harriot Stuart* is a good source of biographical information about Lennox. He speculates that growing up outside London made her slow to learn the proprieties of urban British taste (28). Harriot refers often to the licentiousness of New York society, where Lennox spent at least part of her adolescence.

13. See Whicher 120-22.

14. According to E. Auerbach, the adventures in the old quest romances are connected by the knight's character, though they are directly caused not by himself but by fate (136). This type of logic did not satisfy eighteenth-century readers' more empirical ideas about the way life works, or should work, though it might have been a way of making sense out of the lives of women.

15. Doody discusses the reasons that stories about women followed the pattern of heroic stage tragedy rather than comedy (*A Natural Passion* 112-15). It is worth noting that both Betsy and Harriot make fun of their lovers' theatrical "rhodomontade," but that these men do in fact behave like Rodomonte, the swaggering villain in *Orlando Furioso*.

16. The same type of humor Manley's female characters fail to appreciate. See Doody, *A Natural Passion,* 24; Faderman 96.

17. See Grieder, intro. to Haywood's *The Rash Resolve,* 5; London 112; J.B. Priestley, intro. to Haywood's *The Female Spectator,* xi; Richetti chapters 4 and 5. Doody discusses eroticism in Richardson's *Pamela* (*A Natural Passion* 71, 80).

18. Doody notes *Idalia* "anticipated" *Clarissa* (*A Natural Passion* 147)— though it seems possible it may rather have influenced Richardson's novel.

19. See Brownstein 83.

20. Cf. *L'Astrée:* "Les yeux peuvent bien commencer et eslever une jeune affection, mais lors qu'elle est crue, il faut bien quelque chose de plus ferme et de plus solide pour la rendre parfaite; et cela ne peut estre que la connoissance des vertus, des beautez, des mérites, et d'une réciproque affection de celle que nous aymons" (98). (The eyes may well begin and nurture a young affection, but when it is raw, it needs something firmer and more solid to perfect it; and that can only be the knowledge of virtues, beauties, merits, and reciprocal affection in the woman we love.)

21. See Boone's explanation of this type of paradox (83-86).

22. Jane Barker agreed with this analysis; she named one of her heroines Clelia. See Richetti 128, 233; and Nelson 65.

23. Hunter's comments on the function of novels for young urban readers ("Young") apply especially well to Haywood's and Lennox's novels and the peculiar situation of women in the courtship system; if novels were necessary to help readers identify heroes and villains in their lives, the realistic romance was needed specifically to help young women identify the best prospective husbands.

24. See Faderman 16-17; Vicinus 177-78. Stone laments the lack of "sexual diaries" by women to help historians (490), but Faderman's work makes me feel that a "sexual diary" would hardly depict sexuality as women experienced it. Richetti (rather inconsistently) points out that women writers' descriptions of sex are euphemistic (201, 214); but euphemism is in the eye of the beholder. What he calls "spiritualized eroticism" in Haywood would probably, to her, have been simply "spiritual" (205).

25. Brownstein discusses female narcissism as the basis of women's novel reading (xiv).

26. See also Vicinus 181-82. As with Behn's relationships with women, it is difficult to know how far sentimental friendship was allowed to go. Haywood condemns sex between women in *Memoirs of a Certain Island* (156), but Faderman's book leads me to guess that the relationships she refers to involved transvestitism and other forms of male imitation, which were punishable by death (Faderman 49-52); see also Todd, *Women's Friendship,* 319, 360. The original Sappho, so many women writers' namesake, was a lover of women before deserting them for a man; but as Faderman notes, the English always seemed to emphasize the heterosexual part of her career (27, 47).

27. Cf. Frances Sheridan, *Memoirs of Miss Sidney Bidulph* (London: Pandora, 1987), 60. In Lennox's *Henrietta* and *Sophia*—both of which contain satires of French romance—the word "romantic" is often used with reference to the heroines' high ideals in order to satirize the corrupt reader's possible failure to appreciate them.

28. Cf. the late seventeenth-century devotional diary of Elizabeth Delaval: "The gayety of my humour and the harmelesse mirth in my conversation was pleaseing to those I formerly kept company withall, and what was estimed by them to be wit . . . is look'd upon to be a gidynesse unbecoming a wife" (qtd. in Mendelson 192). Women's devotional diaries of the period associate wit, coquetry, and the reading of romances, all of which were considered acceptable for virgins only (Mendelson 190, 207 n. 60).

29. Cf. Boone's discussion of *Pamela* (88).

30. It was a commonplace of early eighteenth-century love stories that pride in one's virginity comes before a fall. Betsy is a lot like Haywood's earlier heroine Anadea, who fails to make herself love her worthy fiancé and concludes that she has no heart—until she meets the Count de Blessure, when "the Indifference she had for all Mankind, now converted into the most violent Passion for one" (qtd. in Whicher 50).

31. Denial of sex as a means to freedom is a complicated issue. Women such as Mary Astell and Mary Wollstonecraft, regarding love and marriage as forms of slavery, wrote feminist arguments against both; yet as Poovey points out, the sacrifice of sex is also a form of repression (4, 74).

32. At his best, when he surrenders Harriot to Dumont and remains a friend to both, Campbel resembles d'Urfé's Ergaste, who similarly surrenders Bellinde to Célion despite her father's preference for himself (89-90).

33. Even in *L'Astrée* the cynical, "realistic" Hylas is bothered by this lack of distinction between the sexes: "Et quoy . . . vous estes donc Diane? Et vostre chapeau aussi n'est-il pas changé en sa coiffure, et vostre juppe en sa robe?" (165). (What . . . are you then Diane? And isn't your hat also changed into her headdress and your jerkin into her gown?)

34. See Jenijoy LaBelle's *Herself Beheld* (Ithaca: Cornell Univ. Press, 1988), 15.

35. The Garland facsimile edition (NY: Garland, 1979) reads, "those just pretensions to it, which otherwise she had been entitled from the deserving . . . ," which is clearly ungrammatical (3:52-53). The sentence has been silently emended in the Pandora edition in a way that loses the original meaning and creates another syntactical problem. I think the "it" adds something to the meaning and have thus suggested a different solution.

36. Like Sarah Scott's *Millenium Hall*. Boone discusses this alternative tradition in women's fiction (ch. 6)—but I find disturbing his Lacanian identification of the feminine as static rather than questing and communal rather than individual (283-86).

37. A good example of the shepherdesses' heroinely refusal to compete with each other is Stilliane's rejection of Hylas because he has wronged Carlis in *L'Astrée* (61). Congreve satirizes the way such romances almost, but do not quite, end in female friendship in *The Way of the World* when Lady Wishfort dreams of running off to be a shepherdess with Marwood (V, i). Something similar occurs in Lennox's *Henrietta*, when the heroine shatters silly Miss Woodby's pastoral dreams with a realistic description of the life of a shepherd (1:72-73). It is important to remember the source of this almost-sisterly ending, lest we assume that when it appears in later novels it represents something subversive and anti-romantic (see Boone on Brontë's *Shirley*, 15-17).

38. Cf. Schofield, *Eliza Haywood*, 5-6; *Quiet Rebellion*, 10-11, 78. Hunter calls novels in general "rebel" rather than "subversive" "because the resistance is usually close to the surface" ("Young" 266).

39. Harriot herself is comparatively easy about the injustice of being blamed for false appearances (2:188).

40. "Mabel" is the spelling in the Garland facsimile edition; the name is spelled "Mable" in the Pandora edition.

41. See Poovey 35.

42. Cf. Doody, *A Natural Passion*, 19.

43. "Epistle to a Lady," *Epistles to Several Persons, The Poems of Alexander Pope* (London: Yale Univ. Press, 1951), 45. In the poem Pope strategically attributes the statement to his "Lady" correspondent, Martha Blount.

4. *The Female Quixote:* A Realistic Fairy Tale

Epigraph: Austen, "Lesley Castle," *MW*, 111.

1. Richetti uses this phrase with reference to Haywood (126).

2. This philosophy would eventually evolve into what Marilyn Butler calls "antijacobinism" (see *Jane Austen and the War of Ideas*), although one must apply such terms with extreme caution (see chapter 5 of this study). Many writers prefer to emphasize the radical, feminist aspects of Lennox's writings, but seen as a whole they present a strong—though not unambiguous—impression of conservatism. *Henrietta*, for example, depicts the sufferings of an impoverished aristocratic heroine at the hands of various corrupt bourgeois—and the only weapons permitted her are self-humiliation and self-sacrifice.

3. See Staves 193.

4. See articles by M.S. Brownlee and El Saffar in Brownlee, *Romance: Generic Transformations from Chrétien de Troyes to Cervantes;* also McKeon ch. 7.

5. The first phrase is omitted in the Pandora edition. See the facsimile of the second edition (Upper Saddle River, NJ: Gregg Press, 1970), 2:169.

6. Staves notes that most writers of the eighteenth century saw Don Quixote's quest as ridiculous (194-95, 204-5). See Scott on Smollett's *Sir Launcelot Greaves, PW* 3:150. Ronald Paulson notes that Whig writers in general showed more sympathy for such eccentric characters; see *Satire and the Novel in Eighteenth-Century England* (New Haven, CT: Yale Univ. Press, 1967), 60-69. Butler mentions Charles Lucas's *The Infernal Quixote* as an example of an anti-jacobin novel (*Jane Austen* 107-18).

7. See n. 7, chapter 3 of this study. In the facsimile of the 1752 edition (see n. 5 above) the statement is set off by paragraph indentation that has been omitted in the Pandora edition (2:313).

8. See Weinsheimer 11.

9. Cf. Boileau: "Nous la verrons . . . / Conter pour grands exploits vingt Hommes ruinés, / Blessés, battus pour Elle, et quatre assassinés; / Trop heureux!" (67). (We will see her . . . / Count as great exploits twenty men ruined, / Wounded, beaten for her sake, and four murdered; / Too fortunate!)

10. E. Auerbach explains that rank and nobility in romance are "personal" rather than inherited, and that often the two types of nobility are set against each other (139).

11. Behn used a similar romantic trick in *The Dutch Lover.* In *Henrietta* Lennox makes the same point as *The Female Quixote* in a different way—by making the heroine's "fall" the result of her mistakenly running away from the home and protection of a thoroughly evil guardian.

12. See Spacks, *The Adolescent Idea,* 133.

13. See Gilbert and Gubar 22-23, 39. In his review of *The Female Quixote,* Henry Fielding notes that the restrictions on women's lives make it difficult to write interesting stories about them, so that Lennox's novel must in this way be inferior to Cervantes'—though in other respects he praises it highly (*The Covent-Garden Journal* 1:280).

14. See Langbauer 30.

15. See Langbauer (32-33) and Warren (368-69) on the question of whether the turn-around was intended.

16. See Langbauer 47. I have quoted the facsimile edition (2:139) here because I think the Pandora edition's emendation of "posed" to "opposed" (298) is a mistake; Lennox seems to have meant "to puzzle, confuse, perplex, nonplus" (*OED*).

17. See Langbauer 30.

18. See Langbauer 40.

19. Cf. Doody's discussion of house imagery in *Clarissa* (*A Natural Passion* ch. 8). For further discussion of space and enclosure, see Gilbert and Gubar 84; and Ellis x-xi, chs. 2 and 3.

20. Both Langbauer (33) and Warren (368) note the importance of the language of romance to Arabella's self-definition; they also discuss whether this or the Johnsonian language she eventually adopts is really her own (Langbauer 41, Warren 374).

21. Cf. Barrett's *The Heroine:* "I confess I differ from other heroines in one point. They, you may remark, are always unconscious of their charms; whereas I am, I fear, convinced of mine, beyond all hope of retraction" (11).

22. I refer here to *Pamela's Daughters,* by R.P. Utter and Gwendolyn Needham (NY: Macmillan, 1936).

23. On Snow White, see Gilbert and Gubar 37-38. Also cf. Donald Barthelme's *Snow White* (NY: Atheneum, 1982), in which the heroine goes to college and becomes self-aware, discontented, and impossible to live with.

24. In *The Best of Saki* (NY: Viking, 1961), 129-34.

25. See More 1:385; Newton 7-8; C. Johnson 18.

5. Fanny Burney's Novels: Romance with Regret

Epigraph: Thrale, 1:439.

1. Doody's arguments for calling the author Frances Burney are compelling (*Frances Burney* 6). I have persisted in using the presumptuous nickname only because Burney is one of the few women authors who did not have to be "invented," or christened, in the 1980s; I do not wish to seem to ignore centuries of scholarship in one of the rare instances when there is any. She certainly should have been called Frances all along.

2. An example of Burney's royalism is her siding with the court party against her old friend Burke in the trial of Warren Hastings. She even refused to marry until she was sure of the Queen's consent (and the continuation of her court pension). Her most "radical" actions in support of the Juniper Hall émigrés did not take place until those Constitutionalists had come to regret that they had ever wished to limit the power of the monarch (Devlin, *Burney,* 6).

3. Hunter asserts that the eighteenth-century novel is universally about the loss of communal feeling ("Young" 272).

4. See Simons 78; Devlin has a collection of Burney's statements preferring realism to romance (*Burney* 17).

5. See Newton 33-34, 43. Some present writers on romance minimize the importance of the ending in order to emphasize the romance's straining toward infinity, its postponements of closure (see Parker 4). This perspective would have seemed odd to Burney.

6. See McKeon (209) on the "paranoid volatility" of early Tory satirists. On the difficulty of classifying novels as jacobin or antijacobin (the terms come from Marilyn Butler's *Jane Austen and the War of Ideas*) see Gary Kelly, "Jane Austen and the English Novel of the 1790's," in Schofield, *Fetter'd or Free?* 289-94; Devlin, *Burney,* ch. 3; Sarah Smith, "Men, Women, and Money," in Schofield, *Fetter'd or Free?* 53. Feminist concerns do further complicate the issue (Devlin, *Burney,* 66-72).

7. See Croker; also "The Real Fanny Burney," *Times Literary Supplement* 9 Mar. 1972: 160; "Fanny Burney (1752-1840): A Life in a World of Fantasy," *Times Literary Supplement* 6 Jan. 1946: 29.

8. See also Butler, *Maria Edgeworth,* 484.

9. I refer here to Poovey's *The Proper Lady and the Woman Writer.*

10. See Spencer 98, 155; and Simons, 1,7, 76, and elsewhere.

11. The first and most common theory appears in Spencer (95) and to a degree in Spender (286); the second in Simons (87).

12. Now that the "univocal" is out of style, it is important to remember that in Burney's time "singleness of mind" was highly valued (Brunton, *Discipline,* 99). Straub praises Burney for her open-endedness (6, 71), but I think she would have been unhappy with the compliment.

13. Though I believe Devlin underestimates Burney's irony and especially

her satire, which is not necessarily ironic, his comment that she preferred direct statements to risky, ambiguous ones strikes me as correct (*Burney* 62), but cf. Simons 141-42; and Epstein 165.

14. Interpretations of Burney's switch to third-person narration in her second novel reflect various views of Burney's conformism. See Simons 40; Devlin, *Burney,* 91, 95; and Doody, *Frances Burney,* 101.

15. Doody emphasizes Dr. Burney's domination (*Frances Burney* 10, 96). Cf. Butler, *Maria Edgeworth,* 281-82, 295-96, 303.

16. See Aronson 26.

17. Simons's suggestion that Johnson "wistfully" recalled the days of feminine illiteracy is not in keeping with his other comments or general attitude as reported in Simons's own work and elsewhere (3). Johnson's comment, that women "vied with the men in everything," rather shows an unexpected return of the competitive battle imagery Spencer associates with the earlier period of feminine defiance rather than with Burney's period of respectability (92).

18. See Devlin, *Burney,* 63.

19. See M. Brown 33, 35; and Doody, *Frances Burney,* 139.

20. Puzzlement and sometimes disgust have been prevalent in the critical response to Burney's "horseplay." See Chauncy Brewster Tinker, *Dr. Johnson and Fanny Burney* (London: Ratway, 1912), xvii; Muriel Masefield, *The Story of Fanny Burney* (Cambridge: Cambridge Univ. Press, 1927), 32-33; W. Wright Roberts, "Charles and Fanny Burney in the Light of the New Thrale Correspondence in the John Rylands Library," *The Bulletin of the John Rylands Library* 16 (1932):12; Cecil, 86; Emily Hahn, *A Degree of Prudery* (London: Arthur Barker, 1951), 87; MacAndrew, 32; Devlin, *Burney,* 14, 39. See also Doody, *Frances Burney,* 48; Epstein 170-71; Newton 52-53.

21. Both Figes (1-2) and Spencer (75) describe the sharp delineation between the plots of "male" and "female" novels at this time. Kirkham also assumes Burney was seen as a women's novelist by her contemporaries (35).

22. See Simons 20, 80; Spender 285; Figes 40, 42; and Sarah Kilpatrick, *Fanny Burney* (NY: Stein and Day, 1980), 59. Cf. Hunter, "Novels," 497-98; and Spender 92-93 for a more positive view of didacticism.

23. Cf. Devlin, *Burney,* 14-16; and Doody, *Frances Burney,* 32.

24. See Simons 20; and Poovey 40. Spencer (98) associates Burney with the apologetic woman writer.

25. See Devlin, *Burney,* 83; Hemlow 129; and Doody, *Frances Burney,* 34.

26. Devlin notes that the *Critical Review* dismissed *Evelina's* Cinderella plot as merely conventional (*Burney* 87); critics using the text-subtext model who identify romance with the surface text commit a similar oversimplification (see Simons 65, 77; her preface to *Cecilia,* x). See Doody, *Frances Burney,* 33.

27. Fielding's narratives sound "progressive" as Hunter describes them ("Young" 267) and "conservative" as McKeon describes them (401), though neither treats these categories as simple or exclusive. Butler calls Austen an antijacobin (*Jane Austen*), Kirkham a radical feminist (xii, 3). McKeon describes the romantic utopianism of novels such as *Camilla* as conservative (232); Doody treats Burney as a radical. Even according to McKeon's own categories the dislocation of rank and value in *Evelina* is "progressive" (155).

28. Newton describes Evelina's belief that she is more than a piece of merchandise as both a "courtly fiction" that denies the harsher reality (34) and a truth in Evelina's own mind (43). Straub tends to regard the romantic love plot as a patriarchal imposition that leaves the woman powerless (127, 132, 134), but she also notes that this plot could be a source of power (20-21).

29. French feminists such as Toril Moi tend to regard bourgeois realism as reactionary (Todd, *Feminist Literary History*, 75).

30. See Devlin, *Burney*, 93.

31. Simons emphasizes the satirist's frustration, noting that Belfield abandons this career (61); see also Straub (147-50). But then Belfield never follows through on anything.

32. One sees how well Burney succeeded in becoming famous for modesty from Samuel Hoole's paean to women writers, "Aurelia, or The Contest," published after the satirical *Cecilia*, in which she earns the right "to lash unfeeling Wealth and stubborn Pride" by "fly[ing] from the loud applause her talent raised" (*Diary* 2:217; quoted and discussed in Doody, *Frances Burney*, 143).

33. See Devlin, *Burney*, 72, 78.

34. See Spencer 78; Simons 32.

35. Doody's biography misprints "heart-rending" for "heart-hardening" in this passage (203-4).

36. This passage contradicts Devlin's remark that Burney came to define morality differently for men and women (*Burney* 103).

37. For a discussion of the Barlow episode, see Simons 7; Devlin, *Burney*, 43-52; Doody, *Frances Burney*, 42-43; and Newton 24-26.

38. See also *Diary* 3:115-18, 6:399-400; *Journals* 2:20-27, 2:123; Devlin, *Burney*, 64.

39. Cf. Doody on stylistic strain in the *Memoirs* (*Frances Burney* 10).

40. Doody notes that "Burney associates emotional openness with the French language" (*Frances Burney* 330).

41. Doody and many other commentators seem to assume that Piozzi would make Mrs. Thrale happy; like Burney, I am uneasy about her having to almost purchase him (Doody, *Frances Burney*, 164).

42. See Rose Marie Cutting, "Defiant Women: The Growth of Feminism in Fanny Burney's Novels," *Studies in English Literature* 17 (Summer 1977): 520; Devlin, *Burney*, 108; Simons 108-9; M. Brown 36-37.

43. See Spacks, *Gossip*, 24-5, 39-40.

44. See Newton 48.

45. It is not only *female* wits who risk insensitivity, as one may see by Cecilia's mixed reaction to Mr. Gosport's satire—approving his meaning, but "surprised" at his manners (23).

46. E. Bloom quotes a "scrap" from the Burney manuscripts on "levity" as a "hardener of the heart . . . its self-disguises amuse but beguile the fancy till they deaden all sensation" (Introduction to *Camilla* xv).

47. See Straub 197-98. Doody comments that in *Cecilia* Meadows's originality is a kind of conformity (*Frances Burney* 121).

48. The criticism to which Mrs. Arlbery is subjected makes me reluctant to see her as a projection of the author (see Doody *Frances Burney*, 250; and Devlin, *Burney*, 103-5). It is at least a very severe self-portrait.

49. See also 255-56 and 448.

50. See, for example, *Diary* 3:67-68.

51. For other views of Cecilia's individualism, see Doody, *Frances Burney*, 112-13, 117-18, 126-28; Straub 122, 125; Epstein 167; Sulloway points out that the phrase "pride and prejudice," so important to the moral of *Cecilia,* appeared frequently in feminist writings of the time (8, 66-69, 83).

52. Doody notes that reviewers of the time were unsatisfied with the justice of such endings (*Frances Burney* 144-45).

53. Another way Cecilia's romantic delicacy works against realism and

moral clarity is in the way the characters first get together: Delvile must overhear Cecilia confessing her love to a dog, a device which is as providential as Trueworth's overhearing Betsy Thoughtless, and almost as miraculous as the illnesses-unto-death Lennox ridicules in *The Female Quixote.* Frye refers to this convention as "dog knows" (*Secular Scripture* 145-46).

54. See Simons 84.

55. Camilla's original name, Ariella, confirms Burney's intention (xvi). See Doody, *Frances Burney,* 239-40.

56. See Spacks, *Imagining a Self,* 183. If, as Simons suggests, Camilla is designed to illustrate the need for "experiential learning" (84), she also demonstrates the dubious value of such learning. See also Linda C. Hunt, "A Woman's Portion: Jane Austen and the Female Character," in Schofield, *Fetter'd or Free?* 21; Doody, *Frances Burney,* 55.

57. See Straub 184.

58. See *Diary* 2:80-81; L. Bloom, "Fanny Burney's *Camilla:* The Author as Editor," *Bulletin of Research in the Humanities* 82 (1979): 380-82.

59. Straub refers to the heroine as a text to be read and, increasingly, misread (157-60, 172).

60. See Simons 37; and Straub 183.

61. See Devlin, *Burney,* 10-11; but see Doody, *Frances Burney,* 314.

62. See Devlin, *Burney,* 97.

63. "Nearer," perhaps, but not quite independence: thirty years earlier, in her *Cecilia* phase, she had described Bath as *"ton*-led" (qtd. in Devlin, *Burney,* 55). Oddly, according to Southam, Bath became more expensive and exclusive, not less, after the Napoleonic Wars (*"Sanditon,"* 4).

64. See Hunter, "Novels," 493-94.

6. *The Italian:* A Romance of Manners

Epigraph: Smith, 196.

1. See Varma 23; Durant takes exception to this view (519).

2. See Summers 48; and Trowbridge, intro. to Hurd, iii. Todd notes that Longinus had to go through Addison and Dennis to acquire the psychological and emotional emphasis Hurd required (*Sensibility* 29).

3. Pastoral was making a comeback along with the Gothic, to at least one reviewer's chagrin; see *Wollstonecraft Anthology* 223.

4. Varma contrasts baroque and Gothic styles (14-15), as does Charles Ryder in Evelyn Waugh's *Brideshead Revisited* (Boston: Little, Brown, 1945), 81-82.

5. Radcliffe also tended to notice the "baroque" intricacy of design in "Gothic" structures; see Talfourd 58.

6. See also Varma 128.

7. Edgeworth depicts such a modern salon in *The Absentee,* bound with *Castle Rackrent* (NY: Century, 1903): 52.

8. See Poovey 37. Several critics have noted that Radcliffe's humility clothed a serious purpose; see MacCarthy 2:162-63; Murray 17; Chard, intro. to *The Romance of the Forest,* xxiii.

9. Talfourd admires Radcliffe most for seeming to lack an ego in an age of egoist writers (3, 13, 105).

10. On the reputation of French romance during the period, see Summers 26-27; Devlin, *The Author of Waverley,* 14-15. Hurd barely considered French

romance to be true romance (115-16). Walpole did like Scudéry (Varma 53), but he seems to have been conscious of being out of touch with the times in doing so.

11. On Walpole's escapism, see Murray 31; Varma 44-45; Summers sees escapism as the basis of Gothic fiction (17-18, 24).

12. On readers' attitude toward realism, see Haggerty, "Fact and Fancy," 391; David Richter, "The Reception of the Gothic Novel in the 1790's," in Uphaus, 121-22.

13. See Kiely 3.

14. Qtd. in Summers 138; but see a slightly different wording on 187.

15. This is the characteristic of Radcliffe's fiction which has most bothered reviewers, from Scott and Coleridge's time to the present. See Murray 163; and Durant 527 for some examples. According to Summers, reviewers liked such explanations at first, but standards changed around 1795 (139).

16. The passage continues: "The needle, not the pen, is the instrument they should handle, and the only one they ever use dexterously." Cf. this similar statement by the novelist William Beckford: "It might be as well if instead of weaving historical romances the super-literary ladies of the present period would pass a little more of their time at cross stitch and yabble stitch. We should gain some pretty chair and screen covers and lose little by not being tempted to pore over the mazes of their interminable scribbleations" (qtd. in Kiely 43).

17. See Ellis xvi.

18. Recent critics have tended to make light of the distinction between terror and horror, or to redefine it in rather confusing ways that support their own theses. See Twitchell 19, 22; and G.R. Thompson 3.

19. There is some dispute about which style is more "realistic," since Lewis's is more graphic; see Summers 221-22; and Varma 206-7. Lewis has been described as realizing, or concretizing, what is only suggested in Radcliffe's novels—in much the same way I see Radcliffe concretizing Burney (see Ellis 132).

20. For allusions to *The Mysterious Mother,* see *The Italian* 5, *The Romance of the Forest* 15. On Radcliffe's possible male sources for her explanations, see G. Kelly 47; and Varma 123.

21. See also Varma 106.

22. See *Otranto* 5; Summers 183-84; and Varma 45.

23. According to Kent, history was considered a suitable study for girls at this time (61).

24. Todd's *Wollstonecraft Anthology* contains some anonymous fiction reviews, possibly by Wollstonecraft, which make a similar judgment about women's novels (219, 222).

25. See Devlin, *The Author of Waverley,* 26. Haggerty praises Radcliffe for inventing occurrences that resist rational explanation ("Fact and Fancy" 383), as does Tompkins in her introduction to Varma (xv).

26. See Cottom 51.

27. See MacAndrew 122. Both Walpole (*Otranto* 7) and Reeve (*Old English Baron* 3) stated that their intention was to combine old and new romances, or realistic and romantic fiction.

28. Even Twitchell's recent study, which takes Gothic seriously *because* it is "pop culture" (4), retains some "pre-Romantic" bias. The"Great Tradition" viewpoint is still alive as well; see Konigsberg 257-58.

29. Not all critics with a Romantic orientation see Lewis as central; see Varma 206; and Haggerty, "Fact and Fancy," 384-85.

30. See Kiely for a comparison of Lewis's and Radcliffe's euphemisms (75, 113). Even in our own century it seems women are more likely than men to

consider Lewis's novel "pornographic"; see Summers, 213; vs. Howells 76. See also Ellis on *The Monk* (ch. 7).

31. Talfourd praises Radcliffe for the decency—we might say frigidity—of her work, apparently in his own way unable to read her feminine "euphemistic" language of passion (121, 132). For a discussion of Gothic as an exploration of female sexuality, see Cynthia Griffin Wolff, "The Radcliffean Gothic Model: A Form for Feminine Sexuality," *Modern Language Studies* 9.3 (Fall 1979): 98-113.

32. It has been suggested that *The Monk* is a Gothic treatment of the sentimental *Clarissa* (Howells 64; Anderson, intro. to Lewis, xvi). So far was Scott from disliking sentiment that he dedicated *Waverley* to Mackenzie (Devlin, *Author of Waverley*, 19-20). I am aware that "sentiment" is not the same as "sensibility" (Todd, *Sensibility*, 7-9); the difference is important, but the similarities between the terms are more germane to my own discussion.

33. But cf. MacAndrew 3, 6. As distaste for sensibility has grown, critics have stopped thinking of it as "pre-Romantic"; see Todd, *Sensibility*, 9.

34. Durant also notes that Radcliffe was swimming against the tide (520). Walpole discusses the moral of *Otranto* in the preface to the first edition (5). Summers describes the closing didactic passage in *The Monk* that is often left out of modern editions (212).

35. See Platzner, "Robert Hume and R. Platzner, an Exchange," *PMLA* 86 (March 1971):266-74; Wilt 4, 21.

36. Both G.R. Thompson (3) and Wilt (5) consider "dread" the basis of Gothic. But Varma sees a balance of fear and love (70-71).

37. See Wilt 130.

38. See Poovey's chapters on Wollstonecraft.

39. Therefore, as Howells notes, Gothic fiction was a way of treating the same problems found in Richardson or Austen in a more openly fictional manner (7, 11, 28-9, 47-50, 116).

40. See also Mudrick on Austen's *Sense and Sensibility* (86). On some male critics' tendency to reduce rape to symbol, see Todd, *Feminist Literary History*, 123-24.

41. Ellis also cites Charlotte Smith's *The Romance of Real Life*, accounts of sensational trials (79).

42. See Ellis on Reeve's frame device in *The Old English Baron* (61).

43. Cf. Hennelly (8).

44. One gets rather the same sense from reading Waugh's *Brideshead Revisited*.

45. As Hennelly points out, Schedoni really has committed incest of a kind by marrying his sister-in-law (12).

46. See MacAndrew ch. 4; Kiely 122; Murray 99.

47. A lot has been written about Gothic veils, so symbolic of Radcliffe's techniques of mystery and suspense (see Durant 523). But the world of romance is not in essence one in which truth is hidden.

48. Even in life Radcliffe was given to reading real people's faces in much the same way she interpreted portraits (Talfourd 77).

49. On Gothic writers' attitudes toward Catholicism, see Wilt (28) on Walpole; Murray (25) and Hennelly (1) on Radcliffe.

50. See Murray 45-46.

51. See G. Kelly 49-50. The similarity of Radcliffe's and Austen's ideas on sensibility is the premise of Nelson Smith's "Sense, Sensibility and Ann Radcliffe," *Studies in English Literature* 13 (1973): 577-590.

52. See G. Kelly 58-59. MacAndrew discusses fears during this period that

the passivity of sentimental characters would render them didactically useless or harmful (42); Ellis describes Burney's heroines as debilitated in this way (30).

53. See Spacks on gender roles in *The Italian*, "Female Orders of Narrative," in Canfield and Hunter, 171.

54. Scott also liked to observe the rules of chivalry with regard to sexuality in his novels; see Cottom 160-61.

55. Cf. Hennelly on Vivaldi (4).

56. Gothic novels could be used by spokesmen for both sides of this controversy. See C. Johnson 32-33. On radical and conservative women's distrust of sensibility, see C. Johnson 67-68; and Todd, *Sensibility*, 130-37.

57. This is one reason for the father's objection to romances in Hays's *Emma Courtney* as well (20).

58. Reeve goes on to complain that Fielding showed "human nature as *it is*, rather than as *it ought to be*" (*Progress* 1:141), a phrase reminiscent Johnson's *Rambler 4*. But she even "out-Johnsons" Johnson by having one of her characters warn young readers against the harsh morality of *Rasselas* (2:27-29).

59. Cf. Hennelly 13.

60. See Durant 520; Kahane 52; Garber, intro. to *The Italian*, x; MacAndrew 71, 94; Ellis 102-3.

61. Durant argues that Radcliffe's novel is *unlike* an education novel in this respect.

62. Talfourd tells of an incident in which some plays by Joanna Baillie were mistakenly attributed to Radcliffe, who was in agonies lest someone might think she had claimed them (90-3).

63. Scott draws a straight line moving from romance to realism, with Richardson and Fielding—and therefore Burney—as intermediate steps to Austen (*Scott on Novelists* 227, 230); he considers himself as part of this development because of his interest in complex characterization (Devlin, *The Author of Waverley*, 29-31). Wollstonecraft describes a similar line of development (*Anthology* 220, 223). Barrett collapses the categories of sentimental and Gothic by suggesting that all the heroines' names end in "-ina" (12). See McKillop on Austen (59).

7. Jane Austen's Novels: The Romantic Denouement

Epigraph: Edgeworth, *Patronage*, 284.

1. I do not consider Anne Elliot's engagement in *Persuasion* as "secret," but rather as private, or no one else's concern; cf. N. Auerbach, *Imprisonment*, 40.

2. See *Letters* 173; and Bradbrook 90-93.

3. Konigsberg sees Austen as the "culmination" (xi) of a mostly male tradition; he downplays the importance of her more immediate female predecessors (213-14), as does Kirkham (xi, 22).

4. "Exertion" is one of the important "words of Jane Austen" discussed by Tave (98-115).

5. See Todd, *Sensibility*, 17.

6. See Duckworth 131.

7. My argument in this chapter reflects my belief that Austen was a serious Christian all her life. Her contradictory statements—such as the references to evangelicals in her letters (see below)—suggest to me rather the working of an agile mind than any movement in one direction. On Austen's religion, see Fleishman, *A Reading of Mansfield Park* (Minneapolis: Univ. of Minneapolis Press, 1967), 77; Roberts 133-36; Duckworth 28; Butler, *Jane Austen,* 161-67, 284-85; and Poovey 181.

8. For symbolic interpretation of marriage, see Sulloway 217; Wilt sees marriage as a secularized substitute for death in the Christian mythos (144); but marriage has its place in that mythos as well. I rest my argument in this chapter on the belief that Austen's endings did have serious meaning for her and were not merely conventional or forced attempts to provide "aesthetic" solutions for insoluble problems, as some critics suggest see Mansell 73-74; Newton 82; Wiesenfarth 34; Poovey xvii, 206; Sulloway 84-85; Martha Satz, "An Epistemological Understanding of *Pride and Prejudice,*" in Todd, *Jane Austen: New Perspectives,* 178-79, 183. Nor do I interpret her endings entirely as burlesques—either of other novels, or of a society in which such happy closure is impossible (see Lloyd W. Brown, "The Comic Conclusion in Jane Austen's Novels," *PMLA* 64 [1969]: 1582; Koppel 70-71; C. Johnson 48; N. Auerbach, "Jane Austen," 14-15)—though I would not attempt to deny that they have ironic or satiric overtones.

9. See, for example, N. Auerbach, throughout; Spacks, "Muted Discord," 163-64, 168-69; S. Morgan's comparison of Austen and Wordsworth, throughout. Austen is sometimes discussed in terms of old romances, as by Lionel Trilling in the Introduction to *Emma* (Boston: Houghton Mifflin, 1957), xix-xxiv; Frye, *Secular Scripture,* 39-40, 76-79; Steiner 95-96 (discussed below).

10. Wilt discusses a satire by C.L. Pitt (1810) that gives notes on how, by simple substitution, a romance could be turned into a novel (125).

11. See Nelson 49-50.

12. See *Quarterly Review* 24 (Jan. 1821): 352-76; excerpted in the Norton Critical Edition of *Pride and Prejudice* (NY: Norton, 1960); discussed by Mansell (94).

13. See Southam, *Critical Heritage,* 2:8-11, 22-3, 41; Wiesenfarth 22. The romanticization of the eighteenth century continued until quite recently; see David Spring, "Interpretations of Jane Austen's Social World," in Todd, *Jane Austen: New Perspectives,* 54-55. Remnants of this tendency may be seen in some Austen criticism of the 1950s and 1960s as seen in Watt's collection: for example Reuben A. Brower, "Light and Bright and Sparkling," 70; Mark Schorer, "The Humiliation of Emma Woodhouse," 99; Kettle 115; Watt, "On *Sense and Sensibility,*" 42-43.

14. Cf. Konigsberg 214, 216.

15. See Edward Copeland, "The Burden of *Grandison,*" in Todd, *Jane Austen: New Perspectives,* 98-99. See also Charlotte Smith's *Desmond,* discussed in Todd, *Sensibility,* 128.

16. Even now, when "realism" is allowed to mean anything, "probability" is usually what it means. See, for example, Konigsberg 3.

17. Paradoxically Scott connects Austen with Gothic by suggesting that in choosing the commonplace she is merely continuing the search for novelty into the only area in which it has not yet been exhausted (*Scott On Novelists* 230).

18. See Kirkham 138. Scott also complains that Austen's heroines are too shrewd and calculating (*Scott On Novelists* 232, 234), and that modern readers need rather to be stirred up than cooled down; he is thinking of male readers, apparently, since he describes the moral benefits later in life of an unfortunate attachment in youth (236).

19. See Discourses III and VII (San Marino, CA: Huntington Library, 1959), 39-73.

20. This is more or less what Woolf suggested when she wrote that Austen's "powers" were not up to "moons and mountains and castles" ("Jane Austen," in Watt, 21, 17-18).

21. Duckworth and Konigsberg (214) see Austen's "contingent" plots as

empirical and secular, the antithesis of "providential"; but even to Charles Darwin the scientific model was informed with divinity; see *On the Origin of Species* (London: Watts, 1950), 412. Cf. Todd on Sterne (*Sensibility* 101-2).

22. Davis makes a similar remark about allegory in *Robinson Crusoe* (159).

23. See Tave 112-13.

24. See Bradbrook 126-32.

25. See Kahane 51.

26. Discussed in Kettle, 112 n. 1; Bradbrook 98.

27. See Wilt 101. Kirkham speculates that Scott's own sudden popularity as a novelist stunted Austen's career just as it was beginning (72-73).

28. See C. Johnson 34; Fleishman 34-35; Wilt ch. 3.

29. This gender reversal is developed further in *Pride and Prejudice,* in which Darcy, like Clelia and Harriot Stuart and Betsy Thoughtless, feels so besieged by pursuing women that he has trouble developing a free "inclination" for anyone.

30. Ann Banfield discusses sense of place ("The Influence of Place," in Monaghan 31); Brownstein (85) and Konigsberg (13-14) discuss suggestiveness; Tanner refers specifically to "veils" in Austen's writing (67).

31. Catherine's prosaic mind has often been noted by readers who find the abbey scenes inconsistent with her character (McKillop 59); recently Spacks has read the novel as a study of how Catherine's imagination is "redirected" ("Muted Discord" 172).

32. "Marriage" is not the same as "balance" (Moler 220), or "accommodation" (Poovey 173).

33. See Konigsberg 255.

34. See Tave 86.

35. A sample of those who think Marianne is "betrayed" or "killed" by being married off to Brandon: Mudrick, qtd. in Watt, "On *Sense and Sensibility,*" 49; Tanner 100-101; Mansell 76; Haggerty, "Sacrifice," 232, 234, and 221n, where he notes agreement with Gilbert and Gubar; Poovey 185, 189; Angela Leighton, "Sense and Silences," in Todd, *Jane Austen: New Perspectives,* 139-40; N. Auerbach, "Jane Austen," 18-19. An exception in feminist criticism—someone who likes Brandon—is Sulloway (205-6). She pictures him giving Marianne, literally, space to roam around in by herself (204).

36. On female friendships after marriage in Austen, see J. Thompson 165; and Brownstein 109; vs. C. Johnson 91-92. Sulloway remarks that in reality men often did object to their wives' maintaining friendships with women (71-72).

37. See Newton 68-69.

38. Many critics, in different ways, have been talking about "the dialectic of what is and what ought to be" in her novels (J.Thompson 32); see Monaghan, "The Complexity of Jane Austen's Novels," in Todd, *Jane Austen: New Perspectives,* 93; and Zelda Boyd, "The Language of Supposing," also in Todd, 142-54.

39. On the dream problem, Austen refers in a footnote to an essay by Richardson in the *Rambler;* but Richardson himself helped prepare readers to see the absurdity of forbidding women to love first when he created the dilemma of Harriet Byron in *Sir Charles Grandison.*

40. In *The Dramatic Works of Richard Brinsley Sheridan,* 2 vols. (Oxford: Clarendon Press, 1973).

41. Cf. C. Johnson 3-4.

42. See C. Johnson 103-4.

43. For contrasting views of Charlotte's marriage, see Poovey 205; Brownstein 134; and Newton 71-72, 75-76; vs. Tave 136-38; and Koppel 47-48.

44. See Poovey 14-15; in *Sensibility* Todd quotes Christopher Hill's remark, in a review of Stone's work, that *"talk about* marriage for love increased" (16). Ellis notes that the Hardwicke Act of 1753 gave parents more, not less control over their children under 21 (50-51, 74). Cf. Boone 62.

45. See Tave 17-18.

46. See Poovey 193-241.

47. On the question of how private Austen's endings really are, see Duckworth 180ff.; J. Thompson 176.

48. Poovey 234-35; C. Johnson 119; Roberts 53; Lloyd W. Brown, "The Business of Marrying and Mothering," in McMaster, 41.

49. Donald Greene coined the useful phrase "Tory democracy" ("Jane Austen and the Peerage," in Watt, 163, 165); see also C. Johnson xviii-xix; Sulloway 4, 69; Roberts 14-16. Todd notes that feminist readings often make Austen look more radical than she was—oddly, by ignoring the feminine context of her writings (*Feminist Literary History* 100-2).

50. For the first view see Duckworth 28; Roberts 67; for the second, see Poovey 224. See also S. Morgan 127.

51. It was common in old romances for a heroic younger son to rebel against primogeniture and prove his personal worth; see McKeon 141.

52. Cf. Kirkham 127-28.

53. *The Watsons,* probably written around 1805, is as dark as the novels written years later, and in many respects resembles *Mansfield Park.*

54. Major changes in Austen's mood and outlook seem especially unlikely given the overlapping dates of the composition and revision of her novels; see Lascelles 15, 30; D.W. Harding, intro. to J. Austen-Leigh, 269-70.

55. In *Patronage,* Maria Edgeworth has Rosamond Percy observe that "in real life . . . the novel heroine would be the most useless, troublesome, affected, haranguing, egoistical, insufferable being imaginable" (81); though Emma is not that bad, she does seem to illustrate the effects of bringing larger-than-life characters into the "real" world.

56. Austen loved to ridicule the "simple genius" archetype as seen in the novels of Charlotte Smith (discussed by Todd, *Sensibility,* 118) and Lady Morgan (*L* 251); see Lady Morgan's *The Wild Irish Girl* (NY: Pandora, 1986), 73.

57. See Introduction to Bage, xi-xii.

58. In referring to Elinor as heroine of *Sense and Sensibility* I mean (as Tave says, 96) that she is the central consciousness. Cf. Mansell 60-61.

59. C. Johnson remarks that his formula is an oxymoron (150), but I think the novel finally does reconcile the terms.

60. Burney's heroine remarks, "To appearances are we not all either victims or dupes?" (257). Jane Aiken Hodge notes that *Mansfield Park,* like *The Wanderer,* disappointed readers who were expecting something more "light, and bright, and sparkling"; see *Only a Novel: The Double Life of Jane Austen* (NY: Coward, McCann and Geoghegan, 1974): 169-70.

61. Juliet does, when pressed, take part in an amateur theatrical and acquits herself brilliantly (*Wanderer* 82-84); see Margaret Drabble's discussion, intro. to *Wanderer,* xiii.

62. See Trilling, *"Mansfield Park"* (132-33), for the first possible danger of acting; Tave (191-92) for the second.

63. To some readers Fanny triumphs merely by being passive-aggressive rather than strong or right. See N. Auerbach, "Jane Austen's Dangerous Charm," in Todd, *Jane Austen: New Perspectives,* 220; Marylea Meyersohn, "What Fanny Knew," in Todd, *Jane Austen: New Perspectives,* 224.

64. See Mansell 124-25; see S. Morgan (135-37) for comparison of *Northanger Abbey* and *Mansfield Park*.

65. See C. Johnson 109; and Kirkham 102.

66. Mansell sees *Mansfield Park* as revealing Austen's guilt about her own wit, which he sees lurking under the surface in *Pride and Prejudice* (115-122). For contrasts between Mary Crawford and Elizabeth Bennet, see Mudrick 93; Trilling 127-28, 133; Moler 131-32; see also Todd, *Women's Friendship,* 271-72, and Tave's discussion of "liveliness," 164-65.

67. See Mansell 115-16. Often Burney as narrator can indicate her amusement only with well-placed exclamations points, as in a slapstick scene at an opera rehearsal in *Cecilia* (67).

68. See S. Morgan 90; Duckworth 132-40.

69. The last part of the remark is often left off when this passage is quoted. Tave discusses Mr. Plumtre as "amiable" but not "agreeable" (120).

70. Cf. Todd, *Women's Friendship,* 269; and Mansell 142.

71. Mansell sees Emma's failure as the author's comment on the limitations of her own art (153, 184); but there is an important distinction to be made between domination in life and in fiction writing.

72. A great deal of critical argumentation rests on a disputed passage from the text of *Sense and Sensibility.* The question is whether Marianne says to Elinor, "We have neither of us any thing to tell; you, because you communicate, and I, because I conceal nothing," or " . . . because you do not communicate. . . . " The Chapman edition gives the first version (170), Tanner's Penguin edition the second ([NY: Penguin, 1967], 184). Neither editor gives a note on the passage, but Tanner's general note suggests that he has used the corrected second edition instead of the first, and his reading does seem more likely. The passage from the first edition is a major piece of supporting evidence for Haggerty's argument in "The Sacrifice of Privacy in *Sense and Sensibility*" (223-24).

73. Cf. Burney's comments about the amateur theatricals in *The Wanderer* (69, 71).

74. C. Johnson finds very little wrong with Emma (122ff.), as does Kirkham (ch. 18). Spacks (*Gossip* 167), Moler (ch. 5), and Lascelles (69) discuss Emma as a would-be heroine; Brownstein (104) as a failed author.

75. See Duckworth 163.

76. See Duckworth 157.

77. In earlier novels the author supports the heroines' sense of themselves as minds rather than as bodies. We don't find out what Elinor and Marianne look like until Willoughby looks at them in chapter 10 of *Sense and Sensibility;* and though Elizabeth and Catherine are described early, their appearance (like that of Edward Ferrars to Elinor) is so dependent on their personality that one cannot see their faces without also seeing their minds. See Mansell 57.

78. Compare *Emma*—"could Mr. Knightley have . . . seen into her heart, he would not, on this occasion, have found any thing to reprove" (391)—with *Betsy Thoughtless*—"I wonder . . . what Mr. Trueworth would say if he knew the change that a little time has wrought in me!" (568).

79. Not a very good reader of novels, Emma has failed to recognize an even better contender for the role of sentimental heroine, Jane Fairfax (S. Morgan 34).

80. Austen approved Brunton's themes but disliked the lack of "Nature or Probability" in her plots and characters; see *Letters* 344.

81. See Poovey 226-27.

82. It has been pointed out by several readers that Julia is not really so tough, since she acts like a "nut" only to please Wentworth.

83. See Tave 287.

84. Cf. N. Auerbach, *Imprisonment,* 53-54.

85. Cf. Bradbrook 13.

86. See Duckworth 192-93; and S. Morgan 177. She resembles a character in David Lodge's *Souls and Bodies* (NY: Penguin, 1980) whose sad musings are always followed by the refrain, "but then she cheered up." Cf. *Persuasion:* "It was but a passing emotion however with Mrs. Smith, she shook it off" (156).

87. Duckworth's discussion of the symbolic value of trees in the novels adds something to the poignancy of this passage (53-54).

88. On detachment in Austen's humor, see John Halperin, "Unengaged Laughter," in Grey, *Jane Austen's Beginnings,* 29-44; Roberts 88, 93; and S. Morgan 9-10.

89. Cf. Newton 60-61.

90. See Kirkham 152-53.

91. Austen thus recommends an attitude similar to that recommended by some recent critics as the best approach to her novels; Weinsheimer calls it "tact" (*"Emma* and Its Critics," in Todd, *Jane Austen: New Perspectives,* 259); Koppel refers to a "total-response approach" (85); and Duckworth asks for historical flexibility ("Jane Austen and the Conflict of Interpretations," in Todd, *Jane Austen: New Perspectives,* 45-46).

92. Southam discusses the similarity in the way *Sanditon* and *Northanger Abbey* allude to Burney (*"Sanditon"* 7).

93. See Kiely on Austen's belief in "conversation" as a means of linking people (121-22); as we have seen, this is also a theme in *The Italian.*

94. Cf. Kirkham 14.

Selected Bibliography

Primary Sources

Aristotle. *Poetics,* trans. S.H. Butcher. New York: Hill and Wang, 1961.

Austen, Jane. *Jane Austen's Letters to Her Sister Cassandra and Others,* ed. R.W. Chapman. 2d ed. London: Oxford Univ. Press, 1952.

———. *The Works of Jane Austen,* ed. R.W. Chapman. 6 vols. 3d ed. Oxford: Oxford Univ. Press, 1988.

Bage, Robert. [1796] *Hermsprong.* Oxford: Oxford Univ. Press, 1985.

Barrett, Eaton Stannard. [1813] *The Heroine.* London: Colburn, 1813.

Behn, Aphra. [1684-87] *Love Letters between a Nobleman and His Sister.* New York: Penguin, 1987.

———. [1688] *Oroonoko,* ed. Adelaide P. Amore. Lanham, Md.: Univ. Press of America, 1987.

———. *The Works of Aphra Behn,* ed. Montague Summers. 6 vols. 2d ed. New York: Benjamin Blom, 1967.

Boileau, Nicolas. *Oevres Complètes.* Bruges: Bibliothèque de la Pleiade, 1966.

Boswell, James. [1799] *The Life of Johnson.* 3rd ed. London: Oxford Univ. Press, 1970.

Brunton, Mary. [1814] *Discipline.* London: Pandora, 1986.

Burney, Fanny. *Brief Reflections Relative to the Emigrant French Clergy.* London: Cadell, 1793.

———. [1796] *Camilla.* London: Oxford Univ. Press, 1972.

———. [1782] *Cecilia.* New York: Penguin, 1986.

———. *The Diary and Letters of Madame d'Arblay,* ed. Austin Dobson. New York: Macmillan, 1905.

———. *The Early Diary of Frances Burney,* ed. Annie Raine Ellis. London: Bell, 1889.

———. *Edwy and Elgiva.* Hamden, Conn.: Shoestring Press, 1957.

———. [1778] *Evelina.* London: Oxford Univ. Press, 1968.

———. *The Journals and Letters of Fanny Burney,* ed. Joyce Hemlow and Althea Douglas. London: Oxford Univ. Press, 1972-75.

———. *Memoirs of Dr. Burney.* London: Moxon, 1832.

———. [1814] *The Wanderer.* London: Pandora, 1988.

Congreve, William. *The Complete Works of William Congreve.* 4 vols. London: Nonesuch, 1923.

Edgeworth, Maria. [1800] *Castle Rackrent.* Oxford: Oxford Univ. Press, 1981.

———. [1834] *Helen.* London: Pandora, 1987.

———. [1813] *Patronage.* London: Pandora, 1986.

The Female Wits. [1704] Augustan Reprint Society pub. no. 124. Los Angeles: William Andrews Clark Memorial Library, 1967.

Ferrier, Susan. [1818] *Marriage*. New York: Penguin, 1986.

Fielding, Henry. [1752] *The Covent-Garden Journal*. 2 vols. New York: Russell and Russell, 1964.

————. [1742] *Joseph Andrews*. Middletown, Conn.: Wesleyan Univ. Press, 1967.

Hays, Mary. [1796] *Memoirs of Emma Courtney*. London: Pandora, 1987.

Haywood, Eliza. [1744-46] *The Female Spectator,* ed. Mary Priestley. London: John Lane, 1929.

————. [1751] *The History of Miss Betsy Thoughtless*. London: Pandora, 1986.

————. [1748] *Life's Progress Through the Passions*. New York: Garland, 1974.

————. [1725] *Memoirs of a Certain Island*. New York: Garland, 1972.

————. [1724] *The Rash Resolve* (with Penelope Aubin, *The Life and Adventures of the Lady Lucy*), ed. Josephine Grieder. New York: Garland, 1973.

Hurd, Richard. *Letters on Chivalry and Romance (1762)*. Augustan Reprint Society Pub. no. 101-102. Los Angeles: William Andrews Clark Memorial Library, 1963.

Johnson, Samuel. *The Yale Edition of the Works of Samuel Johnson*. New Haven: Yale Univ. Press, 1969.

Lennox, Charlotte. [1752] *The Female Quixote,* ed. Sandra Shulman. London: Pandora, 1986.

————. [1758] *Henrietta*. New York: Garland, 1974.

————. *The Life of Harriot Stuart*. London: Payne and Bouquet, 1751. Micro-published in the Yale History of Women series, New Haven, Conn: Research Publications, 1975.

Lewis, Matthew. [1796] *The Monk*. Oxford: Oxford Univ. Press, 1988.

Manley, Delarivière. *The Novels of Delarivière Manley,* ed. Patricia Köster. Gainesville, Fla.: Scholars' Facsimiles and Reprints, 1971.

More, Hannah. *Strictures on the Modern System of Female Education: The Works of Hannah More*. 2 vols. Philadelphia: J.J. Woodward, 1830, 1:347-466.

Radcliffe, Ann. [1797] *The Italian*. Oxford: Oxford Univ. Press, 1981.

————. [1794] *The Mysteries of Udolpho*. London: Oxford Univ. Press, 1970.

————. [1791] *The Romance of the Forest*. Oxford: Oxford Univ. Press, 1986.

————. "The Supernatural in Poetry." *New Monthly Magazine* 16 (1826): 145-52.

Reeve, Clara. [1778] *The Old English Baron*. London: Oxford Univ. Press, 1967.

————. [1785] *The Progress of Romance*. New York: Facsimile Text Society, 1930.

Richardson, Samuel. [1753-54] *Sir Charles Grandison*. London: Oxford Univ. Press, 1972.

Scott, Sir Walter. *Prose Works*. Edinburgh: Cadell, 1834.

————. *Sir Walter Scott on Novelists and Fiction*. New York: Barnes and Noble, 1968.

Scudéry, Madeleine de. *Artamenes: or the Grand Cyrus,* trans. F.G. London: Humphrey Moseley, 1653.

————. *Clelia,* trans. John Davies. London: Herringman, 1678.

————. *Clélie*. Geneva: Slatkine Reprints, 1973.

Smith, Charlotte. [1794] *The Old Manor House*. London: Pandora, 1987.

Thrale, Hester. *Thraliana,* ed. Katharine Balderston. Oxford: Clarendon Press, 1942.

Urfé, Honoré d'. [1610-27] *L'Astrée: Analyse et Extraits,* ed. Maurice Magendie. Paris: Perrin, 1928.

Walpole, Horace. [1764] *The Castle of Otranto*. Oxford: Oxford Univ. Press, 1988.

————. *The Yale Edition of Horace Walpole's Correspondence*. New Haven: Yale Univ. Press, 1937-.

————. [1768] *The Mysterious Mother* (with *The Castle of Otranto*), ed. Montague Summers. London: Constable, 1924.

Wilmot, John, Lord Rochester. *The Poems of John Wilmot, Earl of Rochester,* ed. Keith Walker. Oxford: Blackwell, 1984.

Critical Sources

Adams, Percy G. *Travel Literature and the Evolution of the Novel.* Lexington, Ky.: Univ. Press of Kentucky, 1983.

Aronson, Nicole. *Mademoiselle de Scudéry.* Boston: Twayne, 1978.

Auerbach, Erich. "The Knight Sets Forth." In *Mimesis.* Princeton: Princeton Univ. Press, 1974.

Auerbach, Nina. "Jane Austen and Romantic Imprisonment." In Monaghan, *Jane Austen in a Social Context.*

————. *Romantic Imprisonment: Women and Other Glorified Outcasts.* New York: Columbia Univ. Press, 1986.

Austen-Leigh, James Edward. [1870] "A Memoir of Jane Austen," 2d ed. In *Persuasion.* New York: Penguin, 1985.

Austen-Leigh, William, and Richard Arthur Austen-Leigh. *Jane Austen: Her Life and Letters,* 2d ed. New York: Russell and Russell, 1965.

Beasley, Jerry C. "Politics and Moral Idealism: The Achievement of Some Early Women Novelists." In Schofield, *Fetter'd or Free?*

————. "Life's Episodes: Story and Its Form in the Eighteenth Century." In Uphaus, *The Idea of the Novel in the Eighteenth Century.*

Bettelheim, Bruno. *The Uses of Enchantment.* New York: Random House, 1977.

Boone, Joseph Allen. *Tradition Counter Tradition: Love and the Form of Fiction.* Chicago: Univ. of Chicago Press, 1987.

Bradbrook, Frank W. *Jane Austen and Her Predecessors.* Cambridge: Cambridge Univ. Press, 1966.

Brown, Laura. "The Romance of Empire: *Oroonoko* and the Trade in Slaves." In *The New Eighteenth Century,* ed. Felicity Nussbaum and Laura Brown. New York: Methuen, 1987.

Brown, Martha G. "Fanny Burney's 'Feminism': Gender or Genre?" In Schofield, *Fetter'd or Free?*

Brownlee, Kevin, and Marina S. Brownlee, eds. *Romance: Generic Transformations from Chrétien de Troyes to Cervantes.* Hanover, NH: Univ. Press of New England, 1985.

Brownlee, Marina Scordilis. "Cervantes as Reader of Ariosto." In Brownlee, *Romance: Generic Transformations.*

Brownley, Martine. "The Narrator in *Oroonoko.*" *Essays in Literature* (Fall 1977): 174-81.

Brownstein, Rachel. *Becoming a Heroine,* 2d ed. New York: Penguin, 1984.

Butler, Marilyn. *Jane Austen and the War of Ideas.* Oxford: Clarendon Press, 1975.

————. "Jane Austen's Sense of the Volume." In Monaghan, *Jane Austen in a Social Context.*

————. *Maria Edgeworth: A Literary Biography.* Oxford: Clarendon Press, 1972.

Canfield, J. Douglas, and J. Paul Hunter, eds. *Rhetorics of Order/Ordering Rhetorics in English Neoclassical Literature.* Newark: Univ. of Delaware Press, 1989.

Cecil, Lord David. *Poets and Story-Tellers.* New York: Macmillan, 1949.

Cottom, Daniel. *The Civilized Imagination: A Study of Ann Radcliffe, Jane Austen, and Sir Walter Scott.* London: Cambridge Univ. Press, 1985.

Crawford, Patricia. "Women's Published Writings 1600-1799." In Prior, *Women in English Society, 1500-1800.*

Croker, J. W. "Madame d'Arblay's *Diary and Letters.*" *Quarterly Review* 70 (June 1842): 245-47.

Davis, Lennard. *Factual Fictions: The Origins of the English Novel.* New York: Columbia Univ. Press, 1983.

Devlin, D.D. *The Author of Waverley.* Lewisburg: Bucknell Univ. Press, 1971.

———. *The Novels and Journals of Fanny Burney.* London: Macmillan, 1987.

Doody, Margaret. *A Natural Passion: A Study of the Novels of Samuel Richardson.* Oxford: Clarendon Press, 1974.

———. *Frances Burney.* New Brunswick, NJ: Rutgers Univ. Press, 1988.

Duckworth, Alistair. *The Improvement of the Estate.* Baltimore: Johns Hopkins Press, 1971.

Duffy, Maureen. *The Passionate Shepherdess.* London: Cape, 1977.

Durant, David. "Ann Radcliffe and the Conservative Gothic." *Studies in English Literature* 22 (1982): 519-30.

Eastlake, Charles. [1872] *A History of the Gothic Revival.* n.p.: American Life Foundation, 1975.

Ellis, Kate Ferguson. *The Contested Castle: Gothic Novels and the Subversion of Domestic Ideology.* Urbana: Univ. of Illinois Press, 1989.

El Saffar, Ruth. "The Truth of the Matter: The Place of Romance in the Works of Cervantes." In Brownlee, *Romance: Generic Transformations.*

Elwood, John R. "Henry Fielding and Eliza Haywood: A Twenty Year War." *Albion* (Fall 1973): 184-92.

Epstein, Julia. "Fanny Burney's Epistolary Voices. *The Eighteenth Century* 27 (1986): 162-79.

Faderman, Lillian. *Surpassing the Love of Men.* New York: William Morrow, 1981.

Figes, Eva. *Sex and Subterfuge: Women Writers to 1850.* London: Macmillan, 1982.

Fleishman, Avrom. *Fiction and the Ways of Knowing.* Austin: Univ. of Texas Press, 1978.

Frye, Northrop. *Anatomy of Criticism.* Princeton: Princeton Univ. Press, 1957.

———. *The Secular Scripture.* Cambridge, Mass.: Harvard Univ. Press, 1976.

Gardiner, Judith Kegan. "The First English Novel: Aphra Behn's *Love Letters,* the Canon, and Women's Tastes." *Tulsa Studies in Women's Literature* 8 (Fall 1989): 201-22.

Gilbert, Sandra, and Susan Gubar, *The Madwoman in the Attic.* New Haven: Yale Univ. Press, 1979.

Goreau, Angeline. *Reconstructing Aphra.* New York: Dial, 1980.

Grey, J. David, ed. *Jane Austen's Beginnings: The Juvenilia and Lady Susan.* Ann Arbor: UMI, 1989.

Guffey, George. "Aphra Behn's *Oroonoko:* Occasion and Accomplishment." In *Two English Novelists: Aphra Behn and Anthony Trollope.* Los Angeles: William Andrews Clark Memorial Library, 1975.

Haggerty, George. "Fact and Fancy in the Gothic Novel." *Nineteenth-Century Fiction* 39 (1985): 379-91.

———. "The Sacrifice of Privacy in *Sense and Sensibility.*" *Tulsa Studies in Women's Literature* 7.2 (Fall 1988): 221-37.

Hazlitt, William. *"The Wanderer: Or, Female Difficulties.* A Novel, by Madame d'Arblay." *Edinburgh Review* 24 (1815): 320-38.

Hemlow, Joyce. *The History of Fanny Burney.* London: Oxford Univ. Press, 1958.

Hennelly, Mark M., Jr. "'The Slow Torture of Delay': Reading *The Italian.*" *Studies in the Humanities* 14.1 (June 1987): 1-17.

Horowitz, Louise K. "Where Have All the 'Old Knights' Gone?: *L'Astrée.*" In Brownlee, *Romance: Generic Transformations.*

Howells, Coral Ann. *Love, Mystery, and Misery: Feeling in Gothic Fiction.* London: Athlone Press, 1978.

Hume, Robert D. "Gothic Versus Romantic: A Revaluation of the Gothic Novel." *PMLA* 84.2 (March 1969): 282-90.

Hunter, J. Paul. "'News, and New Things': Contemporaneity and the Early English Novel." *Critical Inquiry* (Spring 1988): 493-515.

––––––. "The Novel and the Contexts of Discourse." In *Theory and Tradition in Eighteenth-Century Studies,* ed. Richard B. Schwartz. Carbondale: Southern Illinois Univ. Press, 1990.

––––––. "Novels and 'the Novel': The Poetics of Embarrassment." *Modern Philology* (May 1988): 480-98.

––––––. "The Young, the Ignorant, and the Idle': Some Notes on Readers and the Beginnings of the English Novel." In *Anticipations of the Enlightenment in England, France, and Germany,* ed. Alan Charles Kors and Paul J. Korshin. Philadelphia: Univ. of Pennsylvania Press, 1987.

Johnson, Claudia. *Jane Austen: Women, Politics, and the Novel.* Chicago: Univ. of Chicago Press, 1988.

Kahane, Claire. "Gothic Mirrors and Feminine Identity." *Centennial Review* 24: 43-64.

Kelly, Douglas. "Romance and the Vanity of Chrétien de Troyes." In Brownlee, *Romance: Generic Transformations.*

Kelly, Gary. "A Constant Vicissitude of Interesting Passions': Ann Radcliffe's Perplexed Narratives." *Ariel* 10.2 (1978): 45-64.

Kent, Christopher. "Learning History With, and From, Jane Austen." In Grey, *Jane Austen's Beginnings.*

Kettle, Arnold. *"Emma."* In Watt, *Jane Austen: A Collection of Critical Essays.*

Kiely, Robert. *The Romantic Novel in England.* Cambridge, Mass.: Harvard Univ. Press, 1972.

Kirkham, Margaret. *Jane Austen, Feminism and Fiction.* New York: Methuen, 1986.

Konigsberg, Ira. *Narrative Technique in the English Novel, Defoe to Austen.* Hamden, Conn.: Archon Books, 1985.

Koppel, Gene. *The Religious Dimension of Jane Austen's Novels.* Ann Arbor: UMI, 1988.

Langbauer, Laurie. "Romance Revised: Charlotte Lennox's *The Female Quixote.*" *Novel: A Forum on Fiction* 18 (Fall 1984): 29-49.

Lascelles, Mary. *Jane Austen and Her Art.* Oxford: Clarendon Press, 1939.

Litz, A. Walton. "Character and Personality in Jane Austen's Fiction." In McMaster, *Jane Austen's Achievement.*

London, April. "Placing the Female: The Metonymic Garden in Amatory and Pious Narrative, 1700-1740." In Schofield, *Fetter'd or Free?*

MacAndrew, Elizabeth. *The Gothic Tradition in Fiction.* New York: Columbia Univ. Press, 1979.

MacCarthy, Bridget. *The Female Pen: Women Writers, Their Contribution to the English Novel 1621-1744.* Cork: Cork Univ. Press, 1947.

––––––. *The Female Pen: The Later Women Novelists 1744-1818.* Cork: Cork Univ. Press, 1947.

McKeon, Michael. *The Origins of the English Novel 1600-1740.* Baltimore: Johns Hopkins Univ. Press, 1987.

McKillop, Alan D. "Critical Realism in *Northanger Abbey.*" In Watt, *Jane Austen: A Collection of Critical Essays.*

McMaster, Juliet, ed. *Jane Austen's Achievement.* London: Macmillan, 1976.

Mansell, Darrel. *The Novels of Jane Austen: An Interpretation.* London: Macmillan, 1973.

Mendelson, Sara Heller. "Stuart Women's Diaries and Occasional Memoirs." In Prior, *Women in English Society, 1500-1800.*

Moler, Kenneth L. *Jane Austen's Art of Allusion.* Lincoln: Univ. of Nebraska Press, 1968.

Monaghan, David, ed. *Jane Austen in a Social Context.* Totowa, N.J.: Barnes and Noble, 1981.

Morgan, Fidelis. *A Woman of No Character.* London: Faber and Faber, 1986.

Morgan, Susan. *In the Meantime: Character and Perception in Jane Austen's Fiction.* Chicago: Univ. of Chicago Press, 1980.

Mudrick, Marvin. "Irony as Discrimination: *Pride and Prejudice.*" In Watt, *Jane Austen: A Collection of Critical Essays.*

Murray, E.B. *Ann Radcliffe.* New York: Twayne, 1972.

Myers, Mitzi. "Hannah More's Tracts for the Times: Social Fiction and Female Ideology." In Schofield, *Fetter'd or Free?*

Needham, Gwendolyn. "Mary de la Rivière Manley, Tory Defender." *Huntington Library Quarterly* 12 (1948-49): 253-88.

———. "Mrs. Manley: An Eighteenth-Century Wife of Bath." *Huntington Library Quarterly* 14 (1951): 259-84.

Nelson, William. *Fact or Fiction: The Dilemma of the Renaissance Storyteller.* Cambridge, Mass.: Harvard Univ. Press, 1973.

Newton, Judith Lowder. *Women, Power, and Subversion: Social Strategies in British Fiction, 1778-1860.* Athens: Univ. of Georgia Press, 1981.

Palomo, Dolores. "A Woman Writer and the Scholars: A Review of Mary Manley's Reputation." *Women and Literature* 6.1 (Spring 1978): 36-45.

Parker, Patricia. *Inescapable Romance.* Princeton: Princeton Univ. Press, 1979.

Perry, Ruth. *Women, Letters and the Novel.* New York: AMS, 1980.

Poovey, Mary. *The Proper Lady and the Woman Writer.* Chicago: Univ. of Chicago Press, 1984.

Prior, Mary. "Reviled and Crucified Marriages: the Position of Tudor Bishops' Wives." In Prior, *Women in English Society, 1500-1800.*

———, ed. *Women in English Society, 1500-1800.* London: Methuen, 1985.

Richetti, John J. *Popular Fiction before Richardson.* Oxford: Clarendon Press, 1969.

Roberts, Warren. *Jane Austen and the French Revolution.* New York: St. Martin's Press, 1979.

Schofield, Mary Anne. *Eliza Haywood.* Boston: Twayne, 1985.

———. *Masking and Unmasking the Female Mind: Disguising Romances in Feminine Fiction, 1713-1799.* Newark: Univ. of Delaware Press, 1990.

———. *Quiet Rebellion.* Washington, D.C.: Univ. Press of America, 1982.

Schofield, Mary Anne, and Cecilia Macheski, eds. *Fetter'd or Free?: British Women Novelists, 1670-1815.* Athens: Ohio Univ. Press, 1985.

Séjourné, Philippe. *The Mystery of Charlotte Lennox.* Aix-en-Provence: Publications des Annales de la Faculté des Lettres, 1967.

Simons, Judy. *Fanny Burney.* London: Macmillan, 1987.

Small, Miriam. *Charlotte Ramsay Lennox.* Archon Books, 1969, reprinted from Yale Univ. Press, 1935.

Southam, B.C., ed. *Jane Austen: The Critical Heritage*. 2 vols. London: Routledge and Kegan Paul, 1968-87.

_____. *Jane Austen's Literary Manuscripts*. London: Oxford Univ. Press, 1964.

_____. *"Sanditon:* The Seventh Novel." In McMaster, *Jane Austen's Achievement*.

Spacks, Patricia Meyer. *The Adolescent Idea*. New York: Basic Books, 1978.

_____. *Gossip*. Chicago: Univ. of Chicago Press, 1986.

_____. *Imagining a Self*. Cambridge, Mass.: Harvard Univ. Press, 1976.

_____. "Muted Discord: Generational Conflict in Jane Austen." In Monaghan, *Jane Austen in a Social Context*.

Spencer, Jane. *The Rise of the Woman Novelist*. Oxford: Blackwell, 1986.

Spender, Dale. *Mothers of the Novel*. London: Pandora, 1986.

Staves, Susan. "Don Quixote in Eighteenth-Century England." *Comparative Literature* 24.3 (1972): 193-215.

Steiner, George. *On Difficulty and Other Essays*. New York: Oxford Univ. Press, 1978.

Stone, Lawrence. *The Family, Sex, and Marriage in England: 1500-1800*. New York: Harper and Row, 1977.

Straub, Kristina. *Divided Fictions: Fanny Burney and Feminine Strategy*. Lexington: Univ. Press of Kentucky, 1987.

Sulloway, Alison. *Jane Austen and the Province of Womanhood*. Philadelphia: Univ. of Pennsylvania Press, 1989.

Summers, Montague. *The Gothic Quest*. London: Fortune Press, 1938.

Talfourd, T.N. "Memoir of the Life and Writings of Mrs. Radcliffe." In Radcliffe, *Gaston de Blondeville*. London: Colburn, 1826.

Tanner, Tony. *Jane Austen*. London: Macmillan, 1986.

Tave, Stuart. *Some Words of Jane Austen*. Chicago: Univ. of Chicago Press, 1973.

Thompson, G.R. "Romanticism and the Gothic Tradition." In *The Gothic Imagination: Essays in Dark Romanticism*, ed. G.R. Thompson. Pullman: Washington State Univ. Press, 1974.

Thompson, James. *Between Self and World: The Novels of Jane Austen*. University Park: Pennsylvania State Univ. Press, 1988.

Todd, Janet. *Feminist Literary History*. New York: Routledge, 1988.

_____, ed. *Jane Austen: New Perspectives. Women and Literature*, n.s. 3. New York: Holmes and Meier, 1983.

_____. *Sensibility: An Introduction*. London: Methuen, 1986.

_____. *Women's Friendship in Literature*. New York: Columbia Univ. Press, 1980.

Tompkins, Joyce Marjorie Sanxter. *The Popular Novel in England: 1770-1800*. Lincoln: Univ. of Nebraska Press, 1961.

Trilling, Lionel. *"Mansfield Park."* In Watt, *Jane Austen: A Collection of Critical Essays*.

Twitchell, James B. *Dreadful Pleasures: An Anatomy of Modern Horror*. New York: Oxford Univ. Press, 1985.

Uitti, Karl D. "Renewal and Undermining of Old French Romance: Jehan de Saintré." In Brownlee, *Romance: Generic Transformations*.

Uphaus, Robert W., ed. *The Idea of the Novel in the Eighteenth Century*. East Lansing, Mich.: Colleagues Press, 1988.

Varma, Devendra. *The Gothic Flame*. London: Arthur Barker, 1957.

Vicinus, Martha. "'They Wonder to Which Sex I Belong': The Historical Roots of the Modern Lesbian Identity." In *Homosexuality, Which Homosexuality?* London: GMP Publishers, 1989.

Warren, Leland. "Of the Conversation of Women: *The Female Quixote* and the

Dream of Perfection." *Studies in Eighteenth Century Culture* 11 (1982): 367-80.

Watt, Ian, ed. *Jane Austen: A Collection of Critical Essays*. Englewood Cliffs, N.J.: Prentice-Hall, 1963.

———. "On *Sense and Sensibility*." In Watt, *Jane Austen: A Collection of Essays*.

Weinsheimer, Joel. "Fiction and the Force of Example." In Uphaus, *The Idea of the Novel in the Eighteenth Century*.

Whicher, George. *The Life and Romances of Mrs. Eliza Haywood*. New York: Columbia Univ. Press, 1915.

Wiesenfarth, Joseph. *Gothic Manners and the Classic English Novel*. Madison: Univ. of Wisconsin Press, 1988.

Wilt, Judith. *Ghosts of the Gothic: Austen, Eliot, and Lawrence*. Princeton, N.J.: Princeton Univ. Press, 1980.

Woodcock, George. *Aphra Behn: The English Sappho*. Montreal: Black Rose Books, 1989.

Zimbardo, Rose. "The Late Seventeenth-Century Dilemma in Discourse: Dryden's *Don Sebastian* and Behn's *Oroonoko*." In Canfield and Hunter, *Rhetorics of Order/Ordering Rhetorics in English Neoclassical Literature*.

Index